Ranking and Resistance

Ranking and Resistance

*A Precolonial Cameroonian Polity
in Regional Perspective*

RICHARD G. DILLON

Stanford University Press, Stanford, California
1990

Stanford University Press
Stanford, California
©1990 by the Board of Trustees of the
Leland Stanford Junior University
Printed in the United States of America

CIP data appear at the end of the book

Published with the assistance of a grant
from Hobart and William Smith Colleges

FOR JOYCE

Preface

THIS STUDY began in the late 1960s as an attempt to use data about a small-scale precolonial African society to cast light on the initial phases of political evolution, particularly "chiefdom formation." My thought at the time was that, given the considerable variability that such societies had shown in their political organization, Africanist research might be more likely to produce insights into these shadowy developments than inquiry on other continents could.

Although years of analyzing the ethnohistorical data collected in Meta' society have confirmed the fruitfulness of looking to Africa for information on process and change in precolonial non-state societies, they have also wrought substantial revisions in the original evolutionary perspective. As it turns out, even though powerful centralizing forces were at work within the Meta' political system, the Meta' are on balance a better illustration of the vigor of resistance to centralization than of direct "progress" toward chiefdom status. Moreover, they show how a political and legal system may become large, complex, and even specialized without developing fully centralized authority. All of this seems to have been anticipated, albeit in somewhat ethnocentric language, by an early British colonial official who, reporting on the operation of the "indirect rule" system in Meta', wistfully noted that the judicial work of indigenous leaders far outstripped their administrative efforts. Perhaps the lesson of the Meta' (for both this former officer and evolutionary anthropologists) is that the path of political growth is often an unexpectedly complex one in which what constitutes "progress" must be considered from many angles. Adopting this perspective, the present study will explore how much one acephalous African society was able to achieve by way of consensual polity building and the factors that prompted change in this direction.

The fieldwork upon which this study was based was carried out between December 1969 and July 1971. It was funded by a predoctoral fellowship and grant from the National Institute of Mental Health. Igor Kopytoff, Robert McC. Netting, and Thomas Greaves gave essential advice in my preparation for fieldwork as well as during the initial phases of data analysis. Thanks are also due to the late Phyllis Kaberry, Mrs. E. M. Chilver, and the late Edwin Ardener for their suggestions.

In Cameroon itself many scholars and government officials provided support and assistance, including the then Vice President Solomon T. Muna; his Private Secretary Mr. D. T. Atogho; Mr. L. Monfo Soo, Minister of Education; the Reverend Engelbert Mveng, Director of Cultural Affairs; Mr. Mohamedou Eldridge; Mr. H. M. Awazi; Mr. Bernard Ayuk; Dr. M. A. Nkongho; Mr. J. C. Kangkolo; and Mr. Ngole, who was then Senior District Officer for Momo Division. So many people of Meta' contributed to this study in important ways that it would be impossible to mention them all. The most profound gratitude is felt toward my regular informants. In addition, my wife and I are indebted to Chief Akam of Kai Village for his kindness as our first host, as well as to Chiefs Take, Fongu, Fobang, and Fortu of the Bome Valley, where we lived for over a year. I also owe much to Chief Fonbah of Njekwa Village, who worked as my research assistant and became a good friend. Without his great wisdom and ability to bridge barriers to communication, it would have been impossible to understand the more subtle aspects of Meta' political theory.

More recently a number of individuals and institutions have aided my efforts to reanalyze the data on Meta' society and place them in a regional context. Professor Lawrence Rosen helped with my first efforts to formulate a comparative framework during his 1981 National Endowment for the Humanities Summer Seminar at Princeton University. Members of the Grassfields Working Group, especially E. M. Chilver, Christraud Geary, C. H. Latour-Dejean, Michael Rowlands, and Jean-Pierre Warnier, also generously shared their data and their reactions to my work at several meetings during the 1970s and 1980s, and Jean-Pierre Warnier has kindly permitted me to reproduce portions of several of his maps of the precolonial Bamenda region. In addition, both Hobart and William Smith Colleges and the African Studies Center at the University of Florida in Gainesville helped to fund a much needed respite for theoretical reading and reflection during my sabbatical in 1982/83. Hobart and William Smith Colleges have furthermore made possible, through Hewlett and Mellon Foundation funds, a subsidy to cover the costs of drafting illustrations for this book.

I would also like to thank the American Anthropological Association and the Centre National de la Recherche Scientifique of France for their permission to reprint brief passages from Dillon 1980b (pp. 664–669, 671) and 1981 (pp. 361–365). The former is not for further reproduction.

Finally, to my wife Joyce I owe a profound debt for all of her encouragement and assistance. In addition to spending long hours typing notes, sketching maps, and doing photographic work, she contributed her unique perspective on the fieldwork experience and displayed admirable patience with a spouse's long-term involvement in a very time-consuming research effort.

July 1988   R.G.D.

Contents

Maps and Figures

Maps

Figures

A Note on Orthography

ALL TERMS in the Meta' language have been rendered with appropriate phonetic symbols, except that conventional spellings of proper names, where known, have been maintained. The closest familiar equivalents to Meta' vowel sounds and unusual consonants are as follows:

a	As in English "ah"
e	As "ay" in English "say"
ɛ	As "e" in English "bet"
ɜ	As "u" in English "cut"
i	As "ee" in English "see"
ɨ	As "u" in "just" in those American English dialects that do not pronounce this word with an "ɜ"
o	As "o" in English "low"
ɔ	As "aw" in English "law"
u	As "oo" in English "boot"
č	As "ch" in English "change"
ŋ	As "ing" in English "sing"
ɣ	As "g" in German "sagen" ("to say") or in Spanish "hago" ("I make")
ʔ	Similar to the final sound in English "no" when this is exclaimed with force and the air flow is abruptly stopped off

Ranking and Resistance

ONE

Introduction

THIS STUDY seeks to account for the elaborate form of political organization that existed in one acephalous society of precolonial West Africa. The Meta', a sedentary farming people living on the edge of the Bamenda plateau in what is now the Republic of Cameroon, had created a polity that was remarkable for its large size and its relative peacefulness, as well as for the degree to which ranking had developed in what remained an uncentralized political system.[1] Here I hope to gain insight into the forces that produced this impressive polity by focusing upon three kinds of data: (1) information concerning Meta' political ideology, (2) case histories of conflict and political competition remembered from the precolonial era, and (3) data about the articulation of Meta' society with the wider political and economic system of the Bamenda Grassfields region.

A project such as this addresses certain questions of enduring interest. What were the limits of political cooperation for the peoples of African stateless systems? If the members of some such groups did manage to establish substantial political communities, were they positively motivated to do so or simply compelled by circumstances? And was the order that seems to have been achieved in certain of these acephalous societies more the result of consensus on the part of their members, of a balance of power among numerous political actors, or of the operation of informal processes of leadership and domination?

1. Although a more accurate phonemic transcription of the name of the society here under study would be "Mita?," I have retained the spelling "Meta'" since this is by now well established in the literature. The Meta' are sometimes also referred to as the "Menemo."

Questions such as these have long intrigued Western thinkers. Political philosophers have debated about conditions in preindustrial societies and reached quite divergent conclusions. While Hobbes (1651) portrayed life before the state as a war of all against all, Rousseau (1755) envisioned an amiable utopia. During the early and mid-twentieth century, British anthropologists sought through firsthand fieldwork to clarify the bases of social control in African stateless societies. The picture that emerged was that of an "ordered anarchy." Despite strong tendencies toward violence and self-help, numerous mechanisms were seen to contribute to social equilibrium, including the presence of cross-cutting ties and conflicting loyalties (Colson 1953, Gluckman 1956), counterbalancing forces within segmentary lineage systems (L. Bohannan 1958, Bohannan and Bohannan 1953, Evans-Pritchard 1940a, Fortes 1945, Fortes and Evans-Pritchard 1940) and periodic rituals emphasizing societal unity (Fortes 1936, 1945; Goody 1957).

As the foregoing discussion indicates, studies of elaborate stateless systems like that of the Meta' have a long tradition. Some of the best-known groups such as the Tallensi (Fortes 1945), the Lowiili (Goody 1956), the Anuak (Evans-Pritchard 1940b, 1947; Lienhardt 1957, 1958), and certain Ibo polities (Forde and Jones 1950, Uchendu 1965) resembled this Cameroonian society in many respects. However, despite decades of work on this topic, the literature reflects little agreement on how these systems are to be understood.[2] Several recent studies (Muller 1982, O'Brien 1983, Verdon 1980) have emphasized the difficulty of defining leadership roles and the scope of polity organization in acephalous precolonial groups. In addition, Muller (1985) completely discounts the possibility of explaining their organization in causal terms. After describing several complex uncentralized polities of the Jos plateau area in Nigeria as variants on some regional organizational themes, he writes as follows:

Our examination of these four contiguous societies shows that they play the subtle game of creating variations between themselves with

2. General theorists of political evolution have also tended to ignore the complex uncentralized polities of Africa. See Johnson and Earle (1987), for example.

very few basic principles of social organization . . . . [W]e can only say that these populations have devised their political structures with an eye to what their neighbors were doing. If we cannot reconstruct the process, we are at least able to contemplate the result (Muller 1985: 79).

Among those who are more sanguine about the prospects for theory, three contrasting approaches have emerged.[3] Horton (1972), who represents the first, has developed a model that attributes variations in the organization of West African stateless societies to broad patterns of population movement and interactions between groups. Dividing the precolonial societies of this area into three main types (of which only the second and third belong to our category of elaborate acephalous systems), he outlines how differing processes of migration, warfare, and settlement could have produced their sharply contrasting forms of political integration. In areas where farmland was readily available and the population increasing, Horton hypothesizes, West African peoples tended to settle in a pattern of dispersed homesteads, to organize mutual aid among households on the basis of descent, and to augment their territories through uniform outward expansion. This encouraged development of Type One, the classic form of "segmentary lineage system" with its characteristic relativity of group alignments and lack of permanent political offices. Such systems were found among the Tiv of northern Nigeria and the central Ibo. Where geography and population growth had placed uneven pressures on farmland, by contrast, "disjunctive" migration on the part of families and descent groups produced Type Two systems—"dispersed, territorially defined communities" with populations of mixed origin. Under these circumstances, lineages remained the fundamental political support groups, but since it was no longer possible to regulate interactions primarily through descent, more elaborate forms of

3. It must be stressed that this is a study dealing with *precolonial* political organization in stateless societies. Although many excellent monographs have analyzed political dynamics in formerly uncentralized societies under colonial rule (e.g., Bohannan 1957, Middleton 1960, Ruel 1969, Turner 1957), these studies have generally left unclear the relationship between the political processes that they describe and those that characterized the same political systems in precolonial times. I have therefore excluded works of this kind from the present discussion.

political organization began to appear. Among the LoDagaba and LoWiili of northern Ghana, for example, local confederacies of lineages with organizations such as earth cults provided the framework for politico-ritual integration. A distinction between "landowner" and "latecomer" descent groups, with the leaders of the former presiding over rites to the all-important earth spirit, was also fundamental to the organization of most villages. Finally, in societies like the Yako and Mbembe of southeastern Nigeria, where warfare had encouraged clustering of the population into defensible settlements, such towns regulated their affairs through cross-cutting institutions such as age grades, associations, and secret societies. In this third type of stateless system, the "large compact village," descent groups retained much less political significance.

Horton's broad treatment of stateless societies contrasts with the second major perspective on complex acephalous systems in Africa. The scholars who have adopted this line of reasoning find such groups of interest primarily because they may represent the incipient stages of political centralization.[4] Many of them also adopt some variant of the voluntaristic model of change associated with integration theory (Cohen 1978a; Haas 1982; Service 1975, 1978). In this formulation, centralization is believed to occur as community members willingly submit to new authorities because of the benefits that they can provide. One of the earliest examples of this approach can be found in Aidan Southall's well-known monograph *Alur Society*. In this study Southall analyzed the way in which acephalous groups of the Uganda-Zaire border area had sometimes welcomed Alur chieflets to settle in their midst. According to informants from the stateless societies concerned, they had acquiesced in this fashion because they had been awed by the self-confidence and

4. It should be noted that Horton (1972: 111–116) stresses the continuities between stateless societies and states in West Africa. Given such correspondences, he argues, relatively small shifts in patterns of trade or political alignments within a polity could set in motion the transition from stateless society to state. However, there is no inevitability in this, and no single direction of political evolution. Horton (1972: 81, 103–104, 109–119) also observes that approximately 35 million West Africans were citizens of stateless societies, and surmises that the ancestors of these people must have alternated between the basic types of stateless organization for at least the past millennium.

rainmaking powers of the Alur chiefs, but also because they had desired help in regulating violent conflicts within their own groups. Yet another reason was that acceptance of an Alur chief-let secured his subjects some protection from the depredations of more powerful Alur chiefs.

In more recent work, the emphasis has been upon using comparison to isolate the factors that may encourage voluntary centralization processes like those described by Southall. Harris (1962, 1965), for instance, has argued that the differential development of centralized authority in three neighboring Mbembe subgroups of southeastern Nigeria was correlated with several factors, including (1) the severity of the external pressures that each faced, (2) the extent to which their populations had been geographically compressed, (3) how clearly they were divided into opposed village units, and (4) the associated intensity of intra-societal conflict. Netting (1972) invokes some of the same variables to account for incipient centralization among the Kof-yar, the Ibo, and the Tiv of Nigeria, but differs from Harris in that he takes account of the forces impeding centralization as well. Like many stateless societies, the three groups considered by Netting were characterized by competitive egalitarianism and strongly anti-authoritarian values. Ordinarily, this orientation would make it impossible for anyone to consolidate power. However, as Netting argues, a situation of increasing population density could change this substantially, giving the public a greater stake in strong political authority and causing larger polities to coalesce around men who claim special mystical powers. Not only could these leaders adjudicate the conflicts over increasingly scarce resources that are likely to occur in such a setting, but as economic activity becomes more specialized and dependent upon intervillage trade, they can sponsor such commerce in order to assure its safety. Netting supports his centralization model with data from several groups, arguing that the type of sacral authority found in the Alur and Jukun societies represented the fully established version of that seen among the Tiv, the Ibo, and the Kofyar in an embryonic form.

A final example of an integrationist approach to centralization can be found in Cohen's (1974, 1976, 1978b) interpretation of chiefdom formation in northern Nigeria.[5] On the basis of a controlled comparison of the Pabir and Bura groups, Cohen posits that centralization may occur when an acephalous society, threatened by neighboring states, is obliged to shift from dispersed settlement to residence in a compact, fortified town. Under such circumstances, several factors may encourage acceptance of chiefly authority, including the increasing complexity of administrative problems in the now-sizeable community, the need for more effective mechanisms of conflict resolution in a densely settled town, and the necessity of organizing for a common defense. Certain other forces, such as rivalries between potential leaders and the tendencies toward fission that characterize many acephalous polities (Cohen 1978c), may still inhibit consolidation of centralized authority. However, as Cohen (1977) notes, these impediments can sometimes be overcome by complex arrangements for power sharing, such as the establishment of an office of queen mother that members of a dissident faction may be permitted to control.

The third and final perspective that provides possible insights into elaborate acephalous polities agrees with the previous one in treating them as systems in transition to more centralized authority, but differs as to the causes of this process. Adopting the assumptions of conflict theory (Cohen 1978a; Fried 1967, 1978; Haas, 1982) rather than those of the integration model, advocates of this approach regard competition for power as the primary dynamic of preindustrial political systems. From their vantage point, even the simpler stateless societies can be seen to be characterized by hierarchical relations, albeit informal and relatively invisible ones. The more complex polities are simply those in which the authorities have managed to consolidate power more effectively.

The conflict approach has been employed in varying ways by several groups of scholars. Best known are the neo-Marxists such as Claude Meillassoux (1978a, 1978b) and several of his

5. Cohen might object to being identified as a proponent of integration theory in view of how he (1978c) has argued for a complex systems approach to political evolution that incorporates aspects of both this and conflict theory. However, in the particular case study discussed below the interpretation of centralization that he develops relies primarily upon an integrationist model of political change.

French colleagues (Rey 1979; Terray 1972, 1979). Meillassoux differs from most previous analysts of acephalous systems by focusing upon effective structures of control within the kinship system. He attempts to understand these by clarifying the social and economic transactions upon which they rest. Meillassoux's (1978a, 1978b) model of the "self-sustaining agricultural society," for example, portrays the local farming community as a highly competitive system in which elders base their dominant power upon control of economic resources and nubile women, as well as on alliances with peers in neighboring groups.

Meillassoux's formulation is essentially as follows: Given the delayed returns characteristic of agricultural production and the elders' greater experience and knowledge of farming techniques, they will naturally tend to supervise both production and the family granaries in which the harvest is stored. This permits them to consolidate control over resources on a day-to-day basis. However, their small household groups still face insecurities arising from demographic fluctuations and the difficulties of arranging for reproduction of the productive unit itself. As the elders move to redress such imbalances by collaboration with counterparts in neighboring groups, they also come to regulate the exchanges of elite goods that function as bridewealth. This allows them to monopolize control of marriageable women. Warfare further strengthens their hand, since uncertain conditions will tend to limit the contacts of junior males in groups where they might find marriage partners on their own. Finally, on an ideological plane, "ancestor worship" helps to legitimate the power of the elders.

The local lineage-based community thus becomes a gerontocracy in which junior males' chances to establish independent households are severely limited. As for the transition to a more "class-stratified" polity, Meillassoux argues that this could occur as the result of unsettled conditions involving interlineage conflicts over women. Aristocratic clans could emerge whenever certain lineages mobilized sufficient force to impose tributary relations on their neighbors, while simultaneously beginning to marry endogamously themselves. With such transformations of social and economic relations, a new asymmetrical structure of exchange, justified by an altered form of "kinship" ideology, could become established in the society.

The conflict approach to acephalous systems has also been employed in several recent analyses by British social anthropologists. Though critical of the latent functionalism and ahistorical approach that they feel characterizes some neo-Marxist studies, the authors of these papers nonetheless build upon the base that neo-Marxists provide. Brown (1984), for example, explains precolonial Klowe society of Liberia as an informally stratified system in which lineage head-elders prevailed through their control of marital transactions and ties with counterparts in neighboring communities. His model of Klowe accounts, at least provisionally, for several distinctive features of that system, including the preponderance of middle-aged bachelors, the fact that marriage was intratribal while trade and warfare were intertribal, and the pattern whereby iron production and the operation of oracles were controlled by lineage elders in certain areas. Fardon (1984, 1985) has similarly reanalyzed Tiv society from a conflict perspective. He demonstrates that an unstable system of ranking, based upon male agnates competing for wards to allocate in "sister" exchange marriages, underlay social relations among the Tiv. Fardon also compares the Tiv with a wide range of nearby groups in order to show how permanent hierarchy and political centralization could result from an increasing emphasis upon hereditary marriage lordship.

A final variant of the conflict approach seeks to explain political complexity in uncentralized social fields as the result of outside manipulation. Here Ottenberg's (1958) paper on Ibo oracles and intergroup relations provides an early example. In this analysis, Ottenberg demonstrated how an oracle of regional significance with a widespread network of agents had become established in Iboland as the Aro Chukwu village group attempted to expand its trading network and consolidate religious and economic influence over many previously autonomous polities. More recently, Burnham (1980) has tried to account for nineteenth-century chiefdom formation among the Gbaya of northern Cameroon in a similar way. According to his model, centralization occurred when the rulers of nearby Muslim emirates lent their support to certain Gbaya who aspired to chieftaincy. Such client chieflets then served as useful intermediaries in the process of extracting slaves from the Gbaya area.

The foregoing discussion has illustrated the wide variety of viewpoints that scholars have adopted in the attempt to understand the elaborate stateless systems of precolonial Africa. Several distinct lines of inquiry have been explored over the years, and three principal ways of looking at these societies have been developed. Still, numerous questions remain unresolved. Some of the more important can be summarized as follows:

1. Are elaborate acephalous polities to be seen as systems in process of centralization, as both integration and conflict theorists tend to represent them, or as examples of political specialization without "progressive" evolutionary implications, as Horton's model might seem to imply?

2. Was political competition or the need for cooperation the more powerful force in the development of complex stateless systems?

3. How important was the phenomenon of egalitarian resistance to centralization in these polities, and what factors could overcome it?

4. To what extent, if any, was conflict management the focus in complex stateless systems, and to what degree did the need for cooperation in conflict resolution encourage their development of specialized institutions?

5. How are we to understand the impact of broader regional systems and processes upon the more complicated stateless societies?

Many things have of course impeded resolution of these questions. For instance, most scholars have tended to take only one of the three main models into account. Given such an approach, some of the critical issues have yet to be clearly formulated or adequately debated. In addition, a lack of appropriate data has been a serious problem. A full understanding of the questions just listed would obviously require the use of several rather different kinds of information. To determine the precise mix of consensus and coercion that characterized a stateless society's political order, for example, both comprehensive data concerning political ideology and actual case histories of competition and conflict would clearly be needed. These two types of data would also help in assessing the argument of integration theorists that the members of societies experiencing intensifying social conflicts would welcome aspirants to chiefship because of their unique capabilities in dispute settlement. Finally, detailed information about the interactions between particular stateless societies and their neighbors would provide a sounder basis for evaluating hypotheses, such as Horton's, that treat these relations as major influences upon the development of acephalous systems.

However, while the need for a wide range of data is apparent, most existing studies fall well short of this goal. Much of the data is of course derived from research done by scholars with a functionalist orientation during the earliest phases of political anthropology in Africa. Although these researchers excelled in producing lengthy ethnographies based upon their informants' ideal models of political organization, they only occasionally included case histories illustrating actual political behavior. They also tended to view stateless societies as rather self-contained systems. In this context, there was frequently little effort to reconstruct detailed pictures of war and trade with neighboring groups or to analyze the effects of such relations upon the societies concerned.

More recent researchers have of course been less subject to biases of this kind. However, since most must still base their analyses upon data provided by the older studies or upon limited oral and archival sources, their accounts contain little more case-history material or detailed analysis of intersocietal relations than the classic monographs of the 1940s and 1950s (see, for example, Brown 1984; Cohen 1974, 1976; Fardon 1984, 1985; Harris 1962, 1965).[6]

Theory thus threatens to outstrip data in studies of African stateless societies. It is much easier to formulate dynamic models of precolonial stateless systems than to validate these with the kind of fragmentary information that is normally available. In the case of Meta' society, however, oral sources concerning both precolonial political ideology and actual conflicts within

6. Netting (1973, 1974) provides one important exception to this generalization in that he has taken pains to document precolonial and early colonial patterns of conflict among the Kofyar by analyzing a large body of memory cases.

the society are uncommonly rich. Moreover, owing to the research that a number of scholars have carried out on neighboring groups over the past twenty years, our knowledge of the precolonial regional system of which Meta' formed a part is both detailed and comprehensive. Meta' thus offers an unusual chance to explore many issues that previous studies of acephalous systems have found difficult to assess. Here, I shall try to make the maximum use of this opportunity by building up an interpretation of Meta' society that illuminates both its internal political dynamics and the impact of the regional system upon it. My ultimate objective is to do justice to a type of precolonial society, the elaborate stateless system, that has thus far been only imperfectly understood.

TWO

Fieldwork Setting and Research Methodology

IN ANY reconstructive study, it is essential to take account of recent changes that may have altered the informants' understanding of their society's past and to describe fieldwork methods so that readers may evaluate statements about precolonial organization for themselves. I therefore digress briefly to clarify the context of field research. After first summarizing the ways in which twentieth-century changes had affected Meta' society up to the time of fieldwork, I shall then explain the methods that were employed to obtain data about precolonial Meta'.

The Meta' in Cameroonian History

The Republic of Cameroon (see Map 1), of which the Meta' are now citizens, has had a complex history. "Kamerun" was first brought under colonial rule by Germany, but this was the result of a slow process that advanced at an uneven rate in different parts of the territory. A small German patrol under Báron Eugen Zintgraff first visited the Bamenda highlands area of the interior in 1889, but no permanent administrative outpost was established at the time. It was not until 1902 that a military station was commissioned at Bamenda. The primary German motive was to organize a more orderly system of labor recruitment. Since the population of Bamenda was considerably denser than that on the coast, it could supply the labor needed for the plantations that were being established there.[1] In this context, the

1. See Chilver (1963), Levine (1964), and Rudin (1938) for more complete dis-

German approach to colonial administration in the interior of Kamerun was indirect. As a rule, the Germans selected the most powerful chiefs in each locality and administered the people through them. In many cases, however, this had the effect of inappropriately reinforcing leaders who had possessed only ritual seniority among their peoples. A regular system of taxation was not introduced until 1909, and the judicial system under German officers was never formalized.

A hiatus occurred in the colonial administration of Kamerun during the First World War: at this time no European power was in effective control of the interior. After the war, the greater part of the former German colony was assigned to France under the League of Nations, while a small portion was mandated to the British. The latter territory was known as "Southern Cameroons" during this period, and it is within this area that the Meta' reside.

The British managed to establish some degree of administrative control over the Bamenda area in the early 1920s. But since the "indirect rule" model, developed in Nigeria, was followed, their approach was, in some respects, always very loose. Unacceptable precolonial practices such as warfare were proscribed, a head tax was established, and jurisdiction over serious "criminal" cases was taken out of the hands of local chieftains and village councilors. However, because there were very few actual European administrators and technicians, much of the day-to-day political process remained in the hands of traditional leaders. During the British period in Southern Cameroons, a number of missions played an important role, both by converting Cameroonians to Christianity and by establishing local-level schools and teacher-training colleges.

British rule in Southern Cameroons ended in 1961. In 1960, the French-controlled eastern part of Cameroon had gained its independence, and, when a plebiscite was held under United Nations auspices in 1961, the Southern Cameroonians voted to unite with their French-speaking brothers in a federal republic.

During the entire colonial era, the Meta' people were admin-

cussion of the colonial period in Cameroon. Much of the description in this section is based on their work.

istered at least in part through their own precolonial political framework. However, the exact format varied considerably from time to time. Conquered by a German-led expedition in 1903 and once again in 1905, the villages[2] of the Bome and Zang valleys were then declared subject to the neighboring Chief of Bali-Nyonga, who was the principal local ally of the Germans. The remaining Meta' of the Medig valley area were placed under the authority of Nfawminyen (Fonnyen), one of the local village heads. When the people of Bome and Medig continued to prove recalcitrant, they were forced to settle about 10 kilometers away at Bali town, with different villages occupying separate neighborhoods and managing affairs through their traditional leaders. At first, official contact between the Meta' and the Germans was channeled through the Chief of Bali, but when the latter proved incapable of controlling his "vassals," Meta' village heads were permitted to communicate directly with the administration in Bamenda. The Meta' people who had been relocated began returning to their original homes between 1916 and 1921, when the Germans were no longer present to enforce Bali suzerainty, and after some inquiry and negotiation, this move was accepted by the new British administration.[3]

The way in which "indirect rule" was applied in Meta' during the British period varied considerably. In the 1920s, attempts were made to treat the Chief of Zang Tabi village as the "Clan Head" for all Meta'. The British urged the other village leaders to recognize his authority in matters of tax collection and civil dispute settlement. However, since these attempts were based on British misunderstandings of precolonial relationships, administering the entire Meta' group through its "Clan Head" proved unworkable. In the 1930s, the "traditional" political organization of Meta' was carefully reassessed, and it was decided

2. The term "village" is being used here to refer to localized political units, of usually several hundred persons, that were formed through federation of two or more unrelated patrilineal clan sections. It should be kept in mind that, since the Meta' lived in scattered homesteads, the village was in no sense a compact settlement.

3. *Deutsches Kolonialblatt*, 1903, v. 14: 493–494; 1905, v. 16: 667–668. File Ab4, Report on the Political Situation in Bali, 1921 (Buea Archives). File Ab18, Collected Records on Meta Intelligence, 1920s (Buea Archives). C. J. A. Gregg, A.D.O., "Meta: An Assessment Report on the Meta Clan of the Bamenda, Division, Cameroons Province," January 1, 1924 (Buea Archives).

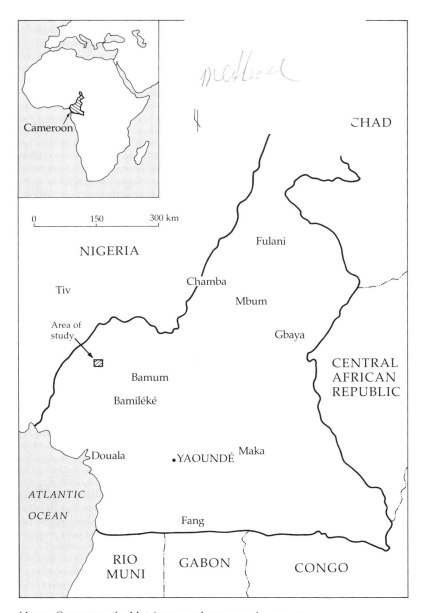

Map 1. Cameroon, the Meta' area, and some nearby groups.

to treat villages as the basic administrative units. A single Meta' "Customary Court," staffed by a large number of village chiefs and other political leaders on a rotating basis, was also established.[4]

With some qualifications, important features of the precolonial Meta' political system can be said to have continued into the present. The move to Bali disrupted both the territorial organization and the prior political relationships of certain Meta' villages. However, when those affected were allowed to return to their homes, most reoccupied previous compound sites. The settlement pattern of precolonial days was therefore largely preserved at the time of my fieldwork (although some people had begun moving their compounds to the roadsides during the 1960s). The former lineage organization had also been retained, and a system of village chieftaincies, resembling the precolonial one in certain respects, persisted.

Some of the important differences between Meta' political organization in 1900 and that in 1970 were that warfare was no longer practiced; that the elaborate precolonial legal system, largely based on supernatural concepts, had been formally superseded by a system of customary and magistrate's courts; and that the political system as a whole was much less fluid. On the one hand, the process of lineage segmentation was operating at a much-reduced rate. On the other, a precolonial system in which new villages were continually being created and some had several "chiefs" had been transformed into one of fixed and permanent units under individual village heads. A principle of "one village, one chief" had somehow become established in the process of organizing "indirect rule." Finally, while descent groups still competed for land, wives, and other resources, this process seems to have become less intense than in precolonial times. Some of the need for competition had been eliminated when wage labor and cash cropping introduced economic alternatives. In short, much of the form of precolonial political organization was preserved in 1970, but some of the functions had been altered.

4. Chilver (1963). C. J. A. Gregg, A.D.O., "Meta: An Assessment Report on the Meta Clan of the Bamenda Division, Cameroons Province," January 1, 1924 (Buea Archives). C. H. Croasdale, A.D.O., "Intelligence Report on the Menemo

The Collection and Interpretation of Data

The reconstruction presented here is based upon both written and oral sources, with far greater reliance being placed upon the latter. The reasons for this are twofold. First and most important, in 1970 Meta' society presented a very favorable environment for oral history. Although the Meta' had no specialized historians, such as are found in some African kingdoms, all Meta' citizens were inculcated with a profound respect for the past. As a result, traditional customs were frequently discussed, and a major objective of most rituals was to recreate exactly that symbolic order that the forefathers had known (see pp. 75–77). The conservatism of the elders with whom I spoke may also have derived partly from their resettlement at Bali. The experience of forced relocation by a colonial authority may have made them more mindful of their cultural heritage and more strongly motivated to reassert that legacy than the members of less disturbed groups were. Among other things, the painstaking manner in which they recreated their former social landscape upon the return from Bali suggests this.[5] Finally, the explicitness with which political prerogatives had been defined in precolonial Meta' also facilitated ethnohistorical work. As Pospisil (1978: 39–40) has noted, where colonized peoples have previously possessed formal offices and titles, it is much easier to reconstruct their precolonial political systems, since the former institutions provide convenient frames of reference to use in discussions with informants. In Meta' not only was this the case, but many of the precolonial political roles had persisted even down to the time of fieldwork.

A second reason for relying more heavily on oral than on written sources was the paucity of early documentary material germane to the subject of research. At the time of fieldwork, the German records of the Cameroonian archives in Buea were

Speaking Families of the Widekum Tribe in Bamenda Division of the Cameroons Province,'' May, 1933 (Buea Archives).

5. A reconstruction of the 1900 settlement pattern for the entire Bome valley revealed that the vast majority of descent groups there continued to occupy their former territories in 1970. Moreover, in three quarters where house-by-house mapping was carried out, most compounds were located on pre-Bali sites.

closed to researchers, and more recent reports indicate that they contain little that would shed light on the topic of this study (Austen 1974; Christraud Geary, personal communication; Warnier 1983: 610–611, 622). In addition, those turn-of-the-century reports that I was able to obtain concerned mainly the process of conquest and the problems of reinforcing Bali control over Meta'. While such accounts can be extremely useful in reconstructing early colonial history, they provide little direct information about the precolonial political system itself.

The British "assessment" and "intelligence" reports of the 1920s and 1930s offer different problems and possibilities. Since the mandate of their authors was to investigate traditional political institutions as a basis for establishing indirect rule, they paid much greater attention to precolonial precedents than did their German predecessors. However, they were also further removed from the precolonial era, and clearly were the focus of intense lobbying by various leaders and interest groups. As a result, their reports are useful only for limited purposes. For example, they provide a sense of how the informants' expectations may have been shaped by earlier experiences of giving testimony to European administrative officers during the conflicts and reorganizations of the colonial era, and they give some rather detailed accounts of clan and village migrations that can be compared with those collected in 1970–71.

A final source of supplementary data was the field journals of other anthropologists and historians who have conducted brief research tours in Meta'. Such notes were available from P. M. Kaberry's 1947 interviews on social and political organization in the Medig valley, from E. M. Chilver's 1963 work on political organization in Bome, from J. P. Warnier's 1973 inquiries on law and conflict in Bome, and from M. J. Rowlands' 1977 research on precolonial trade and economics in all parts of Meta'. These fieldnotes provided very useful information, and I am much indebted to their authors and trustees.

The actual fieldwork on which this study was based was carried out between December 1969 and July 1971. With only brief interruptions to consult the Buea archives and renew visas, my wife and I resided in the Meta' village of Funam during the entire period. The primary unit of study was a group of villages in the Bome valley. The population of this valley was slightly more than 4,000 at the time of fieldwork, and it appears to have been about the same in 1900. A large quantity of data was also obtained from villages in Zang and Medig, the other two main valleys of Meta'.

The fieldwork was essentially divided into three stages in which different approaches were used. During the first three months in Meta', most of my time was devoted to learning the language. I worked for several hours every morning with a language informant and practiced conversation with neighbors in the afternoons. I also attended events such as mortuary celebrations, markets, and village council meetings and took general ethnographic notes.

During the following three months, I worked without an assistant. Informants were interviewed in the Meta' language, and, at the same time, the study of contemporary Meta' ethnography was continued through both directed interviewing and participant observation. This produced some information on precolonial political organization, but it was generally of à superficial kind, and the approach used in this second stage of fieldwork was ultimately abandoned, since it would not have led to fulfillment of the main research goals.

The final stage of fieldwork, to which the following discussion of methodology mainly refers, began in the sixth month and lasted for about eleven more. During this period, I worked with a Meta' research assistant, a man in his forties, and explored aspects of the precolonial system with elderly informants. We alternated between discussing Meta' political concepts and eliciting remembered case histories. In interviewing older informants, the assistant served as an interpreter. This made it possible to examine political concepts and situations on a more sophisticated level, from the Meta' point of view, than would otherwise have been possible. At the same time, the dangers of relying wholly on communication through an interpreter were obviated, because I understood much of what was being said.

Most of the day was usually spent working in this way during the final year of fieldwork. The interviews with elderly informants normally lasted about three hours. I came to each with a concrete idea of the topic that needed to be covered and began by asking directly about it. But the informants were also given as much free rein as possible so that their descriptions of precolonial political institutions and behavior would emerge spontaneously and in a culturally relevant way. Whenever the flow of testimony stopped, I was prepared with many alternative questions from my notebooks and quickly shifted over to these.

On some occasions, the Meta' research assistant was himself used as an informant after a primary interview with an older man. This proved useful whenever there appeared to be ambiguities or contradictions in an elderly informant's account at the close of an interview. In situations like this, the assistant effectively reinterpreted what the original informant had said. (See pp. 22–25 for a further discussion of this aspect of the methodology.)

The assistant, Chief Fonbah, was an ideal person to serve in this capacity. He had a good knowledge of English and, at the same time, was well grounded in the "traditional culture," since he had grown up in an important chief's household. Moreover, he was a chief himself, having been installed some twelve years previous to the fieldwork. Finally, he had served as a judge in the Meta' customary court in which persons knowledgeable in Meta' law decide civil cases in terms of its principles. In general, Chief Fonbah's prestige and good reputation lent credibility and respectability to my inquiries in the eyes of the informants and opened many doors. However, since he was chief of a very small Meta' village, he did not have an important political position to protect, and such considerations did not significantly influence his comments and interpretations. Chief Fonbah also developed a considerable interest in building up an objective picture of precolonial politics by comparing different informants' accounts.

The core of information about the Meta' political system was obtained from elderly informants, many of whom had been alive in precolonial times. Individual interviews were conducted with around eighty such persons from all parts of Meta', and about twenty of these became regular informants.

The system of village-level leadership roles, described in Chapter 6, provides a convenient example of the way in which particular topics were explored with informants. Chief Fonbah and I spent about two months working almost exclusively on this subject. We began by asking numerous informants for descriptions of the ideal roles of various kinds of village-level leaders in the period around 1900—i.e., who the leaders were, how they acquired their positions, what their duties were, etc. After this, we investigated the specific system of leadership roles in about a dozen villages in order to determine how much variation there had been. Finally, numerous case histories of process and change in village organization were obtained from all over Meta' (e.g., remembered conflicts over chieftaincy, cases in which lineage heads had been edged out of their positions on the village council, actual disputes settled by village leaders in the past, and so forth). After two months of this, we had achieved a fairly good understanding of precolonial Meta' village organization, in terms of both ideals and concrete cases. Information on other aspects of the precolonial Meta' political system was obtained in a similar way.

Since Meta' political concepts are discussed at length in this study, it is important to give some indication of how such data were acquired. Put most directly, information about how the Meta' think was obtained by asking Meta' informants. Many of these appeared to be quite aware of their own culture and were always ready to explain specific aspects of it. *Iči ʒbɛŋ* ("the custom of the country") was something that was endlessly debated in circles of men drinking palm wine on market days, in village council meetings, and in many other contexts. Some idea of how the Meta' considered their own culture on an abstract level is conveyed by the fact that the English phrase "native law and custom" had been taken over from former British colonial personnel and was used liberally in public discussions and debates. On a number of occasions, I was solemnly informed by a Meta' friend that I was about to witness some "real native law and custom" as a preface to a ritual or ceremony.

Many examples of how the Meta' discussed specific political concepts and ideas are included in the following chapters. The long analysis of concepts of village chiefship in Chapter 6 probably provides the most detailed illustration of this (see pp. 131–142). However, some explicit discussion of the relation between Meta' informants' statements and the generalizations about Meta' concepts made in this book may also be useful. One convenient example is provided on p. 76, where it is remarked that the hereditary buffalo-horn drinking cup of the lineage head was seen as a means of establishing continuity with the dead fathers of the patrilineage and of drawing upon their mystical power in ritual contexts. This statement is an important part of the overall presentation, because it helps to account for descriptions of certain kinds of behavior that appeared in many of the informants' precolonial case histories and also in their discussions of how the political system ideally worked. At first glance, the point made on p. 76 might appear to be a secondary interpretation, imposed by the ethnographer, on a large body of data concerning lineage organization, successors' cups, mystical power, and other related topics. Actually, however, the statement is an almost direct rendering of Meta' informants' ideas in language very close to their own.

The notions about successors' cups used in this example first became clear in two interviews conducted March 15, 1971. On that day, we began with an elderly informant named Isak. He had recently been in charge of an installation ceremony in which a young man was confirmed as the successor of his dead father, a lineage head. During that ritual, which we observed and tape-recorded, a problem arose about whether the new lineage head would be allowed to use the sacrificial cup associated with his position. Several members of the lineage argued that it was too powerful for him to control, since it had been employed by previous incumbents to kill their kinsmen. It was finally decided that the young man would be permitted use of his cup, but one member of the lineage told us privately that his actions would be carefully monitored by his kin.

When Fonbah and I went to speak with Isak we again asked him whether the youth who had succeeded to the lineage headship would have access to the sacrificial cup of his father and received the following reply:

Jacob will be using his real successor's cup. Why should they install him as lineage head if he were not going to drink from it? The cups are important. If they are doing some sacrifice in the lineage and the successor forgets his cup, they will tell him to go and bring it before they start. A successor with a bad character will be given his father's cup, but if the dead lineage head had two sons, the old men will meet and change the dead man's choice of a successor. If a person in the lineage commits incest with a clan sister, all the fathers [old men] of the lineage take their hereditary cups and make a ritual statement [*njɔm*], and the offender will become sick and die within a year. If somebody steals my father's thing [i.e., land, movable property, or a political office that ego has inherited from his deceased father], I pour from my cup and make a ritual statement, and God [*Ŋwi3*] will protect my right. If I am poor, I ask God and my dead father why the father appointed me to be his successor in this compound if I was going to have nothing to eat. Then I take my father's cup and pour wine or water from it and make the following ritual statement: Since I am going to market, let me sell my things and profit from it. Then God will help me.

These statements by Isak are fairly typical of the kind of information about political concepts that was obtained in discussions with informants who had been alive prior to the German conquest, although, in this case, the point of reference was a recent "traditional" ritual rather than some aspect of political organization in precolonial times.[6] The literal meaning of Isak's statement was clear—i.e., how the cup was to be used, what kinds of powers were associated with it, that its having been given to him by his dead father was important, etc. However, more questions were raised by his account than it answered, and it was evident that he was making many assumptions about the supernatural power of the cup and mystical power in general that he did not explicate. Without an understanding of these hidden premises, it would have been difficult for me to make a generalization about the meaning of a successor's cup that would be at once significant and ethnographically correct.

Faced with these problems, I spent the afternoon talking with Fonbah, my assistant, about the meaning of Isak's testimony. The general question posed to Fonbah was: how does Isak visualize the powers of his father's cup? Fonbah's answer was essentially as follows:

6. Certain elderly informants described concepts and beliefs in a more abstract way; see, for example, the hunting ritual outlined on pp. 158–159.

Since many fathers have been drinking from the cup and dying, their ɜzwi ["spirits/breath"] are in the cup. Therefore, the present successor who uses the cup and calls out the names of the old ones who have died joins with them, and God will quickly hear his request. As people say, "the breath of his fathers is in that cup" [ɜzwi mɨmbaʔ mɨt zɨnga tɔʔ ze]. It is believed that since many fathers have been drinking from the cup and breathing in it, their breath or smell [ɜzwi] is still inside it and will remain there, however much the cup is washed. These cups are like a record or history in which each father is present. If the current successor [i.e., lineage head, possessor of the cup] takes the cup and speaks, others will know that he is telling the truth. He would not take the cup and speak unless he knew that he was speaking the truth. If people had known how to keep written records in the early days, they would not have needed these cups. When you say that the "spirits" of the dead fathers are in the cup, you almost mean that all the beliefs of all fathers are in the cup. The cup of a father is the most important possession of his that can be passed on to his sons. If a father died, having given no indication of which son he wanted for a successor, the first one to get the cup in his possession would be the successor. If the others see that he has the cup, they will have to surrender to his power.

Taken together, the statements of Isak and Fonbah illustrate that the points asserted on p. 76 concerning the power and meaning of hereditary sacrificial cups are not interpretations imposed on the data by me as the ethnographer, but rather fairly close restatements of Meta' informants' own ideas. All of the other political concepts discussed in the following chapters are similarly rooted in the informants' statements, and the only reason that all of this evidence has not been presented is that it would have required a text many times the length of the present one.

This brief example of fieldwork technique brings up several other important methodological problems. First, there is the question of how one can assume that informants' concepts, such as those outlined above, were also important in 1900. This issue was carefully considered in the process of fieldwork and writing. In general, whether data on contemporary Meta' culture can be projected into the past and the degree to which they can are matters to be decided independently for each type of information. In the example just discussed, the ideas about a successor's cup emerged in their clearest form in the summation of

Fonbah, but they also appeared in the accounts of elderly informants. For example, notions about the power of hereditary drinking cups appeared many times in their general descriptions of how rituals with political significance were performed in precolonial times, and they were likewise expressed in a number of the precolonial case histories. Given these facts, it seems justifiable to assume that concepts such as those described by Fonbah and Isak were also important in the past.

The second methodological issue raised by the foregoing example is the question of how different kinds of information can be used in conjunction to build up a fuller picture of the past. It has already been noted that the core of information about precolonial Meta' political organization was derived from the descriptions of informants who had been alive in the period under consideration. However, in the example, an important concept first came to light because of participant observation at a modern ritual and was then elucidated by intensive interviewing with both younger and older informants. The result of using these different types of data, obtained through radically different techniques, was a fuller understanding of an important Meta' concept that had probably influenced behavior considerably in the past. This understanding, in turn, helped to flesh out the facts of precolonial political organization as given by elderly informants. For example, it permitted greater insight into precolonial cases where the different sons of a deceased chief were said to have struggled for the possession of his cup, as well as into rituals in which successors' cups were used to establish mystically-sanctioned prohibitions against intervillage warfare. Thus, if data from contemporary ethnographic work had not been used as an integral part of the historical reconstruction, the significance of many of the historical accounts, in terms of Meta' political concepts, might never have been fully apprehended.

Finally, a word should be said about the character of the informants. The present picture of precolonial Meta' political organization is based on work with a diverse, but carefully chosen, set of persons.[7] The criterion by which informants were selected

7. A list of these informants is provided in the Appendix, along with their village and clan affiliations and dates of testimony.

was whether or not they were knowledgeable in the areas of history and political ideology and process in Meta'. This statement assumes that a person might have become so knowledgeable in any of a number of ways. Some informants were already young adults when the colonial period began for the Meta' around 1903. For example, one informant was estimated to be in his nineties in 1970, and several others were in their mid-eighties. From such men, fairly accurate and detailed descriptions of political institutions and events in the precolonial period could be obtained. However, on some important questions, much younger informants could give more detailed accounts. Thus, a man who had succeeded to an important political office might have been steeped in knowledge about the precolonial duties associated with his post by his elders. The testimony of such a title holder could be very important when used together with the descriptions of the older informants. Similarly, as has already been demonstrated, excellent data concerning rather subtle precolonial political concepts could sometimes be obtained from younger informants. By itself, this kind of information could be suspect, but when it was found to dovetail with that given by older persons, its validity and usefulness in historical reconstruction could be ascertained. In summary, a great number of informants of all ages and a variety of techniques were used in the research on which this study is based, and the validity of each type of informant and each kind of information was established empirically by a process of careful cross-checking. This methodology was devised to make the most of the kinds of data that were available.

The Plan of This Book

The goal of this study is to produce a reconstruction of precolonial Meta' political organization by using the insights and methodological advances of modern political anthropology. I am particularly concerned with illuminating conflicts and political processes, with exploring the complex relationship between political ideology and behavior, and with analyzing the articulation of the Meta' polity with the broader regional system. To facilitate achievement of these goals, I have organized the presentation as follows: In Chapter 3, I describe the overall system of the Bamenda plateau region and the ways in which the societies neighboring Meta' varied in their political organization. After establishing this essential context, I provide an introduction to Meta' itself in Chapter 4—its history, its economic organization, its system of household production, and its fundamental ideological orientations. Chapters 5 through 11 contain the bulk of the data regarding different aspects of precolonial Meta' political organization—patrilineal descent, village organization, and political relations in the intervillage sphere. Here, convenience of exposition has dictated a rather hybrid approach. In some instances, I have separated the discussion of ideology and case histories, while elsewhere it has been possible to include both kinds of data within a single chapter. Chapters 6 and 7, which focus on the ideal model of village organization, and Chapter 9, dealing with process in village-level politics, illustrate the former approach, whereas Chapter 8, analyzing ideal and real behavior in village-level conflict management, exemplifies the latter. Finally, Chapter 12 presents a synthesis in which I draw upon both my own analysis of Meta' and data about the Bamenda regional system to provide an interpretation of Meta' political organization in 1900.[8]

8. A word is in order about the relationship between the interpretation given here and that contained in my doctoral dissertation (Dillon 1973). In that work, I used the model of Meta' political organization in 1900 that I had reconstructed as the basis for interpreting oral traditions regarding the introduction of chiefship to Meta' society. While the evidence concerning these developments has not changed, my own views concerning the limits of ethnohistorical reconstruction have. It is now clear to me that, in the absence of a real baseline in knowledge of the earlier political system (i.e., the one in 1800 or 1750), no discussion of what that system changed into can be meaningful. And the Meta' oral traditions that I collected in 1969–71 do not present a picture of that earlier system that is sufficiently detailed or adequately supported.

THREE

The Bamenda Plateau as a Regional System

OVER THE past twenty years, many anthropological and historical studies have helped to clarify how the precolonial societies of the Cameroon "Grassfields" were linked together in a single regional system.[1] Among others, Brain (1972), Chilver and Kaberry (1968), Geary (1979), Geary and Njoya (1985), Kaberry (1952), Kopytoff (1981), Latour (1985), Masquelier (1978), Nkwi (1976), Nkwi and Warnier (1982), O'Neil (1987), Rowlands (1979), Tardits (1980), Warnier (1975, 1983, 1985), Warnier and Fowler (1979), and Wilhelm (1981) have contributed notably to these efforts. In this chapter, I will summarize some of their findings, focusing particularly on the Bamenda plateau—a portion of the western Grassfields—and its margins. This should not only convey a sense of the political diversity that characterized the region but also provide a more adequate basis for understanding the Meta' polity in regional context.

Linguistic research indicates that the ancestors of the peoples now speaking the various Grassfields languages have comprised a distinct population for many centuries (Warnier 1979; 1983: 16, 341). However, the particular political and economic system that flourished in their homeland during immediate precolonial times had only recently come into being. The change was set in motion when bands of horse-mounted Chamba slave raiders entered the area to establish temporary war camps during the

1. The "Grassfields," a term that derives from the German colonial period, refers to the well watered highland savanna region in western Cameroon. It is bounded by forest to the south and west and drier country to the north.

1820s and 1830s (Chilver 1981, Chilver and Kaberry 1968: 15–19, Kaberry and Chilver 1961).

The Chamba intrusion was itself part of a larger pattern of raiding from Adamawa to the north. Such forays, which were indirectly stimulated by the Fulani Jihad in northern Nigeria, affected various portions of the Cameroon highlands throughout the nineteenth century (Chilver 1981, Nkwi and Warnier 1982: 79–85, Warnier 1983: 296–302). On the Bamenda plateau, however, the Chamba raiders seem to have had their major effect in the early part of this period. By the mid-1830s they had suffered a serious defeat near Dschang and split into several groups. Then, having lost their horses, they began to establish settlements in which they were joined by captives and refugees from the groups that they had raided (Chilver 1981, Chilver and Kaberry 1968: 15–19, Kaberry and Chilver 1961, Nkwi and Warnier 1982: 79–83).

Though brief, the Chamba incursion had profound effects upon the peoples of Bamenda. On the one hand, it led to the foundation by the mid-1860s of Bali-Nyonga—a strong Chamba chiefdom on the plateau itself (Chilver 1981). On the other hand, it prompted indigenous groups to completely reorganize the social landscape. Prior to 1820 much of the population of the plateau seems to have resided in dispersed compounds and hamlets. The Chamba raids thoroughly disrupted this pattern, as people sought security by retreating to inaccessible mountains and clustering around the residences of leading chiefs (Nkwi and Warnier 1982: 86–87, 120–121; Warnier 1975: 89–91, 439–447; Warnier and Fowler 1979). By the mid-nineteenth century, some fugitive plateau groups had reestablished themselves on their former sites. The people of Mankon (see Map 2), for example, had returned from their refuge in Bafut (Warnier 1985: 208). But by now the pattern was everywhere one of clustered settlements. Certain groups also constructed earthworks and ditches or used natural marshes as defensive barriers. Finally, oral traditions suggest that some polities shifted from descent-based to territorial organization at this time, and Nkwi and Warnier have hypothesized that many societies may have abandoned an earlier system of matrilineal descent as well (Nkwi and Warnier 1982: 86–87, Warnier 1983: 354–357).

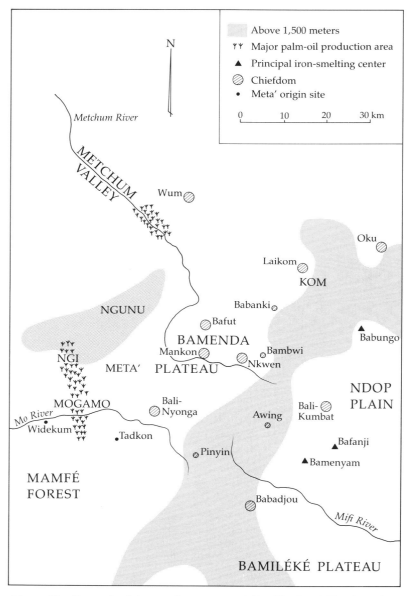

Map 2. The Bamenda plateau region, ca. 1900 (after Nkwi and Warnier 1982; Warnier 1975, 1983, 1985; Warnier and Fowler 1979).

The Regional Economy

The Chamba raids also seem to have precipitated important changes in the economy of Bamenda (Warnier 1983: 27–40, Warnier and Fowler 1979). Before these attacks, for example, a highly technical process of iron smelting in tall cylindrical furnaces was practiced at numerous sites scattered across the plateau and in the mountains to the east. Afterwards, however, such smelting was restricted to several fortified towns in the Ndop plain farther to the east, where it was organized as a large-scale industry. During this time, chiefdoms in Bamenda relied upon trade with the iron centers of Ndop for supplies of new iron to supplement the limited amount that they could reprocess from slag and scrap in simple open-hearth furnaces.

Such changes in iron technology and trade suggest that the Chamba raids must have affected the early nineteenth-century economy of the Bamenda peoples profoundly. Unfortunately, it is at present impossible to reconstruct the prior system in any detail (Warnier 1983: 339–358). What is clear is that, in the absence of further raids from the north, a different regional economy was taking shape on the Bamenda plateau. By the second half of the nineteenth century, the many small and medium-sized polities of this area had evolved complex new patterns of specialization and exchange (Warnier 1985: 11–96).

Trade between these societies was encouraged by the considerable diversity of the local ecosystem. The natural environment of Bamenda (see Map 2) included a central plateau consisting of rolling hills and grasslands; rugged mountains to the southeast, east, and west; and river valleys descending to forests in the northwest and southwest. Although all the groups in this area practiced subsistence cultivation, the involvement of most in production for exchange had given rise to a truly regional division of labor. The primary axis of intra-regional trade was east-west in orientation (Warnier 1985: 11–21, 73–82). Iron and iron products from the Ndop plain villages in the east were exchanged against palm oil that was produced in large quantities in the forest to the west and became a key component in the diet (see Map 2). It has been estimated that 1,000–2,000 metric tons of palm oil were consumed within this system each year (Warnier 1985: 15–17), and approximately 100 tons of iron were produced annually by just one of the iron-smelting villages during the late nineteenth century (Warnier and Fowler 1979). Groups located between the oil and iron belts provided other commodities to the exchange network (Warnier 1985: 22–72). Those in the center of the Bamenda plateau, for example, exported maize and beans, while the small chiefdoms in the mountains to the east supplied livestock, tobacco, and woodcarvings. Most of the foodstuffs moved toward the oil-producing villages of the forest, which were chronically short of starch and animal protein. The carvings and prestige goods, by contrast, usually found their way to the larger chiefdoms of the plateau.

Various Bamenda societies also conducted their trade in different ways. The chiefdoms of the central plateau, for example, dominated the regional system through their many professional merchants (Rowlands 1979; Warnier 1975: 148–158, 310–314; 1985: 82–87). The latter generally belonged to large compounds or lineage segments whose leaders possessed substantial capital in brass-rod currency and the other commodities mentioned above. While the headships of such groups were hereditary once established, unusually successful men could be accommodated by appointing them to new or vacant titles (Warnier 1985: 227–234). Wealthy traders also formed savings and investment societies to mobilize additional capital and organized expeditions to societies distant by up to two days' march (Warnier 1975: 324, 1985: 91–96). Most of the commerce that crossed the Bamenda plateau passed through the trading houses of men such as these rather than through transactions in the marketplace. Although some plateau chiefdoms held small weekly markets, they were generally for retail trade within the town, and outside attendance was discouraged (Warnier 1985: 79–81).[2]

Since the major plateau chiefdoms were economic and political rivals, travel by merchants across the open grasslands was potentially risky. Traders could easily be robbed or enslaved by groups from neighboring polities (Warnier 1975: 304–307). Merchants from the central chiefdoms therefore sought to secure

2. The weekly cycle within precolonial societies of the Bamenda Grassfields was eight days in length.

their safety by maintaining active relationships with partners in other groups. Such links were reinforced by pacts of mutual loyalty backed by supernatural sanctions as well as by ties of kinship and affinity. This in turn gave rise to the fostering of many children with relatives in neighboring polities, multilingualism in such offspring, and a sizable "floating population" that circulated among the various societies of the Bamenda plateau (Warnier 1979, 1985: 84–87).

The commercialism and cosmopolitanism of the Bamenda plateau peoples contrasts sharply with the more passive and parochial stance of peripheral groups. In the societies occupying forest and transitional zones to the south and west, small-scale producer-sellers played a much greater role in exchange, and people did not travel widely. Most often, the members of these groups simply traded with fellow countrymen or visiting plateau merchants at nearby local markets (Kaberry 1952: 23–24; Warnier 1985: 79–81, 83).

One important goal for the central-plateau polities was to improve control over supplies of palm oil coming from the forest. To this end, their chiefs maintained alliances and exchange relationships with the leaders of certain peripheral societies and sometimes also engaged in wars against these groups. Various chiefdoms adopted different strategies (Rowlands 1979, Warnier 1985: 247–285). While Bafut used conquest to incorporate small groups in the lower Metchum valley and harassed the Meta', Bali seems to have maintained peaceful relations with many of its smaller neighbors until it overcame them with German assistance at the beginning of the colonial era. Mankon, following yet another course, alternated between warfare and trade with groups such as the Meta'.

Among themselves the plateau chiefdoms seem to have carried on mainly peaceful rivalries following the Chamba raids. Diplomacy was well developed (Warnier 1985: 127–139, 269–276), and based upon a study of oral traditions, Warnier (1975: 417–419) reports only seven brief wars among these polities between 1835 and 1890.

A final important feature of the Bamenda regional economy was its articulation with the system of long-distance trade. In contrast to the intra-regional networks, the long-distance trade routes had a north-south orientation (Chilver 1961, Warnier 1985: 99–177, Wilhelm 1981). They tied Bamenda groups both to Muslim emirates in the north (via intermediary chiefdoms such as Kom and Wum) and to European merchants in the south (via Mamfe forest groups like the Banyang). Through such links, the Bamenda peoples received cloth, salt, Dane guns, gunpowder, and beads in return for commodities such as ivory, kola, and slaves. However, despite this commerce, several facts indicate that the regional economy was still very self-contained. For example, exchange with outsiders was effected through a relay trade involving many independent polities rather than through long-distance merchants.[3] In addition, palm oil, which was the dominant commodity in the trade with Europeans, was attracted in large amounts away from the coast toward the plateau. Finally, even though slaves constituted one of the major exports to both the north and the south, this had not led to anarchy or large-scale slave raiding in Bamenda (Chilver 1961, Warnier 1985: 129–139). Instead, following the Chamba intrusion of the early nineteenth century, the external slave trade was fed primarily by the sale of relatives, kidnap victims, and offenders. In this context, the authorities of all the plateau chiefdoms carefully monitored transactions through a system of slave-rope "licenses."[4]

Just as in the intra-regional commerce, the larger chiefdoms of the Bamenda plateau dominated the trade in luxury products derived from long-distance exchange. Since the major trading routes passed through the center of the plateau, these groups

3. Warnier (1985: 191) notes that some important Bamenda traders may have occasionally used their contacts to reach as far as Calabar in the mid-nineteenth century. However, the long-distance trade was never organized and dominated by a single group of merchants comparable to the Hausa of northern Nigeria or the Aro Chuku in Iboland.

4. These ropes were usually short (up to 50 cm) strands of human hair plaited with a black vegetable fiber. They were not used to bind captives but to subdue them magically, as they were believed to have a soporific effect. Such slave ropes were typically an instrument through which transactions in human beings were regulated. In some acephalous groups, such as Meta', they were the hereditary possessions of only a few clan sections that specialized in slave dealing and had the sole right to conduct such commerce. In some larger and more centralized polities, they were licenses to deal in slaves that were under the control of the chiefdom authorities (Warnier 1975: 163; 1985: 134–135, 189–190, 245).

were the only ones having direct access to such goods and to the much greater profits that could be gained from transactions involving them (see Map 2) (Warnier 1983: 368; 1985: 92, 182–185).

Political Organization of the Central Chiefdoms

The political complexity of the Bamenda plateau and its hinterland easily matched its physical and economic diversity (Chilver and Kaberry 1968, Warnier 1985: 180–293). In the late nineteenth century, the population of the region was divided into numerous independent groups that spoke distinct languages and organized themselves according to different principles. Although the plateau itself was an area of only moderate population density of about 40 per square kilometer (Kaberry 1952: 3; Warnier 1975: 472–481; 1985: 7, 193), it possessed by far the most impressive polities. These included four large chiefdoms: Bafut with an estimated population of 25,000, Mankon with some 10,000 inhabitants, and Bali-Nyonga and Nkwen with 6,000–8,000 and 5,000–7,000 respectively (Warnier 1985: 7). All had compact patterns of settlement, and the towns at Mankon and Nkwen were enclosed by ditches and earthworks as well.

The four leading Bamenda polities were likewise noteworthy for their elaborate development of chiefship and ranking (Chilver and Kaberry 1962, 1968: 60–63; Kaberry 1962; Kaberry and Chilver 1961; Warnier 1975: 212–221, 342–345; 1985: 238–247). In each case, the *fon* ("chief") was the focus of a large palace complex that was staffed by many royal wives and male retainers. It was common for a *fon* to possess more than one hundred of each type of dependent. As for notables of nonchiefly rank, many of these also possessed sizeable compounds and were distinguished from commoners by exclusive symbols of rank. The latter ranged from architectural embellishments to items of dress and personal accouterments.

The four major plateau chiefdoms differed mainly in their administrative structures, in the degree to which political power was centralized, in the importance attached to the chief's ritual role, and in their modes of articulation with the regional economy. In many respects, Bali-Nyonga was the most distinct (Chilver and Kaberry 1968: 68–80, Kaberry and Chilver 1961).

Having begun as a band of Chamba raiders, augmented by captives and refugees, the polity had an unusually heterogeneous population. In this context, wards rather than descent groups were the primary units of administration, and there was a strong emphasis on the ranking of social categories. Institutions of leadership also reflected the martial origins of Bali society. The Mfon ("chief") was the supreme ruler of a militaristic polity who filled most offices by personal appointment. He also controlled the chiefdom's war lodges and retained the right to dispose of all captives, elephant tusks, and slain leopards. In the absence of a formally constituted legislative body, the Mfon received advice from a war council of trusted personal retainers. Finally, he exercised legal authority very directly, appointing judges in an *ad hoc* fashion to decide any cases that could not be resolved at the ward level.

The vigor of the Mfon's secular leadership was moderated to an extent by his relatively weak ritual role. Although he did have an important part in the annual state ceremonies of Lela and Voma, he was not viewed as a divine ruler and did not preside over a cult of the royal ancestors in the fashion of most neighboring chiefs (Kaberry and Chilver 1961: 364–365).

Bali's position within the regional economic system conferred upon it several advantages (Chilver 1961; Warnier 1985: 169–171, 182–185; Wilhelm 1981). Located strategically at the southern end of the Bamenda plateau, it played a key role in both intra-regional and long-distance exchanges. Furthermore, since it stood astride the major southern gateway of the slave trade, it had become a major entrepôt in this commerce. Along with its efficient military organization, this was a crucial support of the chiefdom's regional power.

The other large Bamenda chiefdoms shared certain patterns of political organization that set them apart from Bali-Nyonga (Chilver and Kaberry 1962, 1968: 19–20, 56–63; Warnier 1975: 82–285, 1985: 207–247). In addition to having powerful *fon*s, all three groups possessed councils with constitutionally established prerogatives and complex systems of titled palace officials. They likewise gave a prominent role to secret societies that fulfilled political and legal functions and attached great importance to the public cult of the *fon*'s ancestors. Finally, each of the three non-Chamba chiefdoms regulated the export of slaves through slave-rope "licenses" that were allocated by either the chiefdom authorities or the leading clan heads (Warnier 1985: 189).

A crucial underpinning of these complex systems of ranking was the authorities' ability to establish control over wealth derived from trade. This was rarely done directly, since none of the three chiefdoms imposed substantial taxes on open commercial transactions (Warnier 1985: 75), and since in most polities there were no exclusive royal trading monopolies. However, the leaders of a chiefdom were still in a good position to divert much of the wealth produced by interpolity commerce. In part they accomplished this by exacting heavy payments from disputants and aspirants to honors, secret society memberships, and chiefdom-level offices, while in part they depended upon fees remitted by licensed slave dealers. Using the capital acquired from such sources, chiefs and senior notables invested in personal trading ventures to further increase their affluence. The foundations were thus laid for semi-hereditary oligarchies in which wealth and political power were mutually reinforcing (Rowlands 1979; Warnier 1975: 241–251, 255–258, 339–371; 1985: 87, 99, 188–192, 227–247).

The three non-Chamba chiefdoms did differ considerably in their ties to the regional system and in certain other aspects of their political organization. Mankon, for example, was quite centrally placed and very active in several exchange networks that crossed the plateau (Warnier 1985: 182–185). It was also a relatively loose confederation of localized patriclans in which hereditary clan heads controlled key leadership positions (Warnier 1975: 82–285, 1985: 207–224). Nkwen occupied a more peripheral location and seems to have been in decline during the late nineteenth century. This trend culminated around 1890 in the defection of a sizable subchiefdom from the town (Nkwi and Warnier 1982: 110–113, Warnier 1985: 267–268). Nkwen likewise differed from Mankon in being organized on the basis of quarters and wards rather than patrilineal groups (Chilver and Kaberry 1968: 60–63). Bafut, the third chiefdom, shared the pattern of ward organization with Nkwen but differed from both of the other polities in several respects (Chilver and Kaberry 1962, Engard 1986, Warnier 1985: 238–259). It was the largest of the plateau chiefdoms and, aside from Bali, the one in which authority was the most centralized. The Fon of Bafut exercised very wide discretion in creating and filling chiefdom-level offices. Bafut had also adopted a unique pose toward the regional system. During the 1870s and 1880s, it seems to have undergone a process of "implosion": as it depopulated its hinterland through raiding and gathered a larger population within the town, Bafut reoriented its economy toward producing goods like palm oil and iron that it had previously acquired through trade. Although this did not completely sever commercial links between Bafut and its neighbors—it continued to be dependent upon the outside for access to certain elite goods—the polity was growing ever more self-contained.

The Peripheral Polities

While the smaller groups that occupied the margins of the Bamenda plateau have been less thoroughly studied than the central chiefdoms, some information about them is still available. In the remaining part of this chapter, I shall summarize the data concerning these peripheral groups and attempt to explain some of the contrasts between them and the larger chiefdoms.

On the eastern and southeastern edges of the Bamenda plateau, there existed numerous polities, including Bambwi, Bambili, Chomba, Songwa, Mbutu, Akum, Ala Tening, Awing, and Pinyin. None of these Ngemba-speaking groups was above 2,000 in population, and most ranged between 200 and 1,000 (Warnier 1975: 67–72, 472–481). Many had responded to the Chamba raids by taking refuge in the Bambutos Mountains, which separated Bamenda from the iron-producing regions in Ndop. Those that remained upon the plateau itself relied upon alliances with the larger chiefdoms or, like Bambwi and Pinyin, constructed fortified sites (Nkwi and Warnier 1982: 120–121; Warnier 1975: 55, 72–79, 418–423; 1985: 270–271).

The political systems of the eastern peripheral societies were small-scale replicas of those seen in the major chiefdoms (Nkwi and Warnier 1982: 120–121; Warnier 1983: 569–578, 1985: 235). They had clustered settlements and organized themselves on a ward rather than a descent group basis. They also recognized hereditary chiefs and nobles, possessed secret societies, and in some instances employed the slave-rope "license" to regulate transactions in human beings (Warnier 1985: 189). Although these small polities were not central to the long-distance trade, they did provide links between the major plateau chiefdoms and the Ndop plain societies that were important in intra-regional exchange (Warnier 1985: 11–53, 61–68, 78, 182–185). In this context, their members are said to have frequently intermarried with citizens of the larger plateau groups (Warnier 1975: 374–376, 1979, 1985: 86).

At the southwestern margin of the plateau, where the grasslands give way to forests and a steep escarpment, were to be found a number of Mogamo-speaking village chiefdoms (Chilver and Kaberry 1968: 13–15, Nkwi and Warnier 1982: 116–117, O'Neil 1987). The population of this area, which was about 20,000 in 1890, occupied two distinct zones. While the villages of lower Mogamo specialized in palm-oil production, their more prosperous brothers in upper Mogamo traded this northeastward toward Meta' and the chiefdoms of the plateau. Upper Mogamo also included several chiefdoms such as Aighwi, Guzang, Ashong, and Bessi with populations of several thousand, whereas most lower Mogamo villages counted their inhabitants in the hundreds.[5]

Though the Mogamo villages were relatively self-sufficient in subsistence terms, their location astride one important route to the coast had caused them to become heavily involved in long-distance exchanges (O'Neil 1987: 8–9, 57–91). Many slaves, large amounts of salt, and a considerable volume of prestige goods passed through their area. Such commodities were typically exchanged privately rather than through the village markets that circulated subsistence products and craft items among the people of local communities.

5. These remarks on village size are based on the 1953 Population Census (Chilver and Kaberry 1968: 123), since earlier village-by-village figures were unavailable. In that year Aighwi (Batibo) had 3,723 residents, while Ashong, Guzang, and Bessi had 2,480, 2,354, and 2,335, respectively. There is also some discrepancy in the estimates of late nineteenth-century population density for Mogamo. Warnier (1985: 193) cites a range of 80 to 100 persons per square kilometer, while O'Neil (1987: 7) puts the density at between 11 and 14.

In the forests of Mogamo, settlement was dispersed. Patrilineages, composed of several compounds occupied by patrilocal extended families, were the basic local groups, and several neighboring lineages typically formed a village federation (O'Neil 1987: 15–20). Those lineage heads who could be counted among the successors of a village's founders normally presided over its affairs with one of their number being recognized as the *fon* or village head. The authority of these leaders was based upon several factors (O'Neil 1987: 14–19, 21, 38, 48–67). In addition to deriving legitimacy from their close association with the spirits of their respective groups' forebears, they fed and entertained fellow villagers, organized and protected village markets, and monopolized the trade in slaves and prestige goods. They also controlled use of the poison ordeal, through which persons accused of witchcraft were tested, and profited by receiving the property of any villagers who died from it.

In the view of O'Neil (1987: 29–31, 75–77, 80–81, 84, 91–92, 356–359), the late nineteenth century was a time when the village authorities of Mogamo were consolidating power. The common folk increasingly looked to them to organize their defenses against the raids that had already depopulated some areas as well as to protect them from witchcraft. This, along with their trade-based wealth, had enabled certain leading village chiefs to extend their influence over neighboring communities. Still, none had as yet emerged as a paramount.

Beyond the range of the village, Mogamo was more a broad zone of linguistic and cultural affinity than a political community (O'Neil 1987: 20–38). While some lineage and village heads, such as those who maintained ancestral shrines at the famous Tadkon market, asserted kinship and common origins, others claimed to have migrated to their present sites from altogether different directions. In this context, there existed no political institutions that unified the entire group of Mogamo speakers.

On the northwestern edge of the plateau, completely different conditions prevailed. In this mixed forest and savanna zone, where the broad Metchum River valley led down toward the Katsina Ala and Benue Rivers in Nigeria, the population was sparse, and small polities faced greater threats to their survival. The lower portion of the valley had been completely depopulated by Bafut raids when that chiefdom began to expand in the 1870s (Nkwi and Warnier 1982: 114, 118–119; Warnier 1985: 193, 247–256). The few small polities that had escaped incorporation—Beba' and Mundum II, for example—managed to do so only by withdrawing into the mountains. A little farther to the north in the middle Metchum region, the indigenous groups remained in place but had been reduced to tributary status by the powerful Aghem federation based in Wum (Kopytoff 1981, Masquelier 1978: 31–45) (see Map 2). Although, strictly speaking, their ties to Aghem removed the middle Metchum peoples from participation in the Bamenda plateau system, they are still worth describing in detail. This is partly because their exchange relations with Aghem paralleled those that linked peripheral oil-producing groups to central trading chiefdoms in Bamenda. In addition, the middle Metchum peoples were closely related in culture to peripheral Bamenda groups such as the Meta', the Mogamo, and the Ngi. Finally, thanks to the research of Masquelier (1978, 1979), they are among the best-documented societies on the western edge of the Cameroon Grassfields.

Perhaps the most crucial difference between the oil-producing polities of the middle Metchum and peripheral Bamenda groups was that the Metchum peoples were unable to control their own palm-oil trade with the plateau (Masquelier 1978: 31–45, 48). The societies of this area did have an outlet to the Benue region through Esimbi in the north (Masquelier 1978: 28–29, 47). However, this route was not heavily used (Warnier 1985: 122), and by the late nineteenth century, the residents of the Metchum valley had been brought firmly into the Cameroon Highlands' regional economy in a subordinate role. Lacking both the specialized trading houses of the Bamenda plateau chiefdoms and the network of popular markets found in Meta' to the south (see pp. 63–65), the Metchum peoples delivered much of their oil as tribute to several powerful Aghem chiefs. They also yielded more of this precious product at bargain rates whenever private Aghem traders appeared with iron implements, livestock, and various craft items. Though nominally independent, the Metchum villagers were subjected to severe reprisals for any show of resistance as the Aghem would launch punitive expeditions or seize hostages in order to ensure their compliance.

In the face of such strong outside pressures, attempts by various Metchum valley polities to achieve wider unity had met with only mixed success (Masquelier 1978: 14, 17–18, 24–31). In the late nineteenth century, the 8,000 to 10,000 population of the middle Metchum region was divided into eight separate political units that shared certain similarities of culture. Individual polities did attempt to establish peaceful relations with their neighbors and received outside visitors at important festivals (Masquelier 1978: 24, 30–31, 184, 298–299). However, all but two of the Metchum groups spoke distinct languages (Masquelier 1978: 17–18), and interpolity warfare was common (Masquelier 1978: 29–30, 47–48, 62–64, 321–322). Marriage between members of different polities was likewise discouraged, and those marriages that did take place were effected through a special kind of transaction that failed to establish an alliance between the kin groups involved (Masquelier 1978: 175, 180–185, 190–191). This was tantamount to the sale of the woman.

Considerations of defense also influenced the settlement pattern significantly. For example, in Ide, one of the best-documented Metchum polities, some 1,500 persons were divided among six grasslands villages clustered within a radius of about three kilometers. All of these were nucleated settlements, and most possessed ditches that were intended to provide protection by controlling the ability of visitors to enter and leave the town (Masquelier 1978: 42, 48–53, 62, 83; 1979).

Internally, the various Metchum polities were relatively open, egalitarian systems based upon both corporate descent group organization and voluntary associations. In Ide, for example, patrilineal descent was a principle that underlay many political relationships even though genealogical knowledge was typically short (Masquelier 1978: 73–137). At the neighborhood level, localized "patriclusters," units of about ten households whose members assumed a common ancestor, were crucial to economic and political cooperation. Although grassland farm tracts and some portions of the forest were managed collectively by villages, patriclusters controlled most other essential resources (Masquelier 1978: 83–88, 99, 123–126, 129–132). Each cluster possessed an exclusive estate composed of oil palms, rights over marriageable women, and valuables like goats, Dane guns, and drums of palm oil. Such assets were generally administered by an elder who was popularly chosen for his wisdom and fairness, and young men were supported in marrying much earlier here than elsewhere in Bamenda (Masquelier 1978: 123–126, 129–130, 161–163, 166, 175–176). Above the level of the patricluster, both the ward and the village were also regarded as patrilineal units. Despite the lack of any precise genealogy, this supplied a sufficient rationale for such groups to mobilize for nonlethal fighting whenever their members became involved in disputes with equivalent units within the same polity (Masquelier 1978: 60–62, 120–121).

Nondescent institutions were also important in Ide villages (Masquelier 1978: 196–225, 272–275, 312–354). These included universalistic groups such as age-sets, war lodges, and hunting societies. By comparison with the associations of most other Grassfields polities, those in Ide were relatively easy to join, even for young men (Masquelier 1978: 317, 335).

Each Ide village had both a male and a female chief or "owner of the land" (*kodong*). Like the authority of the patricluster elders, that of chiefs was essentially representational. They were primarily spokespersons and ritual leaders who embodied the identity of their villages (Masquelier 1978: 226–259, 364–365). Both the male and the female chiefships also rotated between specific lineages located in different wards. The male chief was allowed to nominate his successor from among his own junior agnates, although this had to be confirmed by all the adult males of his ward at the time of installation. The female chief was elected by the women of her ward. Masquelier (1978: 233) reports that there was little conflict over succession to chieftaincy during the nineteenth century.

Ide as a whole was a social field within which relationships were closely interwoven, thus providing the basis for cooperative political and ritual action. Because of the strong preference for intrapolity marriage, most individuals could count numerous maternal kin among the members of surrounding villages. Such ties were given explicit recognition through a system of dispersed matrilineal descent groups that assembled for life-crisis rites and helped to protect their members from sorcery and physical attack (Masquelier 1978: 138–156).

In the Metchum valley, polities such as Ide were normally the largest units that coordinated political and religious activities. In addition to mobilizing for wars with the Aghem and other Metchum groups, the members of the several villages within a polity periodically united for large-scale ritual assemblies. On such occasions, the senior village chief presided over rites that were designed to deal with serious threats of misfortune by using the power of the community's collective voice (Masquelier 1978: 286–311).

The mystical unity of the polity was also expressed in the notion that homicide within this unit was dangerous and polluting. In Ide, this belief laid the foundation for a ritual cleansing process that was supervised by hereditary specialists from four different villages. Though these experts were not themselves of chiefly rank, and though the senior polity chief was not actively involved in the rites, the latter customarily received a payment from the killer and his descent group. This acknowledged his status as representative of the widest possible moral community (Masquelier 1978: 59–64, 275–277, 358–360).

Although they have been only briefly studied (Chilver and Kaberry 1968: 52–54; Kaberry 1952: 16–17, 23–27, 49–52; Warnier 1985: 203–204), the Ngi village polities, which occupied the rugged forested mountains to the west of the Bamenda plateau, provide a final useful example of variability among peripheral groups. Despite the fact that they were linked by occasional slave sales to forest peoples like the Banyang in the southwest, the Ngi were tied even more firmly into the Bamenda regional system. They were in fact large-scale producers of the palm oil that was consumed and traded by the chiefdoms of the plateau (Warnier 1983: 60–66). Ngi oil reached them indirectly after passing through a network of small markets, including some in eastern Ngi itself and numerous village markets in Meta' (Dillon 1981, Nkwi and Warnier 1982: 118, Warnier 1985: 73–82).

In general the Ngi were not enterprising traders and usually did not venture beyond the closest Meta' markets (Dillon 1981, Kaberry 1952: 23–24). Nonetheless, several factors encouraged them to produce heavily for the oil trade. In their densely settled homeland (ca. 80–100 per square kilometer [Warnier 1985: 193]), where the terrain was steep and rocky and the productivity of crops other than palm oil low, exchange with the Bamenda Grassfields provided much-needed supplies of maize and beans as well as protein from livestock (Kaberry 1952: 23–24, 51, 58; Warnier 1985: 20, 29–31, 36–37, 45, 47, 49). Goats that were acquired in this fashion could be used for bridewealth payments that were higher here than in other parts of Bamenda (Chilver and Kaberry 1968: 52, Kaberry 1952: 25, Warnier 1985: 38–39). Finally, the Bamenda plateau was Ngi's major source of iron tools and a variety of handicrafts (Kaberry 1952: 23–24; Nkwi and Warnier 1982: 118; Warnier 1985: 14, 55, 57, 63).

Of all the groups thus far discussed, Ngi possessed the most atomistic form of sociopolitical organization (Chilver and Kaberry 1968: 52–54; Kaberry 1952: 16–17, 49–50). Although an emphasis on hereditary rank as the basis for leadership gave the Ngi system an appearance of formality, corporate organization was only weakly developed. The domestic economy was also much more individualistic than that of the middle Metchum valley peoples. Ngi compound heads, for example, independently administered estates of land and palm groves and could alienate these without the approval of their kin. However, despite such autonomy on the part of male household heads, and the considerable independence of Ngi women (Kaberry 1952: 142), opportunities were not equal for all segments of the population. In many instances, men were obliged to pawn their oil palms or land in order to meet the high cost of bridewealth (Kaberry 1952: 50), and in a context of late marriage for males, there was an institutionalized form of clientship through which unmarried men provided services in exchange for sexual access to the wives of other compound heads and notables (Chilver and Kaberry 1968: 53).

As regards patterns of grouping, Ngi's population of roughly 15,000 was divided into a score of independent villages, most of which had 1,000 inhabitants or less. These were composed of many small compounds scattered along the valley floors and mountain slopes. As in the Metchum valley, political organization was founded upon patrilineal descent, with both the village and its major subdivisions being regarded as descent units (Chilver and Kaberry 1968: 52–54; Kaberry 1952: 16–17, 49–50). However, authority depended upon genealogical position to a much greater extent here, with the first sons of first wives customarily succeeding to positions of village headship. The leadership of both clan sections and villages was in the hands of "notables" (*okum*, sing. *kum*), who were successors to the founders of important descent lines. These men, whose genealogies sometimes went back ten to twelve generations, were the only persons entitled to erect drum platforms in their compounds. Rights to this key symbol of rank were customarily granted in an elaborate series of rituals performed by the *kum* from whose group one's own had segmented. The *okum* of Ngi villages also conducted ancestral rites to promote the prosperity of their groups, organized collective hunting, and presided over village-level moots. However, unlike Metchum valley leaders, their approach to dispute settlement did not rely on concepts of pollution or the use of ritual experts (Chilver and Kaberry 1968: 53). Homicide cases, for example, were usually resolved by the payment of compensation to the victim's kin, and the fines imposed in most other kinds of conflict were consumed by the injured party and his relatives.

Beyond the village level, there was no effective political organization in Ngi. Indeed, intervillage relations appear to have been significantly more conflictual than in any of the societies previously discussed. Despite their traditions of descent from a common eponymous ancestor, the various Ngi villages are said to have frequently attacked one another, and it was regarded as permissible to eat enemy warriors killed in such raids (Chilver and Kaberry 1968: 52).

Conclusion

In this chapter, I have described the Bamenda regional system and the societies of which it was composed. In summarizing, it is tempting to fit the Bamenda peoples into an evolutionary continuum with the archetypically stateless Ngi forest villagers at the bottom and the chiefdoms of the central plateau at the top. "Semi-peripheral" groups such as the Metchum valley polities and the small Ngemba and Mogamo chiefdoms could then be placed somewhere in between. However, in many respects an evolutionary ranking obscures more than it helps to clarify the organization of the Bamenda societies. It also requires sweeping many untidy facts under the carpet. For example, inasmuch as evolutionary anthropologists seem to consider increase in population as a measure of societal success (Harris 1979, Stevenson 1968), Ngi would have to be counted as the most advanced society of the Bamenda region. Its population was roughly twice as dense as that of the Bamenda plateau itself and higher still than in the Metchum valley area (Warnier 1985: 193). Furthermore, Ngi was not simply a well-stocked preserve for slave raiding by the larger chiefdoms, since the evidence suggests that most of the slaves who were exported from the Bamenda regional system in the late nineteenth century came from the plateau chiefdoms themselves (Warnier 1985: 195–197).

Another telling comparison can be made between the Metchum valley polities and Ngi. It is true that the Metchum peoples can be considered more advanced than the Ngi in the overall size of the polities that they established, in the degree of unity that they achieved, and in the diversity of the principles used within their political systems. However, they had also developed hereditary ranking to a much lesser extent. Important Ngi lineage heads, with their drum platforms, their exclusive ritual roles, and their genealogies going back many generations, clearly represented a greater consolidation of social power than did the weak representational leaders of the Metchum valley. In this context, which society is to be considered as evolutionarily the most advanced?

Such comparisons indicate the need for a more open-ended interpretation of political variability in Bamenda. It may still be possible to explain the diverse patterns of organization found among the societies of this area within a common framework. However, each society must be seen as a unique constellation of values in terms of a common set of dimensions or traits.

The data presented in this chapter suggest that two factors may have had the greatest impact upon political differentiation within the Bamenda region. The first of these was the effect of a given polity's location within the regional system upon its members' participation in intersocietal exchange. The second was the influence of the environment (natural and social) upon polity size and settlement pattern. In the rest of this chapter, I will suggest a tentative interpretation of the variations in political organization that existed in nineteenth-century Bamenda, paying the closest attention to these two critical variables.

Looking first at the larger chiefdoms of the central plateau, we see that these groups had the most favorable position in relation to trade. Their location at the intersection of the intra-regional and long-distance trade routes gave them considerable bargaining power in relation to peripheral groups. It likewise enhanced their possibilities for the accumulation of wealth.

As regards the organization of trade, both the large volume of transactions in the central plateau and the danger of making expeditions across the open grasslands must have encouraged professionalism. Sizable households specializing in trade would have been the best able to amass sufficient capital and to arrange for the safety of their agents. Having once emerged, such trading houses doubtless had a significant impact upon the overall organization of their home societies. Most important, they would have contributed to differences in wealth among kinship groups and given increased power to the leaders of the most successful.

In this context, the exposed nature of the plateau environment becomes significant. As we have seen, following the Chamba raids, clustered settlement became necessary to ensure defense. Application of this principle brought together mixed populations and encouraged the use of cross-cutting institutions, such as councils and secret societies, to organize social relations. But it also provided additional opportunities for the heads of major trading houses to consolidate their control over the populace. Once a wealth-based oligarchy had begun to establish itself within a compact town, it would have been difficult for others to escape its control or to create alternative power bases from which to mount challenges.[6] Such, in any event, is the most plausible interpretation of the processes through which the complex social hierarchies of the central plateau came into being.

Only slight modifications of the foregoing hypothesis are

6. Cohen (1977, 1978c) has emphasized that the emergence of anti-fission institutions is a crucial element in political evolution from preindustrial chiefdoms to states. Here, we can note some of the environmental and economic circumstances that may encourage the development of these institutional forms in medium-sized chiefdoms.

needed to explain the patterns of organization encountered in the smaller peripheral chiefdoms such as the Ngemba and Mogamo-speaking groups to the east, southeast, and southwest of the plateau. Taking the Ngemba polities first, it may be noted that they also had nucleated settlement and privileged positions in relation to trade. Yet, unlike the central-plateau chiefdoms, they had direct access only to the intra-regional trade (Warnier 1985: 182–185). They therefore developed more modest versions of the kind of chiefdom organization seen in the central plateau. In the Mogamo villages, by contrast, a set of countervailing forces seem to have been set into play. On the one hand, dispersed settlement within the forest zone favored the autonomy of small descent groups and rendered control by central authorities more difficult than on the plateau or among the Ngemba. On the other hand, direct involvement in the slave trade and long-distance exchange provided an economic basis for the consolidation of power by chiefdom authorities. Moreover, the insecurities associated with slave raiding and intervillage warfare reinforced this trend. In this case, the result seems to have been a series of small but rather authoritarian chiefdoms in which patrilineal descent groups nonetheless retained an important political role.

In the Metchum valley, a rather different set of conditions obtained. While societies here resembled the central-plateau groups in having reacted to an exposed environment by building compact fortified settlements, they stood in a very different relationship to the regional system. As palm-oil producers, they occupied a terminus in the exchange network rather than an intermediary position. This meant that they did not possess a middleman's enhanced awareness of the possibilities of profit from trade. Metchum peoples accordingly played a rather passive role in the regional exchange system. They neither developed strong corporate groups specializing in trade nor used diplomacy and warfare to promote their commercial interests in the fashion of the central-plateau chiefdoms. Such unassertiveness had several consequences. In addition to leaving the Metchum valley groups politically weak in relation to neighbors like the Aghem, it limited the accumulation of wealth and the development of social inequality within their polities. This effectively prevented the consolidation of oligarchic rule.

However, there were also several forces that promoted integration in the Metchum valley polities. For example, living in moderately large nucleated settlements, the Metchum peoples clearly needed institutions cross-cutting their patrilineal descent groups in order to unify their heterogeneous populations. Moreover, the threats posed by powerful neighboring chiefdoms, such as Aghem and Bafut, encouraged cooperation in defense arrangements. The overall result of these factors was the establishment of a number of well-integrated medium-sized polities in the middle Metchum valley. Within these groups egalitarian political relations were encouraged by the lack of significant trade-derived wealth. In the absence of differences in accumulated assets, there was little economic basis for the power of would-be leaders. At the same time, the low population density of the area may have encouraged nonhierarchical relations, since it would have placed a premium on the recruitment of human resources and decreased the need to compete for material ones. This could easily have given rise to the strongly collective control of resources that one finds in the Metchum polities. It may also help to explain why young men were able to marry much earlier here and to achieve leadership roles more rapidly than in other parts of Bamenda.

In Ngi, the last society considered in this chapter, we find a number of contrasts with other groups. Ngi was at once the area with the highest population density in the Bamenda and the only society thus far encountered with a pattern of dispersed settlement. It also had the highest bridewealth, very late marriage for males, and an economic system that granted maximum autonomy to the heads of small households. While the Ngi social system reflected some development of ranking, its political organization depended almost exclusively upon the framework set by patrilineal descent groups. The kinds of secret societies and associations that existed in both the plateau chiefdoms and the Metchum valley groups were apparently unimportant here. Finally, Ngi society was unique in that it had the smallest polities of any group in our sample.

These distinctive patterns become more comprehensible if they are considered in light of Ngi's natural and social environment and its role in the regional system. With respect to the former, it is clear that Ngi differed from all the societies thus far discussed in that it had an environment that favored defense. In the rugged forested hills of Ngi, where the neighbors did not include any large predatory chiefdoms, there was little need for fortified towns. In this context, small localized descent groups could provide sufficient support for individual compound heads to meet any threats to the security of their property and dependents.

As regards Ngi's role in the regional system, this appears to have influenced its patterns of sociopolitical organization in a complicated fashion. Like the Metchum valley peoples, the oil-producing villages of Ngi were located at a terminus in the exchange system. Their members therefore played a rather passive role in trade. At the same time, however, the Ngi were insulated by their environment from the extortionate pressures to which neighboring societies subjected the Metchum valley folk. In this context, they benefited much more from their participation in intra-regional exchange. The large amounts of grain and livestock that they obtained from it were, after all, what enabled them to maintain a dense population in an area that was unfavorable for farming. That Ngi's high bridewealth was payable primarily in goats, a commodity obtained from trade with the plateau, only serves to highlight these relationships.

It is also worth considering whether Ngi's participation in the intra-regional system affected patterns of stratification within the society. As previously mentioned, in the densely populated mountains of Ngi, individual compound heads had assumed relatively autonomous control over productive resources such as oil palms and land. This put them in an excellent position to manage both the outflow of palm oil and the influx of other commodities that Ngi obtained from intra-regional exchanges. This would have given them considerable power over their dependents. Without the support of kin, for example, younger males could only hope to obtain bridewealth through prolonged saving or borrowing, facts that may help to explain why the age of first marriage for males was much higher here than in the Metchum valley.

Once a gerontocratic system had emerged, it could be expected to foster just the sort of political institutions that have been recorded for Ngi. Male elders would tend to collaborate in order to reinforce their control, and this would lead to a hierarchy in which authority and rank were linked primarily to descent status. However, the possibilities for the consolidation of any more elaborate system of ranking would have been strictly limited. Ngi lacked the basis for this in wealth like that produced by the specialized trading houses of the central plateau. Instead, the Ngi economy continued to be organized around small independent households, each of which participated similarly in the intra-regional exchanges. Finally, the dispersal of Ngi's population would have hindered the efforts of any leader to establish centralized authority within a sizable polity. In this context, Ngi society retained a political system that was more atomistic than that of the Metchum valley groups but at the same time less egalitarian.

Consideration of several societies occupying different positions within the Bamenda regional system has illustrated how patterns of political organization and social stratification found in individual societies are often much more comprehensible when viewed in a broader context. One important goal of this study is to analyze the influence of the Bamenda regional system upon yet another group, the Meta'. Located between the Ngi and Mogamo forest villages, on the one hand, and the central-plateau chiefdoms, on the other, the Meta' articulated with the precolonial regional system in a fashion that we have not yet encountered. Meta' society was also distinct from both the Metchum valley polities and Ngi in the degree to which ranking had become elaborate, in the intricacy and effectiveness of its system of conflict management, and in the broad scope of its polity organization. However, as we shall see, the unique organizational patterns of Meta' become the most fully intelligible when an interpretation of the society's place within the wider regional system is combined with a detailed analysis of its internal processes and dynamics.

FOUR

Precolonial Meta'

THIS CHAPTER introduces precolonial Meta' society and lays the foundations for the analysis of village and intervillage politics to follow. After briefly discussing the environment, language, and history of the Meta' people, I will outline their household economy and patterns of exchange. I shall also provide a preliminary statement of several concepts that were fundamental to Meta' political ideology.

Prior to colonization (ca. 1900), approximately 20,000 Meta' occupied an area of some 335 square kilometers on the southwestern edge of the Bamenda plateau (see Map 2).[1] Ecologically, they resided in a transition zone where three valleys linked the lower-lying forest to the southwest with the rolling savannas of upland Bamenda. Elevations ranged from 900 to 1,800 meters. The floors and lower slopes of the valleys were covered with a mixture of natural trees and bush, and economic trees, such as raffia palms, oil palms, and plantains. Grassy hilltops sur-

---

1. The figure of 20,000 for the Meta' population in 1900 is a very rough estimate. I myself have attempted to calculate the size of the population at that time by extrapolating from the number of minimal lineages (*mban* groups) that were reported to have existed in the Bome valley. This indicated a population of about 30,000 for Meta' as a whole. The earliest figure from documentary sources is that of Lt. Hirtler, the leader of the German punitive expedition that conquered Meta' in 1903 (*Deutsches Kolonialblatt*, 1903, v. 14: 493–494). Hirtler estimated the population of 29 Meta' "villages" that he visited to be between 15,000 and 20,000. If a proportional addition is made for the eleven villages that Hirtler states he did not see, an overall population of between 20,700 and 27,600 is suggested. The first detailed census, carried out in the early 1920s, yielded a much lower figure of 13,462 (C. J. A. Gregg, A.D.O., "Meta: An Assessment Report of the Meta Clan of the Bamenda Division, Cameroons Province," January 1, 1924 [Buea Archives]).

mounted these valleys to the north and south, and two of them opened onto the plateau itself in the northeast. Meta' country was well watered. The year was divided into distinct wet and dry seasons, with the rains beginning in March and lasting to October. The valley slopes and floors were also traversed by numerous small streams. Present-day average annual rainfall is around 2,600 millimeters.

In immediate precolonial times, Meta' was one of the more heavily populated portions of Bamenda, with an overall density of about 60 persons per square kilometer. As in Ngi, the settlement pattern was dispersed, with gardens, trees, and bush separating the compounds of neighbors. Many homesteads were located on the valley floors, although the lower slopes were actually preferred because they provided better protection from raiders.

Language

The language of the Meta', commonly referred to as Menemo, is mutually intelligible with the dialect of the Mogamo speakers to the southeast, but distinct from other plateau tongues. Though it belongs to the Momo subgroup of the larger Western Grassfields unit, the relationship of this group to other African language families is still ambiguous (Warnier 1979, 1985: 3–5).

History

Knowledge of the Meta' people prior to 1900 is derived almost entirely from oral sources (Chilver 1965a, 1965b; Chilver and Kaberry 1968: 13–15; Dillon 1981). There are very strong traditions of migration from Tadkon and/or Widekum in the forest to the southwest (see Map 2).[2] According to these accounts, the Meta' travelled progressively northeast through Mogamo, Ngi, and

2. The question of Tadkon versus Widekum as the starting point of Meta' migrations remains open. No detailed account of a migration from either of these sites to the other was given by any Meta' informant in 1970–71. Most simply listed one site or the other as the place of origin for the Meta', and some appeared to use the two place names interchangeably. One possibility to be considered is that certain Meta' clans actually came from Tadkon, while others migrated from the area around Widekum town or still other sites.

the Zang valley in present-day Meta' before reaching villages such as Ku, Funam, Njindom, and Bessi in the Bome and Medig valleys. The Meta' are also depicted as only one of several groups that came forth from Tadkon and Widekum. While the Mankon people and some groups now living near Santa on the other side of the Bamenda plateau are said to have departed earlier and to have been pushed ahead by Meta' warriors, the Mogamo are described as having left Tadkon later and having driven the Meta' ahead in a similar way. The Meta' are also portrayed as the descendants of two heroic founders, Tɜɣɜniča and Tɜmbɜŋjɔ, who were themselves brothers born at Tadkon. Finally, it is asserted that certain Meta' clans customarily travelled together in their early migrations (e.g., Mindik with Bɔgwanɨk, Mɜnɔŋ, and ɜzweɜzuʔ, and Bɔnjɔ with Bɔrangɔp, Mitɨŋ, and Mindam, etc.). Past associations of this sort are cited as the reason that the members of these clans frequently resided in the same villages at the start of the colonial era.

The accounts of Meta' origins that I have just summarized clearly have the flavor of popular legends, and their validity has been questioned on several grounds. I have argued elsewhere (Dillon 1981) that, by evoking the image of a single warring and migratory tribe, they may give a false impression of the length of time that the Meta' polity has been unified. They probably also oversimplify what was in all likelihood a complex series of movements carried out by many groups over a long period of time. Finally, Chilver and Kaberry (1968: 15) have raised the question of whether the traditions of migration from Tadkon are not better understood as ''a symbol of inter-village cooperation'' than as a record of actual population movements. Given Tadkon's importance as a precolonial market, they argue, traditions of origin there may have become a kind of mythical charter that facilitated exchange. The plausibility of this ''trade hypothesis'' is increased by the fact that Meta' citizens did rely upon ties to clansmen to obtain protection in commerce between forest and plateau during immediate precolonial times. It is at least conceivable that the agnatic relationships they cultivated in this situation could have gradually come to be seen as links created by past migrations.

However, several facts argue against this interpretation. First, as Chilver and Kaberry themselves (1968: 14–15) have noted, the oral traditions of neighboring groups such as Ngi and Mankon provide support for a migration of the Meta' from the southwest. Second and more persuasive is the detailed pattern of correspondences that was found in the individual clan histories that I collected in 1970–71. The precolonial migration routes of four clans—Bɔnjɔ, Bɔrangɔp, Mindik, and Mitiŋ—were thoroughly studied by interviewing informants in most localities where segments of them had been present in 1900. This entailed retracing migrations from the most northeasterly points in the Bome and Medig valleys back to the Meta'-Mogamo border area in the southwest. Subsequently, the migration histories of other Meta' clans were studied less exhaustively. The resultant data provided strong corroboration of the type of southwest-to-northeast migration claimed in the popular legends, at least as far as the closest neighboring villages in Mogamo and Ngi. The migrations of individual clans were usually described by informants belonging to them as movements that had originated at Tadkon and proceeded northeast in a number of stages. The ancestors of a typical clan would be portrayed as having stopped in several Mogamo villages before reaching Meta' and then advancing to make successive settlements in villages like Kai, Njah, Njekwa, and Funam. In most cases, segments of the clan concerned were still residing at each location mentioned in its migration history. The list of stopping points given by an informant sometimes represented only part of his clan's overall route from Tadkon. However, since the sequences of sites given by members of related clan sections were usually partially overlapping, it was possible to compare their accounts and to reconstruct longer portions of clan migration routes by going from one informant to the next. Such cross-checking revealed a high degree of correspondence in the testimonies of informants belonging to the same clan but residing in different localities. Although they did not always agree about the relative seniority of their lineages, they usually did concur on the direction of past clan migrations and on the stages through which they had been accomplished.

Additional data supporting the hypothesis of actual migration from southwest to northeast was obtained by reconstructing the settlement pattern for the entire Bome valley in 1900 and by interviewing many informants about its early history. These investigations produced a very consistent and detailed account of how the valley had been occupied, beginning in the west and ending with the foundation of Meta' villages in the easternmost parts of Bome adjacent to the Bamenda plateau.

If actual migration from the forest is tentatively accepted as the most likely interpretation, can anything be said about when the movement occurred? Here we unfortunately have only the indirect evidence provided by genealogies of Meta' lineage and village heads. The fact that these are short—usually including only two to six generations between the first ancestor's arrival and 1900—suggests that settlers probably did not begin arriving in Meta' territory before the late eighteenth century. By contrast, the date by which present Meta' territory was fully occupied is easier to determine. Most groups in the Bome valley, an "advanced" area adjacent to the Bamenda plateau, claim to have been in place at the time that Bali-Nyonga moved to its current site in the mid-1860s. It is therefore probable that the bulk of Meta' migrations from the forest had been completed by this time, even though some pioneer groups were still being sent to settle in outlying farm areas to the northeast.

The mention of Bali-Nyonga raises a final intriguing issue in the reconstruction of precolonial Meta' history—the possibility of correlating Meta' migrations with the Chamba raids of the 1820s and 1830s. As mentioned in the previous chapter, these raids resulted in the clustering of populations on the Bamenda plateau and a reorganization of the regional exchange system in which several powerful chiefdoms came to dominate trade across the grasslands. It is possible that these changes created a vacuum in the area of eastern Meta' from which some of the central plateau peoples are said to have moved. In this context, groups living in the forest might have been encouraged to occupy the Meta' valleys that lay between them and the plateau in order to secure more advantageous positions within the new trading networks. Such a sequence of developments would help to explain the Meta' traditions that their ancestors had "driven" groups such as the Mankon ahead of them through warfare. However, in the absence of additional evidence this interpretation must remain hypothetical.

Relations with Neighboring Peoples

The historical events just described may also help to explain the fact that one finds the clearest differentiation in terms of language distributions and kin relationships between Meta' and the societies on its eastern border. The general pattern is one of a distinct cleavage between the Meta' and chiefdoms like Bafut, Mankon, and Bali on the Bamenda plateau and of closer affiliation with groups such as Mogamo and Ngi in the west. As we have seen, during the late nineteenth century, all of the plateau chiefdoms had clustered settlement patterns with several miles of farmland and bush intervening between them and Meta'. This physical separation was matched by great social and linguistic distance. The peoples of the various plateau chiefdoms spoke languages belonging to the Mbam-Nkam group, while the Meta' were Western Grassfields speakers (Warnier 1979). There also appears to have been little intermarriage between Meta' and these groups,[3] and despite the fact that some eastern Meta' acknowledged ultimate common descent with people of the plateau chiefdoms, they could not cite ties of clanship with specific lineages in those groups. This contrasts sharply with the situation in the west and southwest. Meta', Mogamo, and Ngi all

3. My own somewhat limited inquiries on this topic produced information about the origins of 46 women who had been married to Meta' men in precolonial times. This was obtained by asking elderly informants for their mothers' home villages. None of the 46 women had come from the larger plateau chiefdoms, and 42 were from Meta' itself. The data also indicated that intervillage and intervalley marriages were common within Meta'. Of the 46, nine were intravillage unions, while eighteen were intravalley but not intravillage, and fifteen were intervalley. In the remaining four marriages, two of the women had come from Ngembo and two from Bosa. Jean-Pierre Warnier's research in Mankon (personal communication) gives a very similar picture. Hardly any Meta' women are known to have married into this neighboring chiefdom in contrast with the many recorded marriages between Mankon and other plateau groups. On the other hand, Warnier does feel that there may have been some under reporting of Mankon-Meta' marriages, because they were regarded as low-status unions by his Mankon informants.

spoke languages belonging to the Western Grassfields group, and Meta' and Mogamo were in fact mutually intelligible dialects. The dispersed settlement patterns that characterized all of these societies also served to decrease the social distance between them, even though they were separated in some areas by sizeable tracts of farmland and bush. As regards precolonial marriages between Meta' and its western neighbors, we unfortunately possess no information. However, it is noteworthy that a number of Meta' lineages can trace ties of clanship to specific groups in both Ngi and Mogamo. Some in fact maintained active ritual cooperation with their ''foreign'' clanfellows well into the colonial period (Dillon 1981).

Political relationships between the Meta' and adjacent societies appear to have been rather volatile. Despite the ongoing market trade and notwithstanding the fact that some Meta' village chiefs had exchange partners on the plateau, Meta' frequently became involved in violent altercations with its neighbors. Indeed, with only the exceptions of the rather distant Ngunu villages and the border area between Bali-Nyonga and the Bome valley, some precolonial wars were reported on all sides of Meta'. From the perspective of Meta' informants, the causes of warfare were diverse. Among those cited were the appropriation of an enemy's hunting territory, the intimidation of female farmers, the seizure of resources such as trees used to produce charcoal, incidents of kidnapping, and attempts to exact the payment of tribute. The conduct of warfare also appears to have varied from one border to another. The only reported case of ''war'' (*ibit*) between Ngi and Meta' resembled an inter-village conflict case as much as it did warfare between polities. An Ngi murderer was killed by relatives of his Medig valley victim after boasting at a palm-wine drinking session, and this caused further violence between their kin. To the southwest, where just before the German conquest a war was waged between the Mogamo village of Anong and the villages of Zang Tabi, Tonaku, and Kai in Meta', the pattern seems to have been one of opportunistic raiding by small parties of men. Such groups undertook to capture or kill enemy women working in outlying farm areas as well as to conduct nighttime raids against the compounds of their opponents. By contrast, the armed conflicts between eastern Meta' villages and plateau chiefdoms such as Mankon and Bafut seem to have been much more highly organized confrontations. These wars, which were described by informants as almost a regular dry-season activity, sometimes involved multi-village alliances on the Meta' side and entire quarters or chiefdoms on the other. Although the actual engagements were again usually fought by small parties seeking to ambush the enemy, many warriors were typically mobilized under the auspices of their village chiefs, and societies of war scouts provided intelligence. The use of provocative tactics, such as burning off the hunting tract of an opposing chief, and the informants' descriptions of diplomatic negotiations for the return of important prisoners give these conflicts more of the flavor of international relations between sovereign groups.

Household Economy

The precolonial Meta' depended significantly upon both subsistence farming and trade.[4] The basic economic unit was the polygynous or patrilocal extended family under the authority of a male elder. Such family heads usually controlled several parcels of land scattered in different locations. The compound site was typically two-tenths to six-tenths of a hectare. It had several huts and a central patio of packed clay along with surrounding groves and gardens. Many compound heads also possessed five to twenty oil palms and two to four additional farm plots comparable to their compound sites in size. Such tracts might be located elsewhere within the village itself or in "bush" areas such as the grassy hillsides overlooking Meta' settlements and the border zones with groups such as Mankon, Bafut, and Mogamo. In the latter instance, some farmers would need to pass through neighboring villages to reach their cultivations.

Elderly informants claim that farmland, especially fertile tracts within the village area, was a scarce resource in precolonial times, and several types of evidence support their assertions. The fallow period for village plots could be as short as one to four years, and a fertilization technique, by which dry grass was

4. In this section and the following ones on interpolity exchange, I have drawn upon the 1977 field notes of M.J. Rowlands as well as my own.

turned under during cultivation and subsequently burned, was employed on some farms. In addition, individual inheritance of plots was closely regulated, farmland could actually be sold under certain circumstances, and much of the border area between Meta' and the plateau chiefdoms was quickly taken under cultivation following the suppression of warfare in early colonial times.

Many different crops were produced under the precolonial farming regime. Colocasia, maize, yams, and pumpkins were grown in the cool and moist valley bottoms along with plantains and oil palms. In drier, more open areas, such as the bush farms, the main crops were maize, beans, groundnuts, and yams. Raffia palms, which were tapped for wine and also used in the construction of huts and the fabrication of many household items, were tended in marshy areas on the valley floors.

Animal protein was obtained from both livestock and game, with the principal domestic species being goats, chickens, and pigs. Although goats, which were used primarily for bride-wealth and sacrifices, were greatly coveted, most compounds did not keep more than two to five at a given time. They were tethered during the farming season but allowed to browse freely at other times. Pigs, by contrast, were normally penned. While individuals hunted and trapped game such as antelopes and giant cane rats throughout the year, collective hunts were conducted during the dry season. The owners of sizeable areas of bush invited both village mates and outsiders to help burn them over in order to flush out game. The animals were then killed with Dane guns, spears, and the assistance of hunting dogs.

In precolonial times the household was the basic unit of production and consumption. Operationally, it was divided into subunits identified with the various resident wives and their respective children. Ideally, each woman possessed her own hut with enough space for sleeping and cooking as well as attic storage. In households with little land, however, the co-wives were sometimes obliged to share. Farm plots were similarly subdivided, with each married woman receiving a permanent allocation from the holdings of the compound head. In practice, however, such plots were often shared with mothers, sisters, and other female kin through cooperative farming arrangements.

The precolonial division of labor was based primarily upon sex and age. Men cleared farms, tended trees and livestock, built huts, and engaged in palm-oil production, craft activities, and trade. For their part, the women cultivated, planted, and harvested the field crops as well as doing domestic chores. They also produced some craft items and took part in exchange. The role of children was to carry water and firewood and to learn the skills appropriate to their sexes. From about age seven, girls began to assist their mothers on the farm and boys helped their fathers. In the late teens, the male and female roles diverged even more sharply. While girls married and went to reside with their husbands, their brothers remained in their fathers' households for many more years.

The compound head himself had what is best described as a managerial role. He controlled the household's land, trees, livestock, and other resources as well as its income. While women could store crops grown for consumption in their own huts, they were expected to account to their husbands for anything sold in the market. In return, they were provided with items that had to be purchased, such as meat, salt, and extra palm oil. The compound head also assumed the costs of herbal and ritual curing and saved to obtain bridewealth for additional wives. The latter enterprise was considered vital, since it was only through continuous growth that the household could expect to prosper and provide long-term security for all of its members.

Meta' compounds were ideally perpetual units. At the death of the compound head, his role generally passed to a son whom he had secretly chosen as his "successor" (ɜjɜnɜp). Often one of the younger offspring, the latter inherited both the prerogatives and the obligations of his father. He assumed control of his father's titles and property as well as his wives. He also accepted responsibility for any brothers who remained in the compound. Frequently, however, the successor was still a child at the time of his father's death. In such cases, an elder who was a close agnatic kinsman of the father was usually chosen to serve as "trustee" (wit ni wɛr ɜtɜn) until the real successor had reached sufficient age.

Through the succession system outlined above, established compounds continued indefinitely in existence. Sons not fortunate enough to be chosen as successors were ideally allowed to establish their own households. However, achieving such independence was typically a lengthy process. If a son labored dutifully, his father was expected to provide bridewealth at some point during his thirties or forties. Even then, however, he brought his new wife to live in the father's household. It was only after she had delivered several children, thereby making it clear that the couple would found a continuing line, that the son was allowed to set up his own compound. This could be handled in a variety of ways, depending upon the land holdings of the father. In certain cases, a "young" man built upon some of the land that his mother had farmed, while in others the father's own compound site was subdivided or two or more sons were sent to occupy outlying plots of farmland. If the family assets permitted, a son might also be given some livestock and oil palms.

Interpolity Exchange

Commerce was also important to the precolonial Meta' economy. Exchange with neighboring groups provided a powerful stimulus to production, and both men and women had some involvement in trade. Women, for example, cultivated large crops of beans, maize, and groundnuts and sold up to half of their harvests. In addition, some land-short housewives of the Medig valley area engaged in pottery making as a full-time occupation. For their part, the men produced raffia bags and small amounts of palm oil and palm wine to be traded. They also purchased beans, livestock, and palm oil for resale to neighboring groups. Finally, the members of several clans had blacksmithing as an hereditary occupation. With the proceeds from enterprises such as these, men were able to buy additional food for their families.

Meta' was linked to the regional system in a fashion unique for Bamenda. Like the central-plateau chiefdoms it had a middleman's position. However, this was in a branch of the intraregional exchange network, not the system of long-distance trade. Those trade routes that did cross Meta' also passed through several semi-forested valleys where settlement was dispersed rather than across an open plain dominated by fortified

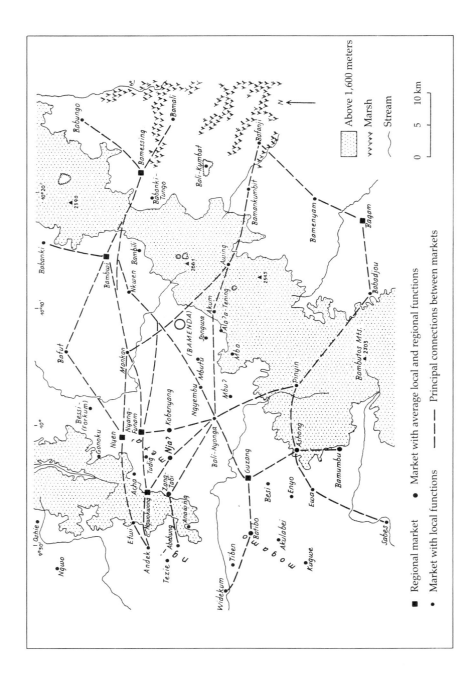

Map 3. Marketplaces of the Bamenda plateau at the end of the nineteenth century. Note concentration of markets in Meta' area, including Ngoo, Ngang-Funom, Mbwekwong, Zang-Tabi, Nja? (Niah), and Kobenyang (Kobenyang). (From Warnier 1985:?)

towns. In this context, a system of weekly markets handled much of the exchange. Map 3 portrays the Meta' market network which was the only one of its type in Bamenda. Several different kinds of agents carried out the transactions in precolonial Meta' markets. These included male and female producer-sellers from Meta' itself and nearby forest groups, male commercial traders from Meta', and professional merchants from plateau groups such as Bali, Mankon, and Bafut. However, in comparison with their counterparts in the latter societies, professional Meta' merchants seem to have been fewer in number and to have operated on a smaller scale.

Since the Meta' profited from a middleman's position in the intra-regional system, they sought to preserve their advantage by restricting travel from neighboring societies. Just as outside traders seeking to bypass the plateau chiefdoms could be robbed and enslaved, no plateau merchants were permitted to pass entirely through Meta' to deal directly with the Ngi and Mogamo. Traders from Mankon sometimes did reach markets such as Zang and Ngwokwong on the far side of Meta', but only if they had close ties to Meta' villagers living along their routes. Contacts such as these escorted and hosted foreign traders as well a providing credit and participating in joint ventures.

Another important channel of commerce was private exchange among notables and chiefs. Meta' village heads, for example, established such relationships with the Chiefs of Mankon and Bafut as well as counterparts in Ngi and Mogamo. A chief initiated an exchange by sending a party with gifts to his partner. The latter then entertained the visitors and dispatched representatives of his own on a subsequent date. As a rule, Meta' chiefs gave commodities that were important in the intra-regional exchange and received complementary products from their partners. However, Meta' village heads also relied upon "big man exchanges" with plateau notables for access to elite goods—like cloth, carved masks, and wooden stools—which they could not obtain through the market.

Slave trading was yet another aspect of Meta' exchange relations with the outside. Though not conducted on a large scale, it was nonetheless an important source of prestige goods such as cloth, guns, and gunpowder. The slaves exported from Meta' were of several types. Some were purchased or captured from neighboring groups on the plateau, while others, like debt hostages and incorrigible criminals, came from Meta' itself. Most were sent in the direction of Bali-Nyonga, with a few going toward Mogamo, and all sales to groups outside the polity were carefully monitored. According to informants in both the Bome and Zang valleys, only the members of a few clans that possessed the slave rope-license were allowed to carry out transactions. The chief and notables of the village in which a sale occurred also had to be informed and given some share of the proceeds.

The Impact of Interpolity Exchange

It is of course impossible to assess how trade influenced precolonial Meta' society in any precise fashion. Nonetheless it is clear that many households were involved with it in one way or another. For some, trade simply provided access to a wider range of consumption products than would otherwise have been available. Others turned to it out of more pressing needs. Some women from land-poor villages in the Medig valley, for example, depended on the sale of their pottery to purchase food in the market. In a similar fashion, men who produced too little palm oil for their families often made or traded craft products in order to obtain it. The use of a brass rod currency, which was freely exchangeable against other commodities, facilitated these transactions as well as enabling men to purchase salt and meat for their households.

Trade was also crucial to the accumulation of wealth in precolonial Meta'. As they built up capital in the form of brass rods, enterprising men reinvested it in savings societies and new trading ventures. This ultimately enabled them to acquire additional wives and land, thereby enhancing further the productive ability of their domestic groups. While the upper limits of this process of household expansion cannot be exactly determined, the number of wives possessed by wealthy men provides at least an approximate index. According to elderly informants, the richest Meta' notables possessed no more than six wives in immediate precolonial times, and important village chiefs were limited to ten or twelve. This is considerably fewer than seen in the larger plateau polities, where some chiefs had hundreds of wives and retainers.

Still, by contrast with those of its neighbors in both the forest and plateau, the Meta' productive system was broadly diversified. More self-sufficient than most Bamenda societies, the Meta' produced enough palm oil for their own consumption as well as all of the key food crops used in the area. They also extracted a middleman's profit from the trade that crossed their territory and contributed significant quantities of maize, beans, raffia bags, and pottery to the Bamenda regional system. On balance, it seems accurate to say that they had a very favorable semiperipheral position within the local exchange network.

Fundamental Political Concepts

While some aspects of precolonial Meta' politics, such as the structures associated with descent and village organization, are best described individually, three broad concepts or clusters of ideas are essential to understanding Meta' political organization as a whole. In this section, I shall outline these basic idea systems and their relations with one another in order to lay the foundations for subsequent discussion of specific political institutions. Each of the three concepts represents a slightly different way of looking at the set of relationships, rights, and duties that made up the Meta' political system in 1900. First, a complex of notions regarding mystical power and danger (*njɔm* and *ndɔn*) provided a system of sanctions that reinforced most political roles and prerogatives. Second, the idea of "historical primacy as a source of legitimacy and power" served to define specific political rights and simultaneously gave such rights a foundation in the value system of the Meta'. Finally, the concept of "*čam*-able property" (exchangeable symbols of political rights and duties) supplied a calculus for expressing the distribution of political entitlements within Meta' society and a set of rules about their transfer from individual to individual and group to group.

My understanding of each of these concepts began with the recording of a simple observation and led to a many-faceted process of exploration that lasted for the duration of fieldwork. The concept of *ndɔn* provides a useful example of this. Several months after arriving in Meta', I suddenly became aware of how often this term occurred in informants' accounts of conflicts within kinship and political groups. They would often explain why a party to a dispute did not take a particular course of action by saying, "If he did, he would carry *ndɔn*," and a knowing look would come over their faces. English-speaking Meta' had originally said that *ndɔn* meant "bad luck," but since this term has such a neutral connotation in American culture (you can do nothing about bad luck but suffer it), I had paid little attention. (I am sure that if they had translated *ndɔn* as "curse" or "witchcraft" my anthropological ears would have perked up at the first mention.)

In any case, the frequency with which the word *ndɔn* appeared finally forced me to take note of it. At this point, further inquiries were made, and I soon learned that *ndɔn* was a kind of curse or suffering with which the traditional God of the Meta' afflicted persons who had violated the rights of others in certain ways. As it turned out, this was only the initial step in a very long and complicated chain of inquiry. In the following months, countless hours were spent expanding the list of reasons for which *ndɔn* could afflict people, investigating the roles that the will of God and the speech of men play in its causation, and discovering the ways in which one can cope with *ndɔn*. I had the sensation of moving ever deeper into a conceptual universe radically different from my own and yet being constantly eluded by the more subtle points. On the last day in Meta', I was still asking questions about *ndɔn*.

There is obviously no practical way to document a process of inquiry such as this, or rigorously prove that the result of it was indeed a "fundamental principle" of Meta' political organization. However, there remains one method by which the reader can judge the validity of such claims for him or herself. As the study of Meta' political organization progressed, the concept of *ndɔn* and the others listed above seemed to emerge as underlying principles in terms of which the more concrete aspects of Meta' political organization became understandable. When viewed as realizations of these general principles, many of the specific features of descent group organization, village structure, chieftaincy, etc. seemed to hang together in a meaningful whole, while without these concepts they remained an assemblage of unrelated facts. For me, then, these three concepts became a key to understanding the Meta' political system, and the consistency with which they rendered one aspect of Meta' political organization after another comprehensible gave me increasingly greater confidence in their value. The reader is free to make a similar test.

Ndɔn and *Njɔm*: Mystical Danger and Power

One crucial component of Meta' political ideology was a somewhat complex and diffuse theory of mystical power. In Meta', such power had both its positive side and its negative side: it could be used either to place a curse on an enemy or to obtain benefits for oneself and one's kinship or local group. Since the negative aspect had a much greater emphasis in Meta' culture, I shall begin by discussing it. Although this approach may be asymmetrical from a logical standpoint, ethnographically it gives a truer picture.[5]

In its negative aspect, the Meta' theory of mystical power can be termed "the theory of *ndɔn*." *Ndɔn* was a form of bad luck or curse that was manifested in illness, death, poverty, and the infertility of women among other things. It was thus the opposite of all the benefits that rituals in most indigenous African cultures were designed to achieve.

Several characteristic manifestations of *ndɔn* can be distinguished, and describing two of these affords a convenient entry into Meta' conceptions of mystical danger. The first type of *ndɔn* occurred in what are best described as situations of ritual pollution. Certain unusual or unnatural events were interpreted as evidence of *ndɔn*. These included death by lightning, death by falling from a tree, suicide, the death of a pregnant woman, the

---

5. To my knowledge, there was no generic term for mystical power in Meta', comparable to *swem* and *tsav* among the nearby Tiv (P. Bohannan 1958). However, some idea of mystical power seems to have been an underlying premise in Meta' culture, since there were terms for the mechanism used to activate it (*njɔm*) and the results of its use (*ndɔn*).

burning of a hut, a fight in which calabashes of wine were broken, acts of symbolic aggression such as throwing a spear at an enemy's roof, and many others. Although Meta' informants did not speculate freely on the causality of *ndɔn* in cases such as these, they treated each event as a serious manifestation of *ndɔn* that could lead to additional suffering if proper rituals were not performed.

Treatment for polluting *ndɔn* involved the intervention of an hereditary specialist (*wit ʒtu ʒfayʔi*). Each such specialist had the exclusive power to remove the *ndɔn* associated with specific unnatural events whenever they occurred within his territory, a monopoly that was itself sanctioned by *ndɔn*. Should anyone fail to summon the specialist after one of the aforementioned manifestations of *ndɔn*, that person ran the risk of suffering additional *ndɔn* from having violated his rights. The procedures by which ritual specialists ended states of polluting *ndɔn* usually entailed the removal of objects identified with the supernatural danger. For example, the *ndɔn* of suicide was removed when a specialist carried off the corpse for burial. Since these procedures were themselves considered to be supernaturally dangerous, specialists were normally well paid for their services.

The second type of *ndɔn* typically occurred when important moral rules had been violated within the kin group or community. For example, if a man fought with an agnate, committed adultery with the wife of a fellow clansman, or failed to pay bridewealth promised to an affine, he might suffer *ndɔn*. Usurping the political position of another, such as a chief or a lineage head, could also bring it on.

In cases such as these, it was first and foremost the speech of the offended party that was believed to cause *ndɔn*. His utterance was described as an *njɔm* ("statement of correct words"), a term applied to supernaturally powerful speech in many other contexts. This was a complaint in which the person whose rights had been violated described the offense in a truthful way. In reality, a great variety of pronouncements were considered as *njɔm*. The purest form of *njɔm* was a carefully worded statement accompanied by ritual acts such as the speaker's pouring palm wine on the ground from his hereditary drinking horn. However, certain community activities in which all the people of the village cried out in unison were also classified as *njɔm*, and even private unguarded comments, not intended as an *njɔm* by the speaker, might have some effect.

In the Meta' view, speech was thus an inherently powerful thing and a force that could be most dangerous. Sometimes, this belief came out in very sudden and (for the ethnographer) unexpected ways. For example, in one case where affines were arguing over bridewealth payments, the father-in-law abruptly stopped and said, "We shouldn't talk so much. All these strong things we are saying might affect somebody." He said this because he did not want his complaints, expressed sharply for the sake of making an impression on the debtor son-in-law, to cause his daughter to become ill or one of his grandchildren to die. For the same reason, people could be fined if they talked about certain types of cases after they had been resolved.

In general, the potency of an *njɔm* or ritual statement was thought to depend on several factors, including the truthfulness of the pronouncement, the seriousness of the offense, the volume of the complaint, and the status of the complainer. A wholly truthful complaint was believed more likely to cause *ndɔn*, and statements by lineage heads and village notables were thought to be more effective than those of ordinary villagers. Similarly, when the person who had been offended complained loudly and was joined by many others, *ndɔn* was more probable.

It should also be noted that God was thought to have an important role in the genesis of *ndɔn*. The Meta' believed in a single Creator Spirit called *Ŋwiȝ* and saw themselves as being in a close relationship with this deity. In the view of many, it was actually *Ŋwiȝ* who heard the complaint of the injured party after a supernaturally dangerous offense and decided whether to punish the offender with *ndɔn*. Both the will of God and the word of man were thus important in the causation of *ndɔn*.[6]

In situations where mystical danger resulted from an *njɔm*, the remedy was usually sought in a negation or reversal of this *ndɔn*-causing speech. In some cases, the offender simply took steps to satisfy the offended party so that he would cease to complain, while in other instances either the latter or his lineage

6. See Haaf (1971, 1977) for additional discussion of Meta' conceptions of God and related beliefs.

head was asked to perform a ritual blessing the offender. As a general rule, one attempted to cut off *ndɔn* at its source by satisfying the person capable of speaking the strongest *njɔm* in the case.

Finally, it should be stressed that *ndɔn* in all forms was believed to be contagious. After a moral infraction, the *ndɔn* was thought likely to spread from the offender himself to related persons, and in cases of polluting *ndɔn*, mystical danger was often seen as something rather like a contagious disease. If one suicide or death by lightning went ritually untreated, another was believed likely to occur in the same compound or locality.

As noted in the beginning of this section, the Meta' theory of mystical power had both positive and negative aspects. The concept of *njɔm* was the link between the two, since an *njɔm* could be either an entreaty that *Ŋwiʒ* punish an offender or an appeal for blessings and assistance from God. The latter kind of request could be made in many contexts. For example, when the men of a lineage prepared to bestow one of their daughters on a man from another group, they rubbed her with camwood and spoke an *njɔm* in which they asked *Ŋwiʒ* to make her marriage successful and allow her to bear many children. Similar requests for the God's blessing were made when a man was being installed as the successor of his father by the members of his lineage. And God could be petitioned in the same way to ensure success in more routine activities, such as going hunting or making a journey. In all of these ways, the same power of *njɔm* that was used to place curses on persons who violated the legitimate interests of others could be used to obtain positive benefits. Individuals could ask for blessings by making a private *njɔm*, descent group segments could do so in formal ritual contexts, and villages and other local groups could do the same. The benefits or successes that were obtained through such positive uses of the power of *njɔm* were normally referred to as *ʒfuʔu* ("good luck") or *bɔrʒ bɔt* ("state of coolness and softness," "blessing").

The general theory of mystical power that has been outlined here played a critical role in the precolonial Meta' political system in at least two ways. First, it helped to define positions of authority and political prerogatives. One useful way of looking at Meta' political organization is to see it as a system in which authority was based on the uneven distribution of mystical power. Most authority roles were in part dependent on the fact that their incumbents had more direct access to God than ordinary persons did. For example, a chief or descent group leader possessed the relatively exclusive power to speak an *njɔm* to *Ŋwiɜ* under certain circumstances. Secondly, the Meta' theory of mystical power played a crucial role in the political system by reinforcing its structure and protecting existing prerogatives. It has already been mentioned that *ndɔn* sanctioned a father-in-law's right to receive bridewealth. In a similar way, most important public rights in Meta' society were protected by the threat of *ndɔn*, since a person who tried to usurp any of them was thought likely to suffer from it. Hence if an ordinary man infringed the right of his lineage head to perform marriage rituals, he risked *ndɔn*. Likewise, if people did not turn over to the village leaders leopards they had killed, or, if certain disputants failed to summon resolution agents appropriate for their cases, they would incur *ndɔn* from the *njɔm* or speech of those whose rights they had violated. The theory of mystical power thus served a dual role in the Meta' political order. Differential access to mystical power was a basis for many authority roles, and, at the same time, the political status quo was sanctioned by mystical forces.

Historical Primacy as a Source of Legitimacy and Power

Another fundamental concept in Meta' political ideology was the idea that history is the source of truth and legitimacy, and therefore, in part, the foundation of actual political organization at any given time. Although this proposition was not stated in such an abstract form by any Meta' informant, it was expressed in many specific contexts and proved to be such a pervasive theme that it can justly be considered as a fundamental principle of Meta' political organization.

This concept appears to have been rooted in Meta' ideas about primary kin relations, particularly the father-son relationship. In trying to explain the essence of this relationship, some Meta' informants posed the question, "How could the son ever know more than the father? The father has delivered the son and is the source of everything that he knows." For the Meta', these statements were logical and coherent, since wisdom in coping with the world and ritual knowledge were both seen as things handed down by tradition, rather than as the products of individual experience. The informants also argued that, since the father had lived longer than his son and lived before him, he had naturally seen more, and his words would thus always have greater force and validity. Accordingly, the son's best hope for success in his own life was thought to lie in learning from his father and approximating, inasmuch as possible, the knowledge of the father himself. One informant brought out these ideas succinctly in a discussion of patricide. In his view, patricide would be unthinkable, since it would be like a group of schoolboys who had just begun to learn killing their teacher, or a branch of a tree pulling out the root.

The idea that a son depended absolutely on his father for the knowledge of how to cope with life was naturally seen as a relative thing. Each father stood in this relationship with his son and in a reverse relation with his own father. Going backwards in time, wisdom was thus thought to increase, and informants often commented that if their forefathers were still alive, they would be able to make ritual statements incomparably stronger than those of any living men.

These Meta' beliefs were of course idealizations that had only an indirect linkage to actual behavior. If the Meta' had always acted upon such premises, it would have meant that cultural innovation was impossible, that father-son conflicts were nonexistent, and that knowledge was continually diminishing over the generations because of imperfect learning and transmission of ideas. However, none of these things was true. The concept of father-son relations set forth above did influence political action profoundly, but it did not determine all political behavior.

Although the Meta' concept that historical primacy is the source of truth and legitimacy was rooted in the model of father-son relations, it found many other expressions in Meta' political ideology. One of these was in a doctrine of testament that provided the basis for numerous political rights and activities. In Meta' belief, the words of deceased fathers had the force of law. Their statements, especially dying testaments, were valid simply because they had spoken them. Since these dead fathers had lived before and knew more than those now existing, there was no appeal from their dictates and no way of evaluating them.

According to informants, testament was often the mechanism through which the reorganization of descent groups was achieved. For example, a man who was the head of a descent group segment from which several others had subdivided might leave dying instructions concerning how these groups should cooperate in resolving conflicts in the future and what prerogatives the various segment leaders would have. Or a dead man's grave might be observed as a hunting shrine simply because he had requested his sons to come there to perform hunting rites. These examples show the multifunctional role of testament in Meta' political order. On the one hand, it reaffirmed existing political structures and authorized certain persons to perform particular ritual roles. On the other hand, it was a source of perpetual change.

The political structure derived from testaments was itself reinforced by Meta' concepts of mystical power and danger. When the instructions of the dead fathers were not carried out, their anger was believed likely to cause *ndɔn* for their descendants. If a subgroup within a unit established by the dead fathers attempted to resolve a conflict on its own, for example, its members might suffer *ndɔn* for two reasons. First, they had usurped the rights of the wider group and its leaders to perform the activity in question, and, second, they had disobeyed the instructions of their dead fathers.

Another expression of the belief that historical primacy was the ultimate source of truth and legitimacy, was the fact that claims of historical priority supported most leadership roles. Lineage heads, for example, derived much of their authority from the fact that they were the chosen successors of their groups' founders. In each generation, the leader of a descent group segment selected one of his sons to act as his successor and thereby created an unbreakable link between the present and the past. Thenceforth, the successor was viewed as the closest approximation to the deceased lineage head. This meant that he would best be able to say the correct thing when speaking of the affairs and history of his group, and that therefore his ritual statements would be the most quickly heard by God.

Since one of the important goals of descent group rites was to create a performance as much like that of the forefathers as possible, many things were done to establish continuity with the past in ritual contexts. For example, the successor normally drank and poured libations from the sacrificial buffalo-horn cup of his forefathers. Because his predecessors had drunk from this vessel, breathed into it, and spoken their words over it, its use was thought to enhance the connection between them and the successor. When he talked, it was as if the dead fathers were speaking with him.

The use of special powdered camwood (*fibik*) in descent group rituals also served to link the participants with their deceased fathers. Each clan segment had its own bundle of camwood, which was said to be identical with that of the clan founder. This was because whenever such a group became ritually independent, its leader was given a portion of the camwood of the parent segment from which his own was separating. Should the new group itself later subdivide, the head of the second offspring unit would be provided with camwood in a similar way, and presumably such procedures had been followed since the beginning of the clan. It was also customary that before any segment head died he spat into his bundle of camwood, thus imbuing it with his breath or spirit (*ʒzwi*). Through these various practices, the camwood of a descent group segment became a powerful symbol. Whenever it was used in rituals, it enhanced the identification of the performers with their dead fathers, added to the credibility of their *njɔm* or ritual statement, and made it more likely that God would answer their requests.

As the foregoing discussion has illustrated, leadership roles within descent groups were based on the instructions and decisions of leaders in previous generations and on the legitimate control of certain ritual objects, such as the sacrificial cup and bundle of camwood, that were identified with the deceased fathers. However, the notion of historical primacy as a source of legitimacy was not restricted to descent group activities alone. Another prime expression of this principle in Meta' political ideology was the fact that the leadership of local communities was based on it as well. Thus, the *mikum si* ("senior village notables"), who were the ultimate authorities of a village, were always said to be the direct descendants of those descent group heads who had arrived first in the history of the place. Meta' informants said that these men "held" (*niŋ*) the village. Since they and their ancestors had been in it longer than anyone else, they knew more of its affairs and history, and better than anyone they were able to "speak the correct thing" concerning their community. Their *njɔm* or ritual statement was therefore more powerful than that of any other person. (The history-based role of the senior village notables will be discussed further in Chapter 6.)

In summary, it can be said that the Meta' concept of historical primacy as a source of legitimacy and power constituted one of the fundamental premises of the Meta' political order. It was used to define the boundaries of specific political groups as well as political rights and prerogatives, and it was the foundation of authority in many leadership roles. All of this stemmed from a rather literal interpretation of the commonsense notion that older people or their representatives had a more precise knowledge because they had existed before those currently living and were seeing things before they were born. But Meta' ideas of history were also integrated with their notions of mystical power. Historically senior persons had greater mystical power because they had lived earlier and seen more. This meant that they were more likely to say the correct thing in their *njɔm* to the God *Ŋwiʒ*, which was therefore more apt to be acted upon. In the Meta' political system, historical primacy was thus a source of both mystical power and legitimacy.

Čam-able Property

To a considerable extent, Meta' political structure seems to have been defined by the distribution of certain physical objects which themselves symbolized the right to perform particular activities. Included within this category were the *sami* ("dancing field") that entitled its possessor to hold independent mortuary celebrations with the members of his descent group; the stone and knife used in butchering a leopard, possession of which authorized the head of a clan segment to receive such animals and consume them with his followers; the instruments and costumes of numerous exclusive dances; and many other items that will be discussed below.

Rights over these objects fell within a single class, because they were all obtained through a similar process. The person or group acquiring the object was said to *čam* ("make payments"), while those granting it were said to *wɛrɛ* ("present"). This type of transaction was clearly distinguished from market exchange (*fɛn—zɔn*: "sell—buy") in a number of ways that will be described. However, the objects that were acquired through "*čam*ing" still did correspond to the English category of "property" in certain respects, so that describing them as "*čam*-able properties" is not misleading. The two attributes of these *čam*-able things that emerged most strongly in discussions with Meta' informants were that they were *possessed* and that they were always potentially *exchangeable*. In addition, *čam*-able properties were also indirectly linked into the system of subsistence production and market exchange: the things that were most often "*čam*-ed" (i.e., given as payment for such properties) were goats and brass rods, and both of these items could be obtained through barter with subsistence products in local markets. In this context, what served to distinguish *čam*-able properties from other goods was the special rules that governed their transfer and the fact that many of them were highly prestigious possessions.[7]

Rights over *čam*-able properties were normally described as if they belonged to individual men, but in reality they were held by and transferred between descent group segments of different sizes. It was only the head of an *mban* group or minimal lineage segment who could acquire a *čam*-able property, and when he did so, he acted on behalf of his group. Even though he exercised the greatest control over it, the other members of the group cooperated in its use (e.g., performed the exclusive dance that had been purchased by their leader) and had some say about when and how it would be employed.

7. It is possible to conceive of Meta' *čam*-able properties as existing within a special "sphere of exchange," such as the sphere of prestige goods that Bohannan (1959) describes for Tiv society. However, the various "spheres" of the Meta' economy were not nearly as insulated from each other as Bohannan claims their counterparts among Tiv to have been.

Possessing rights to *čam*-able properties simultaneously served to define descent groups and authorized them to carry out exclusive activities. For example, a given segment might enjoy an independent identity because its leader had a dancing field at his compound, and, at the same time, it was only possession of this *čam*-able property that enabled the group to perform the activities associated with it, such as mortuary celebrations involving dancing.

The conditions under which *čam*-able properties were transferred were briefly as follows: The head of one clan segment (the size and composition of the group varied from case to case) made payments to the leader of another. In most instances, these included at least one goat, several brass rods, and a quantity of palm wine. In return for such payments—the things that had been *čam*-ed—he and his group received full authority to use the property concerned as well as the power to grant it to other descent group segments under the appropriate circumstances. These use and transfer rights over the property in question became the possessions in perpetuity of the clan segment that had *čam*-ed them, to be controlled by each successor of the original leader. In addition, the entire transaction through which a *čam*-able property was acquired had the character of a permanent contract that was mystically sanctioned. Other descent group segments could not appropriate the new owners' rights (e.g., use their dance without having *čam*-ed it). Likewise, the members of the group that had granted the *čam*-able property could not attempt to rescind this, and the new owners could usually not convey the right to still other groups for a higher fee than they themselves had paid. All such rules pertaining to the transfer were sanctioned by *ndɔn*.

Within the large category of exchanges designated by the term *čam*, there were several subtypes. Most of these variations stemmed from the fact that certain *čam*-able properties could only be exchanged by descent group segments that stood in specified relationships to each other. For example, some had to be transferred between two segments belonging to the same clan. The granting of *čam*-able properties in this category (e.g., *mban*, "sacrificial hut"; *sami*, "dancing field"; and *ɔtɔn inyam*, "the seat of an animal," see pp. 93–99) represented part of the normal segmentation process in every clan. Newly emerging segments *čam*-ed properties such as these from already established ones and thereby acquired the right to perform specific descent group activities. Other kinds of *čam*-able properties were controlled by the chief of one's village (e.g., the right of *mbɛŋ*, "woven raffia mats," and the right of *iču ɜnɜp mibe*, "two doors," see pp. 162–163), and granting these was a prime expression of his political role. Finally, a third group of *čam*-able properties (like the various exclusive dances and the right of receiving leopards) could theoretically be exchanged in an unrestricted fashion. Items in this category could pass between segments of the same clan or different clans, as well as between segments residing in different villages and valleys. However, the transfer of such *čam*-able properties was often limited in practice, since they were exclusive items that enhanced the prestige of the groups possessing them. Hence the members of a group that had an exclusive dance might be reluctant to allow either their own clanfellows or unrelated persons to acquire it.

In general, the concept of *čam*-able property seems to have been essential to Meta' political organization. In the following chapters, I hope to show how Meta' ideas about the use and transfer of these properties marked off the boundaries of political groups of all kinds, helped to structure their activities, and served to define roles of leadership and authority.

Conclusion

As the preceding discussion has conveyed, the three concepts of historical primacy, *čam*-able property, and mystical power were among the most fundamental aspects of Meta' political ideology. Although by no means determinative of social action, they comprised a unified system that provided the conceptual foundations for most political behavior. As will be seen in Chapters 5 through 11, the precise form of both descent groups and local groups appears to have depended to a great extent on the Meta' notions of historical primacy and *čam*-able property. Authorizations to perform particular activities came from the dictates of the dead fathers and from the process of exchange known as *čam*-ing. Having such an authorization seems to have defined the group that possessed it: its identity depended, at least in part, on its right to conduct the activity in question. Leadership roles also appear to have rested on these authorizations, since a group's acquiring one was described as a process in which its leader was given or *čam*-ed the particular right. Finally, the Meta' concepts of supernatural power and danger (*njɔm* and *ndɔn*) provided a set of sanctions that sustained the entire political structure created through the use of the other two concepts.

FIVE

Patrilineal Descent

ALTHOUGH the household constituted the basic unit of the precolonial Meta' economy, descent provided the foundation for the Meta' political system. In this chapter, I will outline the concepts and values associated with patrilineal descent and describe the various ways in which descent groups sought to organize themselves. Before embarking on this task, however, it is necessary to clarify certain limitations inherent in the data. Despite its fundamental importance, patrilineal descent organization is the part of the precolonial Meta' system for which it is least possible to analyze the relation between ideal and real behavior. The primary reason for this is that since the precolonial era, Meta' society has experienced greater continuity in the realm of kinship and descent than in village or polity organization. As a result, memories of recent conflicts among kin have displaced recollections of similar precolonial events to a much greater extent than is the case with village and polity-level disputes. In addition, behavior within descent groups is generally less public and broadly consequential than political action at the other levels. It therefore provides fewer striking episodes that are likely to be recalled after the long passage of time.

Given such obstacles to reconstruction, I have chosen to present my material on the Meta' patrilineal system in the following way. I shall first describe the various concepts and values associated with patrilineal descent in Meta' culture and the ideal model of lineage and clan organization. All of these data are based upon the informants' idealized accounts. Next, I will analyze the organization of one particular clan section, beginning with its precolonial history and describing some of the subsequent restructurings that it underwent. This example is being presented, not because it is assumed that the more recent changes described in it are fully reflective of processes in the precolonial system of descent, but because they do convey in a concrete fashion some of the patterns of organization that are touched upon in discussing the ideal model of that system. Following this, I shall outline the characteristics of the clan as a whole and finally comment upon some possible political implications of the kind of patrilineal descent organization seen in Meta'. Although the latter interpretation cannot be supported by case-history material like the hypotheses regarding village and polity organization to be presented later, it is nonetheless important to formulate such a model. Failure to attempt this would distort the overall analysis of precolonial Meta' political organization by giving insufficient attention to the possible discrepancies between ideal and real behavior in one crucial sector of the political system.

Concepts and Values Associated with Patrilineal Descent

Meta' concepts of descent can largely be subsumed under the single word *nibi*. This term expressed the idea of a patrilineal descent group in general, and it was applied to all such groups equally, regardless of their sizes, the types of activities that they carried out, and their temporary or permanent character.

Anthropologists have tended to think structurally about African "lineage systems" and have developed a complex vocabulary for use in describing them. Terms such as "minimal lineage," "maximal lineage," "sub-clan," and "clan" are used to distinguish "different-order" descent groups (Evans-Pritchard 1940a; Fortes 1945). While this approach may help to clarify operational units, the Meta' practice of using a single term to designate all possible subgroups within a lineage structure contrasts sharply with anthropological usage. There are at least two reasons for this. First, the members of societies like Meta' lived their systems rather than analyzing them in abstract terms or comparing them with those of other groups, and second, the Meta' concept *nibi*, unlike the anthropological terms cited above, had more of a qualitative than a structural connotation.

It expressed certain features that all groups called *nibi* shared, rather than differentiating between them.

A *nibi* was essentially a social group whose members all claimed patrilineal descent from a common "father" or ancestor. "Claimed" is the key word here. With such a belief, a group was a *nibi*, and without it, it was not. Moreover, the names of *nibi* groups often underscored the premise that the members were the "children" of one "father"—e.g., Bɔnjɔ ("Children of Njɔ") or Bɔrangɔp ("Children of Tingɔp").

The other essential features that distinguished a *nibi* seem to have been:

1. The concept that its members "ate" or "consumed" things together,

2. The idea that they were obliged to interact in a moral way and provide support for one another, and

3. The belief that they faced a common supernatural predicament.

When it was said that the members of a *nibi* "consumed things together" (*jigɜ non*), the reference was complex. Not only did such persons share the meat of sacrificial goats and game provided by their fellows but they also possessed common interests in certain types of property and either did, or potentially could, benefit from the realization of these jointly held rights. The *nibi* was almost always an exogamous group, and marriage and sexual relations between male and female members were thought of as mystically dangerous offenses. Conversely, all of the male members of a *nibi* were thought to have some legitimate claim over both their fellows' wives and their daughters. Such rights were expressed in a formal way in the smallest unit that could be referred to as a *nibi*, the minimal lineage or *mban* group, composed of about five household heads and their dependents. Within these groups, the bridewealth received for daughters was allocated in a prescribed way, and members also had priority over outsiders in inheriting each other's wives. However, such sharing of interests in marriageable women was not limited to the *mban* group. Actually, the members of any group called a *nibi*, even geographically dispersed ones of several hundred households, were seen as having certain potential rights in one another's wives and daughters. In theory, these would continue to devolve on ever more distantly related agnates as the men in one segment of the *nibi* after another died without sons to inherit. This residual interest of all *nibi* members in rights over women was sometimes also expressed in bridewealth payments. Normally, most of a woman's bridewealth was reserved for the men of her own *mban* group and that of her mother's father, along with select female kin. Yet in even the largest groups called *nibi*, each man had the right to receive a fowl from the husband of a woman of his *nibi* when he traveled outside of his own village and happened to meet her in her husband's compound.

A final aspect of "consuming things together" was that all members of a *nibi* possessed common interests in other important types of property, including farmland, compound sites, raffia and oil palms, livestock, and brass rods. Normally, immediate rights over such property were exercised by individual men who passed them on to their sons through inheritance or by grant during their own lifetimes. However, when a man died with no son to succeed him, his property reverted to the leader of his *mban* group, who was expected to dispose of it in accord with the needs of other group members. Moreover, in cases where all the men of a *mban* group died without sons, their combined estate passed to more and more distant agnates, just as with rights over marriageable women.

Another important characteristic of the *nibi* was that its members all bore a permanent moral responsibility toward each other. Being of the same *nibi* established a bond between two individuals such that they were obliged to support each other in ways beyond what was expected of neighbors and friends. In precolonial times, when a man traveled to distant places he could always count on members of his *nibi* to offer him hospitality and guarantee his safety. If he met with misfortune on the road or was attacked and gave out the alarm cry of his group, any member of it was expected to come to his rescue without question. Likewise, at home a man could expect the members of his *nibi* to fight on his behalf if his wife was abducted or he was seized as a hostage for a bridewealth debt. In modern times, the same supportive values are expressed when the *nibi* brothers of a man contribute toward his court fines or when those who are working at the coast help with the medical expenses of one of their fellows.

Of course, the actual group that provided assistance in such situations varied according to circumstance and necessity. When a man's localized *nibi* segment was able to muster sufficient strength to support him in a fight, other clanfellows would not join in, but would rather try to separate the combatants. However, if the opponents were beating a segment of one's own *nibi* badly and refused to desist, all agnates were obliged to respond. The moral obligation to aid a *nibi* brother was thus not a rigid rule, mechanically applied to all situations, but rather a statement about the potential relationship between all members of the same descent group. What Meta' informants stressed was not that agnates never quarreled or that they always supported each other, but that if no other help was available, the members of a *nibi* had an absolute duty to assist.

The same relationship was also expressed by the fact that certain offenses within the *nibi* were viewed as leading to supernatural sanctions. Thus, failure to come to the assistance of a *nibi* brother who was threatened in any of the above-mentioned ways was thought to lead to *ndɔn* or mystical danger. Once again, the actual need of a brother was subject to interpretation, but if it turned out that one's failing to help was what had caused him to suffer seriously, *ndɔn* was thought to follow automatically, and it could only be removed by an appropriate sacrifice. For example, if a man failed to assist an agnate who collapsed on the road and the man quickly recovered, he might or might not suffer *ndɔn*. But if the kinsman died because he was left lying unattended, the brother who failed to respond would surely bear this affliction. As noted earlier, a number of other specific offenses, such as physical fighting with a *nibi* brother, adultery with his wife, betraying him to thieves or slave catchers, and having sexual relations with a fellow *nibi* member were similarly defined as mystically dangerous.

Being of a single *nibi* also conveyed the idea that people faced a common supernatural predicament (i.e., that they were exposed to the same mystical dangers and simultaneously depended on the same sources of supernatural power for protection against them). This concept was not expressed as a general principle by Meta' informants, but it seems to have been implied in many of their specific statements. Its negative side was contained in the notion that mystical danger was contagious within the *nibɨ*. According to Meta' beliefs, there was a link between agnates such that a mystically dangerous act performed by one could lead to his fellows suffering *ndɔn*. Hence when stressing the seriousness of incest and homicide within the *nibɨ*, informants often claimed that an entire descent group might die out if the correct rituals of purification were not performed.

The positive side of the idea that the members of a *nibɨ* faced a common supernatural predicament can be seen in the belief that they depended on the same forefathers for mystical power and protection in many situations. As noted in the preceding chapter, one's mystical power was thought to depend on his capacity to make a strong statement (*njɔm*) to *Ŋwiʒ*, the traditional God of the Meta', and to his forebears. Delivering such ritual statements allowed the members of the *nibɨ* to protect their legitimate interests by giving *ndɔn* to those who had offended them; to promote the success of activities such as marriage, childbirth, and hunting; and to cure members of their group who were suffering illness through *ndɔn*. Moreover, the basis for making a strong ritual appeal was the collective knowledge that had been passed down by the dead fathers of the group. Thus, according to Meta' concepts of mystical power, persons who shared one ancestor also shared a common source of knowledge and power that allowed them to meet the many threats and challenges that arose in the course of everyday living.

Another concrete expression of the unity that the *nibɨ* derived from having a common source of mystical power is found in the set of customs surrounding camwood (*fibɨk*). As noted previously, each *nibɨ* possessed its own bundle of camwood for use in rituals, and this was among the most potent symbols of the luck and prosperity for which its members wished. It was also regarded as a legacy from the founders of the *nibɨ*, since elaborate ritual procedures served to identify each present-day segment's camwood with that which the forefathers had possessed.

In supernatural terms, all the members of a Meta' *nibɨ* were thus joined and faced a common predicament. Their acts could expose each other to common mystical dangers, and, at the same time, they depended on common sources of knowledge and power in combatting these and promoting the success of their affairs.

In summary, the concept of *nibi* was an idea fundamental to Meta' political order. It was a general category of social group that had many specific manifestations. It provided a basis for dividing the social world into those who shared a common and irrevocable commitment by virtue of their birth and those who did not. Groups called *nibi* had extremely important functions, including organizing rights over property and women and offering assistance to members in times of unusual need. Finally, belonging to a *nibi* placed a person in a common supernatural predicament with his fellows.

An Overview of Meta' Patrilineal Organization

As the preceding discussion has shown, Meta' folk conceptions of patrilineal descent were rather flexible. In the absence of a hierarchy of named different-order descent units, various groups mobilized and then disbanded in the process of achieving specific goals. What defined these units were several kinds of authorizations, such as those provided by the testaments of the forefathers or by exchanges of *čam*-able properties, that empowered given segments of the *nibi* to perform particular activities or to use restricted items.

However, despite the apparent looseness of the concepts of patrilineal grouping used by the Meta' themselves, three broad levels of descent units are readily apparent to an outside observer. Such empirical regularity makes it possible to present a concise analytical overview of descent group organization in Meta'. Accordingly, before beginning to outline the ideal model of *nibi* organization as given by Meta' informants, I shall briefly describe these three levels of grouping. While such a tripartite division of the *nibi* would probably be seen as too rigid by the Meta', who had no terminology corresponding to such a classification, it will hopefully make their ideal model of patrilineal organization more accessible to the non-Meta' reader. The basic types of groups were as follows:

1. The *mban* group. This was the building block of the Meta' patrilineal descent system and the group that controlled marriage and property rights most directly. The *mban* group was a multifunctional localized lineage.

2. The clan section. This was a more or less localized segment of the *nibi*. The members of such units often resided within the same village or at least within the same valley. The internal relations of clan sections were formally structured, with various segments cooperating in important descent group activities on a regular basis. However, the organization of localized clan sections was quite variable.

3. The clan or *nibi* as a whole. As noted above, this was a broad category of persons who recognized common patrilineal descent and the rights and obligations that this entailed. The clan was usually exogamous. It did not have a precisely defined structure, and its members engaged in cooperation and mutual support only on an individual basis, as the appropriate circumstances arose. Subgroups within the clan that did have some kind of formal structure will henceforth be referred to as "clan segments" when not identified more precisely as *mban* groups or clan sections.

The Ideal Model of Descent Group Organization

Organization and Activities of the *Mban* Group

The smallest unit referred to as a *nibi* was the group with its own *mban* ("sacrificial hut"). While informants usually described the *mban* group as being composed of a father and his grown sons, it could in practice consist of any small set of male household heads who traced their descent from a common ancestor, one or more generations removed. Frequently, though not necessarily, the *mban* group was a closely structured residential unit. Although the overall Meta' settlement pattern was one of dispersed homesteads, the compounds of the junior men of an *mban* group tended to cluster around that of their leader. This resulted more from inheritance patterns and circumstance than from any rigidly observed rule that the *mban* group should be localized. As noted earlier, a man normally acquired his compound site by grant or inheritance from his father, and fathers often subdivided their land holdings in the area adjacent to their compounds to make room their sons. Also, if a man died without a successor, an *mban* brother's son would often be installed in his vacant compound. These rules of inheritance, together with a general preference for living among close agnates, encouraged localization of the *mban* group. But in cases where no nearby land was available, younger members who wished to build their own compounds might locate at distances of a kilometer or two.

The identity of the *mban* group was symbolized by the *mban* itself. Having this sacrificial hut allowed the members of the group to perform important social and ritual activities independently of outsiders. The *mban* was a hut built in the same manner as others in the compound. Inside it was a special site called the ɜɣɜm, where the *wit mban* ("man of *mban*," i.e., head of the *mban* group) poured libations of palm wine as he invoked Ŋwiɜ and the spirits of his forefathers. The ɜɣɜm took the form of a small clay pot buried in the floor so that only its lip was visible. Inside the pot, which was usually filled with palm wine, was a small round stone. During rituals, this stone was removed, rubbed with camwood, and dowsed with palm wine. In general, the ɜɣɜm was described as a "channel" or "way" (nɜndzi) that facilitated communication with Ŋwiɜ and the spirits of the dead fathers. These spirits were thought to be present, though invisible, in the area surrounding the ɜɣɜm, and Ŋwiɜ was believed to hear the njɔm that a man spoke more clearly in this place than in any other.

The actual rituals performed by the *mban* group were of two kinds: those done to promote success in important undertakings and others designed to ward off misfortune. Rites of the first type included those associated with marriage and childbearing by daughters of the group as well as the installation rites for male successors, and hunting and warfare rituals. All of these activities were thought unlikely to succeed without proper support from a person's *mban* mates. Whenever a daughter married, for example, it was believed that ill will on the part of any group member who had not received his fair share of the bridewealth could cause her to suffer ndɔn (illness, barrenness, or even death). Therefore, all members had to express their approval by participating in a ritual in which they rubbed the woman's body with camwood (the symbol of happiness, luck, and fertility) and asked Ɲwiʒ and the spirits of the forefathers to make her stay happily with her husband and deliver many children. Similar rituals were necessary before a man could be recognized as his father's successor and begin to enjoy his properties and privileges.

The second type of *mban* group rite was one performed after ill will among members of the group, or between them and outsiders, had caused someone to become ill or die. This might happen, when, as in the preceding example, one of the members of the group had received insufficient bridewealth upon the marriage of a colleague's daughter. Such a man would continually complain of having been slighted, and his bitter talk would lead to *ndɔn* for the woman. After she became ill or her children began to die, her husband would visit a diviner to determine the cause of the *ndɔn* that was plaguing them and be advised to pay at least some of the outstanding debt. He would then ask the men of his wife's *mban* group to perform a sacrifice to end the *ndɔn* that his family had been suffering.

As mentioned earlier, *ndɔn* could also manifest itself in many other situations (e.g., if two men of an *mban* group quarreled seriously, if one betrayed another to enemies, or if a member of the group failed to carry out the instructions of a dead father). In all such cases, the offender's only recourse was to pay fines to the leaders of the *mban* group so that they would perform a ritual to end the curse and restore harmony. Every individual was thus dependent on his own or his spouse's *mban* group leaders to protect him from the malicious speech of living agnates, deceased fathers, and affinal kin.

The nonritual functions of the *mban* group were often intimately connected with its rites. In addition to conducting actual marriage rituals, for example, the men of the *mban* group collectively regulated the distribution of the bridewealth payments that were given for their daughters. For although a suitor was expected to present the various members' shares privately, only a ceremony performed by the entire group could end a state of *ndɔn* caused by any recipient's dissatisfaction. Moreover, whenever the men of such a group met in the sacrificial hut to bless one of their daughters for marriage, they simultaneously collected some token payments of bridewealth to share amongst themselves.[1] Similarly, the properties and rights that a man inherited from his father were formally conferred upon him at the same time that he was ritually installed as a successor in the *mban*. In this fashion, the *mban* group was able to control some of the most vital economic transactions within the Meta' kinship system.

As noted previously, the *mban* group was also involved in the allocation of property in cases where a man died without a son to succeed him. In such cases, the group leader assumed control of his estate. Then later, when another *mban* member was unable to provide land for all of his sons, one of them could be installed in the compound of the deceased. In this way, the *mban* group served as an economic pool to which all excess properties reverted and from which the extraordinary needs of its members could be met.

The claim of the *mban* group on the property of its members was expressed in still other ways. For example, a man could not bypass his *mban* brothers to name someone else as his heir without causing serious conflicts within this group. Also, while a man theoretically had full control over the property he received from his father, he could not sell his land to an outsider unless his *mban* mates agreed.

Finally, the *mban* group was also the primary unit of mutual assistance in Meta' society. If a man was being beaten by others or had been seized as a slave, he could expect his *mban* brothers to come to his aid before any others. He could likewise count on

1. The total amount of bridewealth that changed hands at the time of marriage was high in terms of the wealth of the average man, but it could be paid in a number of different commodities, including goats, brass rods, guns, salt, palm oil, cowries, cloth, and fowl. It was necessary to complete a substantial payment that had been agreed upon before the bride went to live in her new husband's compound. However, other kinds of payments continued throughout the couple's lifetime. Although it is impossible to give a single figure for the first major bridewealth installment in immediate precolonial times, informants suggested 20 or 30 goats together with 20 to 50 brass rods as suitable amounts. Subsequent payments most often took the form of goats to be sacrificed by a woman's agnates on behalf of her and her children, or livestock, palm wine, and other commodities given in ceremonial contexts.

them if he had killed someone and needed money to pay for the costly rituals that served to resolve homicide cases. Furthermore, a man relied upon help from his *mban* brothers when he faced big tasks such as housebuilding or clearing new farms, and any person who lacked primary kinsmen depended on the members of his *mban* group to fulfill their roles. Thus, if a young man's biological father was dead, he would turn to the other senior men of his *mban* group to aid him in finding a wife and negotiating the bridewealth with her kin. Conversely, aged men without sons of their own expected younger *mban* group members to protect them and provide for their material needs.

The Formation of New *Mban* Groups

The process by which new *mban* groups were formed was expressed by Meta' informants in two idioms, one of biological descent and another of *čam*-able property. Normally, they described the relationships between newer and older *mban* groups in terms of the relations between the individuals heading them. The leader of the old group would say about the head of the new, "He is my *wan kyɛŋ* ['big son']. He became big, and so I sent him out to be with his own *mban*." When asked to explain the process in more detail, informants would usually describe the "son" making payments (*čam*-ing) so that the head of the *mban* group from which he was separating would come to consecrate an *ʒɣʒm* ("libation hole") for him. At first, this would only be relied upon for minor matters such as curing slight illnesses among the members of the new group. But later they could begin to "rub" their daughters with camwood (*zɔʔri bɔn*) prior to marriage in the new *mban*. At this point, they had become fully independent and no longer needed to share the bridewealth received for their offspring with the members of the original *mban*.[2]

2. Some informants claimed that it was not correct to describe the process through which the right of *mban* was acquired as an instance of "*čam*-ing," even though some payments or gifts were presented to the head of the original group. According to them, the "father" simply presented (*wɛrɛ*) the right of *mban* to his "son." However, this contradiction in testimonies makes little difference in the overall analysis of Meta' descent organization, since both rights that were obtained through *čam*-ing and those handed down by the fathers are subsumed under the analytical category of "authorizations."

The new *mban* head was rarely the actual biological son of the original *mban* group leader. A new *mban* was created when an old one had grown too large to distribute bridewealth shares among its members without complications and quarreling. (According to virtually all Meta' informants, the *mban* group was ideally composed of a core of five male household heads, together with their sons and daughters. If it grew larger than this, disputes over bridewealth shares would continuously be breaking out. On the other hand, a group of less than four or five households was considered too small to have its own *mban*.) The head of a new *mban* group would be any man (other than the original *mban* holder) who was the successor of an ancestor from whom five or so men of the old *mban* group traced direct descent.

The way in which the segmentation process in *mban* groups normally took place is illustrated in Figure 1. This shows *mban* group segmentation occurring in the most recent generation (5). In the previous generation, there had been a single *mban* group composed of H, I, J, K, L, M, and N, all of whom were direct patrilineal descendants of the founder of the *mban* group, A. As the unit continued to expand, it became uncomfortably large from the Meta' point of view and finally divided. This segmentation was accomplished when the head of the new *mban* group-to-be, S, *čam*-ed to P (the living successor of A) and received the right of having his own *mban* in his compound. S was the appropriate person to do this because he was the successor of G, the ancestor to whom all members of the new *mban* group trace direct descent.

As is apparent in the diagram, the segmentation of the *mban* group was not based on actual genealogy. If it had been, the single *mban* group of generation 4 would have divided into two groups, each tracing its origin to a different son of the founder, A (i.e., in the current generation, there would be the *mban* group of B, headed by P, and the *mban* group of C, headed by R). One important consequence of this segmentation process is that men who are genealogically senior may remain as subordinates in *mban* groups headed others. This is illustrated by the case of R. He is genealogically senior to S, since the ancestor of whom he is the present successor (i.e., C) was the actual father

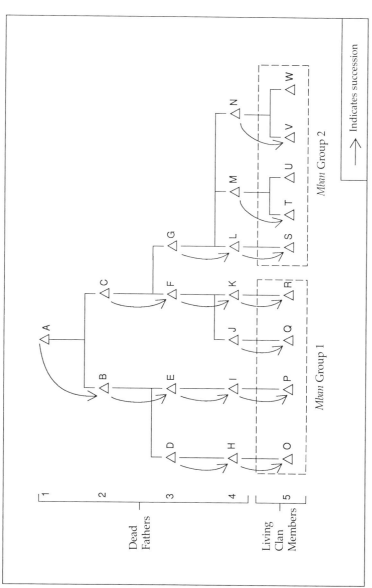

Fig. 1. Segmentation of an *mban* group.

of G, whom S succeeds. But since the descendants of G multiplied more rapidly than those of F, S was able to *čam* for his own *mban* while R was not. Meta' informants sum up such a situation by saying that R is a "big man who still remains in the house" (*wit kyɛŋ ni čibi nga nɜp*).

The entire segmentation process described above established a new relationship between the two *mban* groups and their heads. As noted earlier, the leader of the group that had separated from the old *mban* was spoken of as the "son" (*wan*) or "big son" (*wan kyɛŋ*) of the original *mban* head. Similarly, the leaders of any other new groups that separated from the old *mban* at a later time would be referred to as the younger brothers of the first man to receive his own *mban*. Actual relations of biological descent were thus of no relevance in stating the relationships between the heads of various *mban* groups within a localized clan section. While real descent links would continue to be traced within each separate *mban* after the new one had been established (and actual descent relations beyond the range of the *mban* group were sometimes remembered), the relationship between closely related *mban* groups was expressed in a genealogical idiom that did not correspond to the genealogical facts.

On the lowest level, the structure of the *nibi* must therefore be described in terms of two different kinds of "genealogies." The first kind recorded actual descent relationships and defined the internal structure of each *mban* group. The second described relations among groups signified in the relative positions of their leaders. Relations among the heads of *mban* groups depended on who had received his independent right of *mban* from whom and in what order. On the basis of this criterion, a series of "father-son" and "brother-brother" relationships was established among the leaders of the various *mban* groups in the localized clan section. Granting *mban* was thus the equivalent of "delivering" a son in the "genealogy" that ordered relations among the heads of separate *mban* groups. This second kind of genealogy will hereafter be referred to as the "*mban* genealogy."

The Structure of the Wider *Nibi*

The Meta' *mban* group can be easily comprehended by anthropological readers, since it corresponds closely to the model of a "localized lineage." Its membership was based on actual descent relations. It tended to be a residential unit that was regular in size. It also had a number of functions, including the fact that it served to organize rights in property and arrange the marriages of its members. And it was responsible for many important rituals.

However, beyond the range of the *mban* group, the Meta' *nibi* is much less easily described. The clan as a whole was a rather amorphous social category that was organized in a number of different ways according to the context or situation, and what constituted a cooperative social unit on one occasion might not on another. Of course, some order was given to relations by the "*mban* genealogy." But aside from this, how a given clan was actually structured appears to have depended most on two basic Meta' political concepts discussed earlier: (1) the principle that the clan and its activities could be organized by the distribution of *čam*-able properties, and (2) the belief that the dictates of dead fathers of the clan could authorize the performance of certain activities by particular segments of it.

The *mban* group itself provides the prototype for a clan segment whose identity depended on the acquisition of a *čam*-able property—the *mban*. However, many other *čam*-able properties served to define groups and organize activities within the wider *nibi*. These included *sami* ("dancing field"), ɜtɜn *inyam* ("the seat of an animal"), and a number of exclusive dances, dance costumes, musical instruments, and magical paraphernalia. The *sami* or dance field was a circular clearing located at the compound of its possessor. Having it authorized him and his group to hold public celebrations involving dancing, the most significant of which were funerals. This was important to sociopolitical relations, inasmuch as the feasting and ceremonials associated with mortuary rites were among the most elaborate aspects of Meta' culture. Individual compound heads sought to enhance their statuses by planning elaborate funerals for themselves and their dependents, and descent group segments competed vigorously to carry off the grandest displays.

The dancing field was normally acquired by a dual process of *čam*-ing, the potential *sami* holder making substantial payments to both the heads of closely related segments within his own clan and the chief and senior notables of his village. If these transactions were not completed and a man attempted to hold dances at his compound, he and the members of his group would be likely to suffer *ndɔn* from the speech of the men who had not received their payments.[3]

The *ɔtɔn inyam* ("seat of an animal") was a stick that was hung on the outside wall of the *mban*. It was called the "seat of an animal" because the carcasses of wild game such as antelopes were suspended on it for butchering. Aside from this utilitarian function, the "seat of an animal" served as an authorization for a clan segment to butcher and divide such animals independently. Without it, the members of a segment were forced to take any animals they had shot to the *mban* of the group from which their own had subdivided, provided its leader himself had the "seat of an animal." Like *sami*, the "seat of an animal" had to be *čam*-ed from those senior segment heads in one's own clan who already possessed it, and their exclusive right to give it was sanctioned by *ndɔn*.

Numerous dances, masks, and musical instruments also served to define concrete subgroups within the clan. Certain segments were groups because their members all had common interests in one or more of these. However, unlike the right of *sami* and that of *ɔtɔn inyam*, the authority to use a particular dance rhythm or mask did not have to be acquired from another segment of one's own clan. Even though passing such rights to outsiders was discouraged, they could sometimes still be *čam*-ed from completely unrelated groups.

3. Many more *čam*-able properties were mentioned by informants than are described here. Those discussed represent the common denominator—the kinds of properties that were found in almost all clans and that seem to have been transferred in essentially the same way in all groups. Even so, the case of *sami* ("dancing field") is problematic. Although it was most often granted after *mban*, it was occasionally obtained at the same time as the right of *mban*. Moreover, some informants stated that *sami* could be acquired before *mban* was. It may be that these differences in the informants' accounts were due to variability from clan to clan. Or it may have been that only the first stage of *čam*-ing for *sami* was completed in cases where a man got it before *mban* (i.e., that the person *čam*-ed to segment heads of his own clan but not to the chief and the village notables). In any event, a survey of all the clans in one entire Meta' valley revealed very few cases in which a segment head had acquired *sami* without first having obtained *mban*.

The distribution of all these *čam*-able rights and the patterns of clan organization that this created are most easily understood if one visualizes the clan as being composed of a number of *mban* groups. These were the basic structural units or building blocks of the *nibi*. The organization of the clan as a whole was, in large part, determined by the pattern in which rights to dancing fields, "seats of animal," and dances were held by *mban* groups and combinations of these. In some cases, all of these rights coincided, thereby contributing to the identity of a single clan section. In such instances one segment of five to ten households would possess *mban, sami*, and the "seat of an animal" as well as its own exclusive dance, dancing costume, and set of musical instruments. In other cases, the distribution of these *čam*-able rights would define a hierarchy of ever larger and more inclusive clan segments. For example, four *mban* groups might combine into two *sami* groups, and finally unite in a single ɜtɜn *inyam* group that was also a unit possessing its own dance, set of costumes, and musical instruments. Here the largest unit would assemble as a clan section for only some descent group activities. Thus while *čam*-able properties such as *sami*, "the seat of an animal," and exclusive dances served to define effective segments within the clan, the way in which these were distributed among the *mban* holders was highly variable. In this context, whatever regularity existed in Meta' clan organization derived from common acceptance of the principle of *čam*-able property and agreement on how rights over *sami*, "the seat of an animal," and other such properties could be held rather than from any universal pattern through which these rights were allocated to the various segments of a clan.

While the distribution of *čam*-able properties was an important parameter of clan organization, it was not the only one. The internal organization of the clan was also partly derived from the dictates of deceased fathers and from traditions of how its various sections had been organized previously. As explained in Chapter 4, the boundaries of particular *nibi* segments and their rights to perform certain activities were also established through application of the concept of "historical primacy as a source of legitimacy and power." The most important non-

čam-able rights were those authorizing a group to perform installation ceremonies for the successors of *mban* holders, to organize funerals for important men and women, and to resolve serious disputes within the clan section. Such rights derived from several sources. In some cases they depended on the *mban* genealogy that stated the relationships between various *mban* holders, while in other instances they were based upon covenants or the testaments of the deceased fathers.

The procedures for resolving serious disputes within the clan section provide one of the best examples of how these rights were distributed and how they organized relations among clan segments. The general principle expressed by informants was that a "father" should settle conflicts among his own "sons." In the case of minor quarrels within the *mban* group, this often meant that its leader would preside over the resolution. However, when conflicts were more serious, for example when they had led to physical violence, it was not considered appropriate for the *mban* head himself to judge them. Informants gave some practical reasons for this, for instance, saying that the man would not be likely to fine his "sons" enough to make the resolution effective. Yet privileges sanctioned by *ndɔn* were also involved, since the heads of certain other segments were thought to have the exclusive right to settle serious disputes within any given *mban* group. This was of course to their advantage, since they could dictate the fines to be given (e.g., sacrificial animals like goats, bundles of salt, fowl, brass rods, etc.) and reserve the major portions for themselves. The authorized judges therefore had a strong vested interest in presiding over the resolution, and it was believed that if this right was not recognized, their *njɔm* or complaint might lead to even greater *ndɔn* for the disputants than the quarreling itself had caused.

Generally, the "father" of the *mban* holder in whose group the dispute had occurred (i.e., his father in the *mban* genealogy) was considered the appropriate person to preside over its settlement. However, in some cases, the "brothers" of the *mban* holder in question (i.e., "brothers" in the *mban* genealogy—other *mban* heads whose groups had segmented from the same original *mban*) might also be called to participate and receive honorable shares of meat. The number of such persons who attended de-

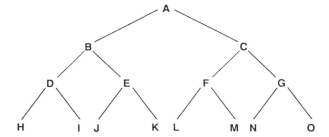

Fig. 2. Intraclan relations.

pended on the seriousness of the case as the people saw it. A more severe conflict required a "stronger" *njɔm*, spoken by a greater number of closely related *mban* holders, to end the *ndɔn* that it had produced.

Figure 2 shows how relations were ideally arranged among the segments of a single clan section in regard to resolving serious disputes within *mban* groups. As the diagram, which is an *mban* genealogy, indicates, the clan was structured as a series of partially overlapping groups extending backwards in the genealogy toward the *mban* of the clan founder. In the diagram, the letters represent *mban* holders, and the lines show "descent" relations between them. According to the diagram, disputes in the group of G should be resolved by C, with perhaps the cooperation of F, since C is the "father" of G. A would have no hand in the matter, since one does not settle quarrels in the place of his "son's son." B, D, and E would also be excluded because of their indirect relationship with G. Similarly, if the dispute were in the group of O, G and N would be the parties concerned with resolving it.

The kind of organization of relations among segments of the clan shown in Figure 2 represents the ideal form, the way in which informants felt that they ought to be structured. Taking this model at face value for the moment, one can see that the clan would be divided into a series of partially overlapping activity groups, in this example ones that cooperate in the resolution of disputes. Since this structure is based on the *mban* genealogy, the group that assembles and cooperates in any given case depends entirely on the locus of the conflict. However, one word of caution should be added here. The diagram presents the *mban* genealogy of the clan as a whole and may seem to imply that this overall structure of relationships among *mban* holders would be known to at least every such leader within a clan. Yet in reality only exceptional informants would have an approximate knowledge of these relationships for the clan as a whole.

Several factors prevented the ideal model of the wider *nibi* that has just been outlined from being realized in many cases. Lack of spatial proximity was one of the most important of these. Where segments that were closely related in terms of the *mban* genealogy of a clan all clustered in a single locality, they tended to cooperate more closely in matters such as resolving internal conflicts. Sometimes geographical closeness like this even overrode the dictum that a "father's father" has no concern in the affairs of his "son's son's" group. In such cases, the "father's father," since he was a close neighbor, would attend as a senior person and help his "son" resolve the conflict in his own "son's" group. On the other hand, *mban* groups that were geographically separated from their parent segments tended to exercise greater independence in descent group activities. Sometimes, nearby "brothers" might be called to preside at the resolution of a conflict instead of the "father" who lived at a distance. Such spatially influenced modifications of operational clan structure were often the result of short-range migrations in search of available land.

Another important factor that influenced the ideal model of relations between clan segments was the rate of segmentation in different branches of the clan. When a single *mban* group had given rise to several others, cooperation between the senior *mban* holder and his own "father" might be discontinued in matters such as conflict resolution, leaving the former to handle such matters with his own "sons." In such cases they would become a closed unit, cut off from relations with other segments of the clan.

Finally, rearrangements of relations among the segments of a clan could be precipitated by conflicts among their heads. Since descent group rituals and activities involved the use of prestigious *čam*-able properties as well as the receipt of rich payments and fine food, there was ample scope for jealousy and quarreling between these leaders. Such tendencies were exacerbated whenever uneven demographic growth had brought about imbalances in human and material resources among the branches of a clan.

A variety of factors could thus establish artificial boundaries and lines of cleavage in the *mban* genealogy of the entire clan. The resultant inconsistencies between ideal and real clan organization were accounted for by several other principles in Meta' descent group ideology. The doctrine of testament, which has already been discussed, was one of the most important of these and was used to explain many irregularities of structure. For example, when numerous *mban* groups had segmented from a single original one and some had gone off to settle at a considerable distance, the "father" or head of the senior group in the "*mban* genealogy" could give a testament in which he declared relations between himself and his "sons" to have been "cut" (*sobi*). In such a case, he might instruct that his various "sons" in the new location should cooperate among themselves in matters such as the installation of *mban* heads and the settlement of disputes. He usually also paired his "sons" so that each would reciprocally act as the "father" to another in important ritual contexts, for example, designating which of them would come to preside over the resolution of a serious conflict in each of the fraternal segments, to perform the necessary sacrifices, and to receive the most honorable shares of meat. Finally, the original "father," who had specified such a pattern of relations in his testament and thereby given a charter to a new clan section composed of several of his segment-head "sons," could also arrange priorities of succession among them, stating which segment had the right to inherit the property of another, should its members die out.

In cases such as this, the dead "father's" testament would serve to justify the given patterning of relationships within the new clan section. As we have seen, the Meta' believed that the testaments of the deceased fathers had an absolute validity. Moreover, the fact that the various *mban* groups continued to survive and prosper over the generations while they followed

the instructions of their forefather further legitimated their practice. If this had been wrong, they would have presumably died
from *ndɔn*.

Irregularities in relations within a clan section were also occasionally based on covenants or agreements made among the
segment heads themselves. While meeting to resolve a conflict
or to install a successor, for example, various segment heads
might decide that their clan section had grown too large and
agree that they would no longer cooperate in such activities.
After making such a decision, they could jointly speak an *njɔm*
describing the pattern that future relations within their branch
of the clan would take. This gave their covenant the force of a
law, sanctioned by *ndɔn*. The justification for such a covenant
made by living segment heads was essentially the same as that
by which a dying segment leader made changes in the structure
of the clan section through his testament. Since the segment
heads were the legitimate successors of their deceased fathers,
they were thought to be speaking for them. Therefore, in the
eyes of junior clansmen, their statements had the same sort of
absolute validity as those of the ancestors themselves. However,
those who sought to reorganize their descent groups always
faced some risk of *ndɔn*, so that changes of this sort were never
undertaken lightly. In fact, such new arrangements were likely
to be suspended and rituals would then be performed to reunite
the formerly cooperating segments, if there was evidence that
they were suffering *ndɔn* from having offended the dead fathers
through their innovations.

An Example of Clan Section Organization

Thus far, I have presented the model of precolonial Meta'
descent organization in rather abstract terms. The principles
of lineage segmentation, the distribution of *čam*-able properties, and the redefinition of relations through covenant and
testament have all been explained, and their somewhat variable realization has been noted. At this point, both for purposes of summary and to give the reader a better feel for how
Meta' descent units looked "on the ground," I will outline the
organization of a particular clan section as it appeared at the

time of fieldwork.[4] Of course, a good deal has changed since precolonial times in the functioning of Meta' descent groups. For example, clan sections have lost considerable political autonomy and much control over their members' lives. However, because Meta' clan sections continue to base their organization upon the same principles as before, it is possible to use a contemporary group to illustrate the formal precolonial patterns. Furthermore, since there had been only one significant postcontact change in the structure of the particular clan section to be discussed (and that one well remembered), the relationship between its current and prior organization was easy to ascertain.

Map 4 shows a localized settlement of a section of the Mibu? clan.[5] This group has been chosen because its present-day settlement pattern closely resembles that of the precolonial period. The main difference between the two is that the area shown in the map is less densely settled than it was before. Over half of the adult males of this Mibu? group are living outside Meta' territory, so that there are fewer compounds now than there were in 1900. However, all of those men who currently reside in the area of precolonial settlement have built their compounds on the sites of their fathers so that the skeleton of the previous residential pattern has been preserved. Moreover, all *mban* holders in the group, save one, live on the sites of their fathers. (The precolonial compound site of this exception is shown in the map without houses—compound site number 10.)

At the time of fieldwork, the segment of the Mibu? clan section shown in Map 4 was fully independent in terms of all regular descent group activities, such as installing the successors of *mban* heads and resolving internal conflicts. The only occasions on which other nearby segments of the clan would cooperate in *nibi* activities with the members of this group were ones such as important mortuary celebrations when any clan segment could attend on a voluntary basis. The portion of the Mibu? clan

---

4. Two additional case histories of clan section organization can be found in Dillon (1973: 141–200).

5. Pseudonyms for descent groups, villages, and individuals are used throughout this study to protect the identities of the persons and groups discussed. The only exceptions to this are found in Chapter 11, which deals with political organization in the intervillage sphere.

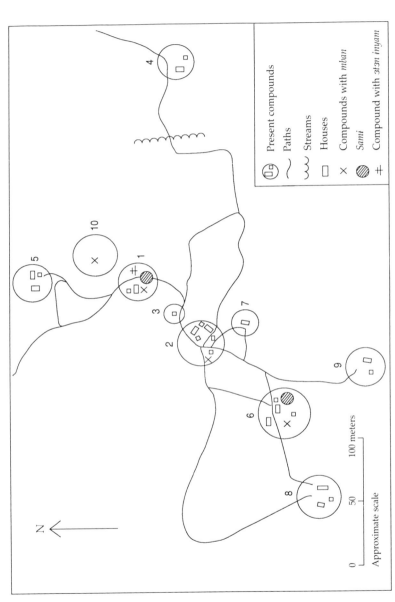

Map 4. A settlement of the Mibuʔ clan.

Present compounds

Paths

Streams

Houses

Compounds with *mban*

× *Sami*

+ Compound with *ətən iŋam*

shown in Map 4 thus constituted a "localized clan section" in the analytical terminology that has been developed here.

The identity of this section depended on genealogy in the minds of informants belonging to the group. But like most Meta' genealogies, the one that was given appears to be an "*mban* group genealogy" at the upper levels and one reflecting biological descent only at the lower levels (see Figure 3). All members of the group claimed descent from a common "father" (11 in the genealogy of Figure 3) who is said to have lived four generations prior to his present successor, 1.⁶ The genealogical traditions of this Mìbuʔ clan section assert that all of the various *mban* and *sami* ("dancing fields") shown on Map 4 derive from 11, the founder of the entire group. The head of compound 6 is said to be the "big son" (*wan kyɛŋ*) who first received his *mban* and *sami* from 11. Subsequently, the ancestor of 10 (who is trustee of the position of 12) received *mban* only, and finally, the forefather of 2 was given his own *mban*.

For activities appropriate to the *mban*, the group shown on Map 4 would thus split into four independent units, those headed by 1, 6, 10, and 2. The other compound heads on the map—i.e., those who do not possess *mban*—would join with the *mban* head with whom they have the closest descent relation for activities in the *mban*. Thus, 7, 8, and 9 would assist 6 in his *mban*, since he is the successor of their common father, while 5 would participate at the *mban* of 10, and 3 and 4 would be with 2. No other compound head shown on the map would join in

6. Actually, 1 is not the successor of 11, but merely the trustee for his position. When 13, the first successor of 11, died, his son 15 was named as his successor. However, 15 was later captured as a slave, and 14, who was the trustee for his position, became the permanent incumbent. When 14 himself died, his son's son, 16, was named as his successor, and 17 was named as the temporary trustee of the position. But 16 left the Meta' area in the context of quarreling within the clan section and never returned. Once again, the trustee of the position became the permanent incumbent, and when 17 died, the trusteeship devolved on his own son, 1. At present, whether 1 is the actual successor (*ɜjɜnɜp*) or merely the trustee (*wit ni wer ɜtɜn*) of 11 is a disputed issue. Also, as shown in the genealogy, 10 is not the true *mban* holder, but rather the trustee of this position for 12, who is a child. The men who head compounds 3 and 9 in Map 4 are not shown on the genealogy, since they are attached to the Mìbuʔ group through maternal links. However, they are included in the following description of clan section activities, since they did participate in these.

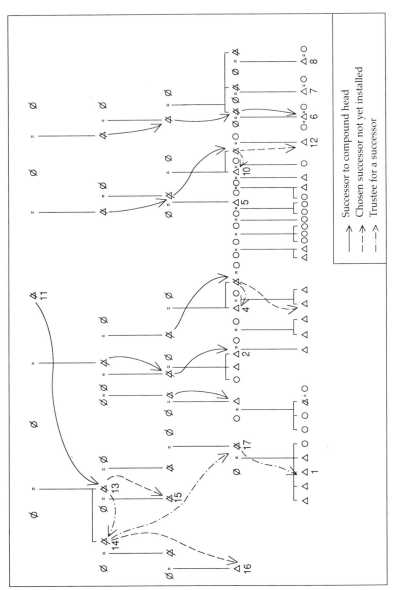

Fig. 3. Genealogy of the Mibuʔ clan section.

the *mban* of 1, since all of the adult males who belong to it are on the outside for wage labor.

Since there are only two *sami* ("dancing fields") held by persons of this Mɨbuʔ clan section, the group would divide into two separate groups for ceremonies on the dance field. Thus, if 6, 7, 8, or 9 died, the mortuary dances would be held on the *sami* of 6, while if 1, 2, 3, 4, 5 or 10 died, the dances would be held on the *sami* of 1.

Because 1 is the only segment head possessing the "seat of an animal" (ɜtɜn *inyam*), an antelope shot by any member of this Mɨbuʔ section at a communal hunt would be brought to his compound and butchered there. All compound heads in the entire section would attend on such occasions and receive shares of the meat. A similar arrangement would be followed with the dance and dancing disguise of the group, *kwebit*. The dance is said to be owned by 1. However, all of the other men of the section cooperate with him in using it, since none of the other segment heads possesses a dance of his own (6 would be the only one of them capable of acquiring a dance, since he alone has a dancing field). Also, even though the dance *kwebit* is said to be owned by 1, all other members of the section have certain rights in it. Thus, if mortuary celebrations were to be held for 6, 7, 8, or 9, *kwebit* would have to come when requested, because all of these men are "sons" of 1. Likewise, if any compound head shown on Map 4 was obligated to bring a dance to the funeral of his father-in-law, he would petition 1 so that *kwebit* might be brought. He would have to make appropriate payments for this service, but after he had done so, all the men of the Mɨbuʔ section would be obliged to assist in their brother's mourning.

The Mɨbuʔ group shown on Map 4 was also an independent unit for the observance of many other descent group activities, including the installations of *mban* and *sami* holders, the resolution of internal disputes, and the organization of mortuary celebrations for important men and women. For example, if the successor of 1 was to be installed, his important "sons" (2, 6, and 10) would be the ones to "put him on the chair of his father," conduct the appropriate rituals, and receive the important named shares of meat from the sacrificial goat given by 1. If any of the other *mban* holders (i.e., 2, 6, or 10) was to undergo installation, his "father" (1) would be the man to preside at the ceremonies and receive the most honorable portion of meat. Likewise, if a dispute broke out within or between any of the *mban* groups in the section, the man at compound 1, as the "father" of the entire Mɨbuʔ group, would supervise the resolution. Should 1 himself be a party to the dispute, all three of the other *mban* heads would attend, with 6 presiding.

The Mɨbuʔ clan section shown on Map 4 was thus a closed and independent unit for all formally structured descent group activities. According to informants, it had only been autonomous in this way for about 30 years. Before that time, its organization had been essentially the same, except that the head of 1 had maintained more direct relations with the heads of several other Mɨbuʔ clan segments in the same valley. Thus, according to the previous arrangements, when 1 himself was to be installed or was involved in a serious conflict with a member of his group, these other segment heads, described as his "brothers," attended and received honorable shares of meat. During the same period, 1 himself reciprocated when they had similar activities taking place in their own groups. However, in most other respects the earlier organization of the Mɨbuʔ section under 1 had been the same. Thus, in the previous period, if 10 and 2 were involved in a fight or if 6 was to be installed, the matter was seen as one among 1 and his "sons," and the "brothers" of 1 were not involved. According to informants, relations between 1 and his "brothers" had been severed by mutual agreement during a mortuary celebration for one of them. At that time, it was decided that the *nɨbɨ* had grown too large to cooperate in such activities, and that, since 1 had "delivered many sons," he should separate from the others and do everything on his own. The structure of the Mɨbuʔ clan section thus changed from the kind described on pages 101–102, in which an overlapping series of groups exists and the cooperation of segments in formal activities depends on the position of the host group in the clan's *mban* genealogy, to a structure in which this regional branch of the clan was divided into several fully independent sections, composed of several *mban* each. Through this process the operational clan sections had also become geographically much less dispersed.

The Clan

In the preceding sections, the organization of *nibi* at an intermediate level, that of the clan section, has been considered. Now that discussion will be placed in the context of the clan as a whole. This was normally an exogamous group[7] whose members shared putative common descent in the male line. It could include as many as two hundred separate households dispersed over a wide area. Some clans, in fact, had members residing in each of the three main Meta' valleys as well as outside Meta' territory.

The discussion of the concept of *nibi* at the beginning of this chapter has outlined many of the characteristics of the clan, and it is not necessary to restate them here. Let us simply note that the clan did not possess a single formal structure, agreed upon by all of its members, which organized relations within it. Rather, belonging to a clan placed a person in a social category within which there was always the potential for cooperation. Clanfellows shared residual rights in common property as well as the duty to defend each other from attack and the obligation to interact in a moral way. Although the entire clan never united for a single activity, this was theoretically possible under certain conditions: informants said that if one-half of the clan was faced with annihilation, the members of the other might rally to its defense. In practice, the closest approximation to this seems to have been certain instances of valley-wide participation in clan activities. For example, since incest was regarded as a heinous offence from which *ndɔn* might spread to the entire clan, representatives of many localized clan sections normally assisted in the ritual resolution of such cases. And in some clans members of all the sections resident in a valley would come to dance at the mortuary celebrations of very old men and women.

---

7. The level at which exogamy was enforced varied in some cases. Although, in most instances, the clan was strictly exogamous, there were a few groups, including the very large Mindik chiefly clan, in which the component segments had "cut" (*sobi*) their relations and begun to intermarry. In such cases they usually retained the original clan name, and their organization corresponded to that of other clans in most other respects.

However, it was usually only within groups smaller than valley-wide clan populations that agnates cooperated regularly. The largest such formally organized segments of the clan appear to have been units of less than 50 households. These tended to be localized, and only in rare cases did some of their members live in different valleys. Although there was no Meta' term for large localized descent groups of this sort, I have here designated them as "clan sections," and all of the preceding description of formal descent group organization is meant to apply to such groups.

The Political Significance of Meta' Patrilineal Organization

In this chapter, I have outlined the concepts and values that were emphasized in the Meta' ideology of patrilineal descent. The political implications of this distinctive ideological system were complex and multifaceted. First, it should be noted that agnatic kin were the main group to which individuals, facing a precarious situation, turned for political support. In precolonial times, Meta' society was a rather volatile social field. As will be shown later, arbitrary enslavement and interpolity warfare were common threats. Moreover, in this densely settled region, competition over resources, such as livestock, farmland, bridewealth valuables, and marriageable women, frequently led to physical fighting.

Inasmuch as localized descent groups were the basic units that organized themselves to counter these threats, many of the values stressed in Meta' descent ideology begin to seem more intelligible. For example, the emphasis placed upon loyalty among agnates and upon the mystical dangers posed by betrayal of these kin clearly promoted the solidarity of descent groups and enhanced their ability to deal with opposition. Furthermore, both the doctrine that agnates "consumed things together" and the belief that they depended upon the same sources of mystical power reinforced their mutual commitments. Powerful forms of symbolic expression thus conveyed the reliance of all categories of Meta' citizens upon descent group organization, not only for their physical survival, but also for the protection of their property, and for their success in life's most important undertakings.[8]

As the preceding discussion illustrates, individual and group interests were linked through some of the main themes of Meta' descent ideology. Nevertheless, many of the same concepts also had divisive implications. In fact, the entire ideological system can just as easily be read as a formula for political and economic domination. Thus, while the concept of history as the basis of mystical power promoted descent group unity, it also laid the foundations for exclusive claims to authority on the part of descent group leaders. As successors to their groups' founders, they were seen as the most direct links to the power of the past and were, at least in theory, unassailable. Together with the authorizations that they derived from testaments and *čam*-able properties, this enabled them to control most of the important rituals and economic transactions within their groups. For example, they supervised the marriage of each daughter of the lineage and the allocation of her bridewealth. They also oversaw inheritance and succession to compound headship, as well as the rituals of curing and conflict resolution and the lineage-segmentation process. In all such instances, descent group leaders received substantial payments from those requiring their ritual services or aspiring to new statuses and estates, and their right to these benefits was sanctioned by *ndɔn*. Thus, given the principles of Meta' descent ideology, a small group of elders was able to dominate most significant economic transactions within the kinship system. Viewed from this perspective, Meta' patrilineal organization was a rather closed order of ranking.

A final important feature of Meta' descent ideology was the fact that it guaranteed all parties a modicum of procedural regu-

8. In this context, I would like to register disagreement with the position of Engard (1986: 109) that it makes little sense "to describe any Western Grassfields society as a primarily descent based society." Although Meta' conceptions of *genealogy* clearly departed from those encountered in classic segmentary lineage societies, such as Nuer and Tiv, descent *group* membership was of profound emotional and practical significance to the individual (see the discussion of the concepts and values associated with patrilineal descent [pp. 83–88 above], for example). Moreover, as we shall see in the case histories of conflict to be presented in Chapters 8, 9, and 11, fundamental power lay with the clan sections in Meta' rather than with the regulatory societies and chiefdom institutions. In this respect, Meta' differed greatly from most chiefdoms of the Bamenda plateau.

larity in the decisions that served to allocate positions of authority and key resources. For example, the elaborate rules concerning succession and the formation of new descent group segments not only protected the prerogatives of existing leaders, but also established formal pathways through which junior males could rise in status. Likewise, since all marriage and succession rites had to be conducted in the *mban*, agreements concerning the distribution of bridewealth shares, the inheritance of estates, and other similar matters were always publicly expressed. And because the assent of all *mban* group members was believed essential to make the career of a bride or a successor prosper, any complaints of unfair treatment had to be considered before the rituals could begin. Finally, even senior elders were believed likely to suffer *ndɔn* if they abused their authority in order to appropriate what rightfully belonged to their junior colleagues. The elaboration of formally specified rights and ritual procedures, as well as the notion that these were sanctioned by mystical danger, thus provided a framework of rules to which all lineage members could appeal during important rituals and transactions within their groups.

The significance of these procedural safeguards is not difficult to ascertain. Although absolutely loyal to their lineage mates in theory, male agnates were often among one another's keenest competitors. The primary reason for this was that they possessed common interests in land, livestock, and marriageable women. However, the potential for conflict was also increased by the manner in which senior elders typically used their positions to consolidate power and control over resources. In this context, the procedural rules that were built into Meta' descent ideology served to protect the rights of junior males, which in turn would have increased their perceptions of the system's fairness and their commitment to it. On an abstract level, then, the elaborate rules and procedures are perhaps best interpreted as a response by descent group members to the dangers posed by uncontrolled intragroup competition in a predatory social environment. Such standards could have evolved quite naturally as lineage members invoked agnatic loyalty and cautioned one another about the mystical dangers of betrayal in urging restraint upon their more competitive fellows.

In summary, the Meta' ideology of patrilineal descent had a wide range of political implications. The same set of concepts provided a basis for the mobilization of political support, for the development of hierarchy and ranking, and for the reinforcement of procedural regularity in kinship rituals and transactions. On the whole, the Meta' patrilineal system was patriarchal and genontocratic in nature. However, it also provided physical security for all Meta' citizens and safeguarded, to a certain extent, the property rights of every adult male. Perhaps the most noteworthy aspect of Meta' descent ideology was its multivalent character. Not only did political actors rely upon it in order to cope with a wide variety of threats and problems, but it simultaneously appealed to the self-interests of both juniors and elders.

SIX

Village-Level Leadership:
The Ideal Model

THE PRINCIPLES of descent and local grouping supplied the two fundamental axes of Meta' political organization. Since patrilineal descent groups have provided the focus in the first part of this study, the remainder of it will be devoted to territorially based relations.

Meta' concepts of local organization closely resembled their concepts of descent in that a single elastic term (bɛŋ) was used to designate a wide range of groups. Just as nibi ("patrilineal descent group") might refer to anything from an mban group of several households to a dispersed "clan" of several hundred, bɛŋ could indicate a range of local groups associated with different political functions. In precolonial times, a bɛŋ was anything from a "village" of 100 or so persons to the entire Meta' polity, a group of some 20,000. The exact meaning of bɛŋ seems to have varied with the speaker's frame of reference. Addressing a member of a neighboring village, he would use bɛŋ to designate his own, while in conversation with a non-Meta' person he might employ the term to refer to Meta' society as a whole.

According to informants, the essential meaning of bɛŋ was "a discrete place where one people live and build their houses." It was thus the conceptual opposite of mbɛŋ ("bush" or "farm area"). Some informants also said that a bɛŋ was a place "under one chief." Accordingly, a localized clan section of 50 persons would not have been called bɛŋ, while an equally large residential group that was mixed in terms of descent and had its own chief would have been. However, the larger manifestations of bɛŋ, such as entire valleys and the Meta' polity as a whole, did not conform to this second definition, since they had never been under centralized political control.

By contrast with the concept *nibi*, *bɛŋ* seems to have had little affective meaning. Whereas a person's identity was emotionally linked to the fact of his descent group membership in a powerful way, *bɛŋ* was more a matter of practical necessity. A person cooperated with fellow members of his *bɛŋ* because neighbors naturally shared certain problems. People of other areas might try to seize their lands, capture them as slaves, or use mystical powers against them. It was therefore important to organize as a community to meet outside threats.

An Overview of Meta' Village Organization

In the next several chapters, the primary concern is with describing the organization of the units that I have called "villages." These were dispersed groups ranging from about 100 to more than 1,000 in population within which a certain set of property rights and social relationships were concentrated.[1]

Meta' villages were normally federations of several clan sections under a single political leadership. Since at least some of these descent group segments were usually unrelated, the village itself did not constitute a patrilineal group. The basis for the association of such diverse elements within one community was in most cases oral tradition. The men of the various clan sections might be said to have "traveled together" to reach their present location or to have fought alongside one another to drive the enemy off their land. Although the number of descent groups found in Meta' villages varied considerably, there were typically between four and eight units of sufficient size to be classed as clan sections in the terminology of Chapter 5, along with splinter groups composed or one or two *mban* each.

Precolonial village government was representative in that it was jointly conducted by the hereditary heads of the principal clan sections, the *mikum si* or "senior village notables" (sing.

1. The maximum size of precolonial villages is somewhat uncertain. Although the village of Guneku in the Medig valley may have had as many as 2,000 inhabitants, detailed study of precolonial population and village structure was not carried out in that area. The range of village size given above is based on in-depth investigation of these questions in all villages of the Bome valley.

kum si). While all of the members of this group based their authority upon the possession of certain mystical powers, the role of one was greatly elaborated in its symbolism, and he was accorded far greater prestige and prerogatives. This pre-eminent *kum si* was referred to by the title *fɔn* ("chief"), and his office provided the focus for a centralized village-level political structure. The special characteristics of the chiefly role will be discussed further in a later section of this chapter. At this point, it is only necessary to underscore the fact that he was regarded as a *kum si*, first and foremost. His powers were, at least in part, derived from the same sources as those of his colleagues, and in most cases he was unable to act without them.

The structure of a village was most often described by Meta' informants in terms of the relations among its larger clan sections. Normally, each of these resided within its own "side of the village" (*ba bɛŋ*) and was represented by its senior *mban* holder (*kum si*) at the meetings of the village notables. By custom, the people under him could not approach the chief or the other village notables for important business without his assistance. The members of splinter groups were usually associated with the clan section that was dominant on their side of the village and under the jurisdiction of its *kum si*. However, in cases where the founders of such groups had been among the village pioneers, their leaders might still be accorded the status of *mikum si*.

At any given time, the internal organization of a village was expressed in two basic ways. First, the entire village cooperated in certain activities that were designed to secure common interests. For example, wars were fought to defend the village territory and to prevent outsiders from enslaving its people. In addition, villagers collaborated in rituals to seal off their boundaries from outside sorcerers who could magically steal the fertility of the land. Finally, the chief and *mikum si* of each village operated a complex conflict-management system in order to maintain the peace and protect essential rights over persons and property.

The second expression of the internal structure of the village was through what Ruel (1969: xv) has termed "constitutional ordering" in his study of Banyang political organization. The

Meta' village was a unit with a carefully worked out "constitutional" structure, based upon the distribution of certain public rights and prerogatives among its leaders. The treatment of leopards that were slain by village hunters provides a useful illustration of this. Since the leopard was regarded as the physically and mystically most dangerous of animals, the organized leadership of the village came to be used as a safe mechanism by which the beast's power could be harnessed for the benefit of society. Rights to receive and butcher such animals were sanctioned by *ndɔn*, and only chiefs acting together with their senior village notables could legitimately carry out such functions. It was therefore in the presentation, butchering, and consuming of a slain leopard that the rights of the various village leaders and the relationships among them were openly expressed. Rules about the proper channels through which a leopard, taken by a village hunter, should pass, about who should operate on it, and about who would receive shares of its meat or skin—all these had political significance. Such rules served as a tangible charter for the structure of the village. "Constitutional" relationships were similarly expressed in many other activities, ranging from the resolution of conflicts to communal hunting and the ceremonies for granting titles and honors to outstanding villagers.

In the remaining part of this chapter, the various positions of leadership within an ideal Meta' village and the network of relationships among its leaders will be described. After this, in Chapter 7 the many political activities in which this statically conceived set of roles and relationships found active expression will be considered. Taken together, Chapters 6 and 7 present an ideal model of village organization that has been synthesized from informants' general statements on the subject. Finally, in Chapters 8 and 9, which deal with conflict management and political processes respectively, the relationship between this ideal system and the realities of village-level politics will be explored.

Mikum ("Notables")

The *mikum*, representing their various clan sections, provided centralized leadership for the village and a symbol of its unity.

While in some respects, they were like a society of title holders, in others they resembled an hereditary village council. There also existed several kinds of *mikum*. It has already been noted that, although the chief was considered a *kum si*, his role was in some respects unusual. Further distinctions can be made between the *mikum si* themselves and certain lesser notables. I shall therefore begin by describing the role of a *kum si* and then contrast it with those of the other types.

Mikum Si ("Senior Village Notables")

The *mikum si*, who were referred to by other names such as *mikum ɜbɛŋ* ("notables of the village") in some Meta' communities, were the most important local-level leaders. The number of such notables generally depended on how many descent groups had pioneered a village. In theory, a *kum si* was always a man whose predecessor had arrived in the village at the time of its foundation, being already then the head of a distinct clan section. Because of this, each *kum si* was considered the correct person to "say something" concerning his "side" of the village. Knowing the most about its history, he was able to speak an *njɔm* ("ritual request or complaint") that was more accurate, and hence stronger and more likely to be heard by the God *Ŋwiɜ*, than any other. This superior knowledge was also believed to be transmitted to each successor of the *kum si*, so that, relative to other men of his generation, his powers of speech were greater.

Such inherited mystical potency was of course crucial in many kinds of situations. If a conflict erupted within the area controlled by a *kum si*, for example, he would have a key role in resolving it, since he best knew the way in which his predecessors had settled such matters and the historical basis of any contested rights. Accordingly, *mikum si* sometimes tried to resolve disputes within their domains independently, referring only the more difficult cases to the combined notables of the village, and even in the latter instance, the *kum si* of the area in which a dispute had occurred would still have had a major hand in its settlement.

Because of their mystically based authority, the *mikum si* were shown much deference and respect. Most had hereditary stools reserved for their personal use, and while fellow notables of equivalent rank might sit upon these when invited to do so, lesser men would be fined for such an attempt. At public gatherings, such as mortuary celebrations in both their own and other villages, the *mikum si* were usually seated together in private as befitted their dignity. Furthermore, whereas ordinary men were served palm wine out of a large common pot, separate calabashes were placed in front of all the *mikum si*. Finally, when the *mikum si* prepared to leave such gatherings, their hosts were expected to present them with small gifts to "wake them from the chair" and express thanks for their attendance.

As noted earlier, the original *mikum si* of a village were considered to have achieved their positions by being local pioneers. Thus, in theory, no payments were made for the position of *kum si*, and it could not be obtained by *čam*-ing. Moreover, the heads of latecoming clan sections could not become *mikum si*, however much wealth or power they acquired. Such restrictions on a pivotal office established an important element of stability in the Meta' political system that was otherwise in constant flux.

As a group, the *mikum si* were said to "hold" (*niŋ*) the village, since their combined mystical powers covered it fully. They possessed the right to handle many local problems and to profit from doing so. For example, they had the exclusive authority to resolve any disputes that led to interclan fighting and to fine those responsible. They also organized the rites that sealed off the village from foreign sorcery; butchered important animals, such as leopards, that were slain in the village; and arranged for the execution of habitual offenders.

The role of the *mikum si* in all such activities was defined by Meta' mystical concepts. They used their hereditary powers of speech to safeguard the community when other means failed, and they depended upon these powers to protect them while performing supernaturally dangerous tasks, such as butchering leopards and authorizing executions. Ordinary persons who attempted these deeds were thought certain to die from *ndɔn*, and the right of the *mikum si* to perform them was itself sanctioned by *ndɔn*.

While the authority of the *mikum si* was ultimately based on their historical primacy, they were also strongly identified with the portion of ground upon which their forefathers had settled.

Their title meant literally "*mikum* of the earth" and conveyed the idea that they were both responsible for and powerful over all events within their particular zones. For this reason they were the ones to consume important things such as leopards and other restricted animals that were found upon the earth.

The *mikum si* can also be seen as a society to which men aspiring to recognition made payments (*čam*-ed). Although the status of *kum si* was based upon birthright, lesser hereditary titles such as "*kum*" could be acquired by any descent group leader who presented valuables such as goats, brass rods, salt, and palm wine to the *mikum si* of his village. In addition, each successor of a *kum si* or *kum* had to *čam* a goat to his peers in order to be recognized. The valuables received from such sources were used by the *mikum si* for their own feasting and entertainment.

In summary, the *mikum si* occupied the most prestigious positions within the precolonial Meta' village. They possessed unquestioned authority and awesome mystical powers that they used both to defend the community and to punish offenders. They also had many special prerogatives and engaged in lavish feasting for which they were greatly envied by ordinary people.

Mikum 3gɔ ("Lesser Notables")

Every village had some *mikum* who did not possess the same authority as the *mikum si*. In such cases, the title and status of *kum* were divorced from the *kum si*'s special mystical powers. The actual designations of these lesser notables seem to have differed from place to place. They were variously called *mikum kwa* ("small *mikum*"), *mikum 3gɔ* ("ordinary *mikum*"), and—lumping them together with the *mikum si*—*mikum 3bɛŋ* ("*mikum* of the village"). However, in every instance the statuses of these men were essentially the same. They were persons whose names were known to the public and who were therefore respected.

In many ways, the lesser *kum* was accorded prestige similar to that of a *kum si*, although in situations where both were present, he received fewer honors. Thus while the *kum 3gɔ* was served from a private calabash at gatherings of ordinary men and sometimes presented with gifts to "wake him from the chair," such gestures might be omitted when *mikum si* were present. Moreover, just as the *kum si*'s stool was forbidden to ordinary persons, it was denied to the *kum ʒgɔ*, and the *kum si* himself would never wish to occupy the seat of his junior counterpart. According to one informant, he would regard this as "the chair of a dog."

Another important distinction between the *kum si* and the *kum ʒgɔ* was based on concepts of mystical power. As a latecomer to the village, the *kum ʒgɔ* lacked mystical power stemming from historical primacy and legitimacy, and his ritual statements were therefore weaker than those of the *kum si*. Because of this, the *kum ʒgɔ* played less of a role in resolving village-level disputes and in the rites performed to ward off foreign sorcery.

The *mikum ʒgɔ* also received fewer valuables than the *mikum si*. In some villages, they simply did not partake of the goats that were given to the *mikum si* by disputants and title seekers, while elsewhere they were granted only minor shares. In still other places, the *mikum ʒgɔ* had to *čam* goats to the senior *mikum* in order to receive hereditary rights to certain portions of "village beef" (*nyam ʒbɛŋ*).

The participation of the *mikum ʒgɔ* in local government likewise seems to have varied. In some villages, it is said that they met at the compound of the chief to drink wine once each week, just as the *mikum si* did, sitting in a separate hut and receiving their own share of the chief's wine tribute. Elsewhere, informants denied that the *mikum ʒgɔ* regularly came to the compound of the *fɔn* at all and asserted that they never played an active role in village affairs unless the matters discussed concerned their own clan sections. In generalizing, it can only be said that the *mikum ʒgɔ* were more likely to participate in village leadership activities than were ordinary men.

As noted earlier, the *mikum ʒgɔ* were holders of titles that, though hereditary, had been established after the formation of the village. These came about in several ways. Sometimes a man settled in an established village after already becoming head of his clan section and *kum* in another place. In such a case, he could be recognized as *kum ʒgɔ*, but never, theoretically, *kum si*. A man might also become *kum ʒgɔ* if he was the head of a clan section that had been formed through the segmentation of an original settler group some time after the foundation of the village. The new segment's leader then sought the position of *kum ɜgɔ* by *čam*-ing to the *mikum si* and the chief of the village, typically paying more than one goat. There was considerable variation in the informants' accounts of the process by which such titles were created. Some saw the position of *kum ɜgɔ* as equivalent to that of *sami* holder (man with a dancing field). According to such informants, when a man *čam*-ed his dancing field he simultaneously became a *kum ɜgɔ*. However, others stated that the title of *kum* and the dancing field had to be purchased with separate goats. In any event, it is certain that a man achieved his title as *kum ɜgɔ* by *čam*-ing to the *mikum si* and the chief, and that, once acquired, it was hereditary. In addition, the new *kum ɜgɔ* in some cases became part of a society of village notables (including both *mikum si* and *mikum ɜgɔ*) that operated as a self-sustaining group. Its members gave and received goats to validate their own successions and accepted payments from those aspiring to titles.

Mikum Nga Nɜp ("Compound Notables")

A third type of *kum* was referred to as *kum nga nɜp* ("*kum* in the house" or "compound notable"). This indicated that he was only recognized as a *kum* within the "side" of the village where he resided. Accordingly, compound notables did not attend meetings regularly at the residence of the chief and possessed no rights to a share of "village beef." Since "sides" of the village were often the exclusive settlement areas of single clan sections, a man generally *čam*-ed just to his own "fathers" (i.e., the senior segment heads of his own descent group) to acquire the title of *kum nga nɜp* and not to the chief or *mikum si* of the village. His position was thus quite analogous to that of *kum ɜgɔ* but on a lower structural level, and he was only accorded honors in meetings of his own clan section.

Persons referred to as *mikum nga nɜp* invariably had dancing fields in their compounds. However, the use of these was restricted, since masked dancers with anklets were forbidden to appear upon them. Some informants referred to such a dancing field as a *sami*, but others characterized it as a *sange nuʔu nɜp* ("yard about the house") to distinguish it from the dancing fields of the other types of *mikum*. From these facts it appears likely that the position of *kum nga nɜp* was merely a stage on the way to the status of *kum ʒgɔ*. As noted earlier, a man was required to *čam* to both the senior segment heads of his own descent group and to the chief and *mikum si* in order to acquire a *sami* and be recognized as *kum ʒgɔ*. Since the *kum nga nʒp* had already made payments to his "fathers" for his dancing field, all that remained for him to be recognized as a *kum* in the village at large was to *čam* to the chief and the *mikum si*.

Kum Wa Tɔʔ ("Notable of the Chief's House")

Yet another kind of notable was known as the *kum wa tɔʔ*. This term, which may be translated as "*kum* who is a son of the chief's house," indicated that the possessor's descent group had segmented from the chief's own sometime after the founding of the village. Such a cadet held a position that was basically comparable to those of the *mikum ʒgɔ* and *mikum nga nʒp*. The main differences lay in the greater prestige that accrued to the *kum wa tɔʔ* and in the fact that he had to adopt a rather passive role politically in order to avoid any impression that the chiefly descent group was dominating the village.

Like the other lesser notables, the *kum wa tɔʔ* could never become a *kum si*, since he was, by definition, not descended from an original settler. (If his predecessor had been a village founder, he would have been described as a "brother of the chief" rather than as a "son of the chief's house" and counted as a *kum si*.) Yet there remained one channel through which a *kum wa tɔʔ* might rise in status. According to this process, when his lineage had grown very large he might be allowed to *čam* the position of chief. If he did so while remaining in his home village, he would not be able to exercise any of the chiefly political prerogatives, since this would reduce the authority of the original village head. However, when such a person moved away with his supporters to found a new settlement, he could become a full chief in his own right. (The process through which this occurred will be described more fully in Chapter 9.)

The Role of *Fɔn* in Meta' Society

It is difficult to describe the position of a *fɔn* ("chief") in Meta' society succinctly, since the things that distinguished him from his fellow village notables were at once subtle and critical to Meta' political theory. It is perhaps best to begin by saying that the *fɔn* was, first and foremost, viewed as a *kum si* in the village. Like the others, he represented a clan section whose ancestor was counted among the village founders, and he possessed all the privileges and powers of an ordinary *kum si* in regard to his exclusive territory and the people within it.

However, unlike his colleagues, the *fɔn* transcended the normal social and political order in many ways. While the *mikum si* as a group represented the entire village and possessed a certain authority over it, the *fɔn* stood as a symbol of the village and exercised the combined mystical powers of its people. The difference was one of representation versus identification.

The *fɔn* also differed from an ordinary *kum si* in that he normally had an assistant, the *ndi fɔn*. Most commonly, this was a half-brother of the *fɔn* from a different mother. He was customarily chosen by his father at the same time as the successor to the chieftaincy itself, and he assumed office simultaneously with the new *fɔn*. Ideally, anyone from outside the *fɔn*'s household who approached on business was supposed to present himself first to the *ndi fɔn,* who would then take him to the *fɔn*. In practice, however, the significance of the role of *ndi fɔn* varied greatly from village to village. In addition, in a few Meta' villages, still other brothers of the *fɔn* were given titles such as *moma* and *kwɛti* that had been borrowed from Grassfields chiefdoms, but these do not seem to have been important offices in precolonial times.

It is difficult to give a list of chiefly political duties and prerogatives that were distinctly different from those of the *mikum si*, since in most important matters these leaders acted together. I shall therefore defer discussion of many of their joint functions until the next chapter, where the focus is on the activities themselves. In the present section, only those aspects of the *fɔn*'s role that served to distinguish him from the other *mikum si* will be discussed. I begin by considering the special economic situation of the *fɔn* and conclude with an examination of the symbolism of Meta' chieftaincy.

The Economic Position of the *Fɔn*

*Fɔn*ship conveyed numerous economic advantages, since a chief could expect both service and tribute from his people. Thus, for example, the *fɔn* was entitled to summon all the villagers to prepare farms for him on one day each year during July or August, as well as to call for workers whenever huts were to be built or rethatched in his compound. *Fɔn*s also received a regular tribute in palm wine, although the way in which the collection was organized seems to have varied from place to place. In most, the *fɔn* is said to have obtained some wine from the territory of each *kum si* on the rest day of the village. This was the one portion of the eight-day week during which women were forbidden to work on their farms and everyone spent time relaxing and visiting. It was also the time when the *mikum si* met at the *fɔn*'s compound so that much of the wine collected was consumed by them. While some informants claimed that this wine was taken directly from the tapping bushes by *mičɜŋɜnɜp* ("page boys") who served the *fɔn*, others said that delivery was arranged for independently by the *mikum si*.

The amount of wine actually given by the men of any "side" of the village varied according to the needs of the *fɔn* and the production of the tappers. One informant said that if the men of his neighborhood of about twelve households had collected no wine by the day of tribute, they would give nothing, whereas if they had tapped forty calabashes, they might send ten to the *fɔn*. Most informants also agreed that when the *fɔn* needed extra wine and food for public entertaining, perhaps one to four times each year, he would receive greater amounts from the people. On such special occasions, his pages might collect all the wine that had been tapped in the village as well as four or five hips of plantains from the area of each *kum si*. Finally, precolonial markets likewise provided a tribute in palm wine to the chiefs of those villages in which they were held. Informants estimate that a marketer selling twenty calabashes of palm wine would send one to the *fɔn*. Accounts vary on whether this was collected by representatives of the *fɔn* or merely sent to him by the vendors.

The *fɔn* also received tribute of an informal sort in that the villagers tried to present some of the best of everything to him. For example, a man might voluntarily reserve a special kola tree, *ikwɛbi tree*, or plantain stalk for the *fɔn* and bring him its products whenever they ripened. Or the *fɔn* himself could point out a tree whose fruits he desired. The amount and value of this type of "tribute" is of course impossible to estimate.

An additional source of chiefly income consisted of the fines (*ičwi*) given by disputants. If the thief of a goat was fined seven such animals, for example, one normally went to the *fɔn*, while another was divided amongst the *mɪkum si*, and the rest were surrendered to the close agnates of the thief's victim. (The way in which the two goats are divided among the *fɔn* and the *mɪkum si* in this example is typical of cases where they received valuables jointly. The *fɔn* usually took the lion's share, even though he was frequently not as directly involved in judging the cases.)

The *fɔn* and the *mɪkum si* sometimes also received hidden payments (*nɜmɜ*) to encourage their intervention in cases that they would otherwise not have considered. Thus, a deserted husband who sought the refund of his bridewealth might give the chief several brass rods or some fowl and palm wine so that he would urge the *mɪkum si* to judge the case and try to influence their decision. In such an instance, the *fɔn* might also be paid by the other party who would suspect and want to offset the favoritism.

As noted earlier, the *fɔn* derived considerable economic benefits from his control over *čam*-able properties. Whenever a villager wished to be recognized as a *kum* or to open a dancing field, he paid the *fɔn* a goat, along with other valuables, and the *fɔn* received a goat from the successor of each *kum si*. Moreover, the members of clan sections that had not previously enjoyed the right of *mbɛŋ* ("raffia mats used to screen a compound") or that of employing two doors were required to pay him similar fees in order to obtain these prerogatives.

Finally, a *fɔn* had certain advantages in relations with his affines in that he could acquire new wives by sending his page boys to capture them. However, this was mainly a symbolic gesture. Unlike some neighboring plateau chiefs, Meta' village heads did not obtain wives without giving bridewealth, since it was thought that the father-in-law's resultant anger would cause the new spouse or her children to suffer *ndɔn*.

The foregoing discussion has outlined the economic advantages of a Meta' chief. Goats, brass rods, fowl, palm wine, and other kinds of produce were continually being brought to him, and when the bridewealth that he received for his many daughters is also considered, his resources begin to seem great. However, these benefits were counterbalanced by almost as many obligations. The foremost duty of a *fɔn* in the mind of any Meta' person was to feed his people. This was done most lavishly when he provided several grand feasts at the time of his installation. Yet the *fɔn* also entertained more modestly on a regular basis. Each time that the villagers worked for him he was obligated to feed them when they had finished their task, and he hosted the entire village whenever he held an annual celebration involving dancing. Likewise, if the village went to war, it was said to be fighting on its chief's behalf, and the *fɔn*, who stayed away from the battlefront, had to provide the returning warriors with an appropriate reception. But even if no such activities had taken place within a year, the people sometimes still expected the *fɔn* to give them a feast simply because he was their leader.

Besides hosting the entire village on special occasions, the *fɔn* frequently entertained individuals and small groups. He was expected to have wine ready for such visitors at any time, as well as for the *mikum si* when they met on the village rest day. Moreover, if there was a market in his village, he held court in a house just outside of it, providing palm wine for both the local notables and important visitors. Finally, just as individuals were to reserve some of the best of everything for the *fɔn*, the *fɔn* himself was expected to reward those who had honored him with gifts. No exact equivalence was required. However, in the eyes of the people, what the *fɔn* bestowed often symbolized much more than its everyday value would imply. Thus, one informant described an imaginary case in which the chief had rewarded a loyal supporter by giving him a small hen. The latter then used it to produce many more. After selling these fowl, he bought a goat from which he bred a large herd. Then he used the goats for bridewealth and, finally, had many children with his new wife. The point of the story was that the *fɔn*'s small gift was a great blessing that ultimately allowed the man to marry and have a large family.

A further meta-economic significance of the exchanges between a *fɔn* and his people was that they often constituted an indicator of ranking within the village. The Meta' were very sensitive to subtle discriminations reflected in hospitality, and one man's attitude toward another might be significantly altered, depending on whether he had made a special effort to serve him or offered only lame excuses. People attending important gatherings also noted how various guests were treated, depending on their statuses and relations with the host. Speaking of a man who was seated in a private room and given special attention, they would say, "he is a person" (*wi yɛ wit*). By contrast, one placed in a more public space without elaborate food and drink was not considered a "real person."

Since the *fɔn* was continually receiving visitors—on week days, on village rest days, on special occasions, and on market days—he was in an excellent position to use the norms of hospitality as a political tool. He could honor and reward allies as well as cultivating the nonaligned. At the same time, he gained prestige with the entire community by feeding it well. Thus, to a considerable extent, the significance of the role of *fɔn* in Meta' society was due to the sheer number of valuables coming in to a *fɔn* and the control that he exercised over their subsequent distribution. Meanwhile, the people themselves curried the *fɔn*'s favor by using similar techniques (i.e., by presenting him with special gifts, by quickly bringing tribute from their areas, and by making hidden payments when they required his assistance).

A final economic feature of *fɔn*ship was the special relationship that existed between the *fɔn* and the land (*si*). One expression of this was his tribute, since, as we have seen, the chief normally possessed tributary rights over several items. These included both noble game, such as leopards, and products like palm wine that were found within the residential area (*si ʒbɛŋ*) or zone of farmland and bush (*si mbɛŋ*) belonging to the village. (This tribute was justified by saying that the *fɔn* had provided leadership and fed the people while they were driving previous settlers off the land.) In addition, most chiefs also had larger personal farm tracts than other descent group leaders. From this reserve, they were expected to provide plots for any male villagers who could not be accommodated by their own kin. Permanent hereditary rights were transferred in this way, not merely temporary usufruct, and no return payment was required. Of course, the *fɔn* was not the only one sharing land with others. Temporary use rights were granted by notables possessing large tracts without regard to the recipients' clan affiliations, and a man unable to provide his adult son with farmland might petition the head of his descent group segment. However, only the *fɔn* bestowed farmland permanently on members of other clans. He likewise had the sole right to present wandering strangers with homesites and farm plots and to reclaim their property (together with improvements) if they subsequently left the village. Such chiefly prerogatives were prime expressions of the *fɔn*'s territorial dominion as well as of the Meta' concept that the *fɔn* is "over the people" (*gwɜ bɜt*) and responsible for all of them. As such, they were jealously guarded.

The Symbolism of Meta' Chieftaincy

In this section, Meta' concepts of *fɔn*ship will be considered as a symbolic system. The analysis is based on several kinds of data, including observed and reported ritual behavior involving chiefs, interviews with several excellent informants in which the concepts surrounding precolonial chieftaincy were explored, and numerous incidental observations from everyday life in the field.

It has already been noted that the *fɔn* was credited with extraordinary mystical powers capable of affecting the village as a whole and that he therefore served as its focus of unity. However, these concepts were themselves based upon more fundamental notions concerning mystical power, two of which will be discussed here: the belief that during his installation the *fɔn* was invested with the mystical potency inherent in his villagers' voices and the concept that he achieved legitimate power through identification with the leopard.

In Chapter 4, Meta' mystical concepts that portrayed speech as a potent and dangerous act were examined. It was also noted that the *njɔm* ("ritual complaint or request") was the means by which the potency of speech was activated and that the distribution of speech-based power was uneven in Meta' society. Persons representing the closest links with the forefathers and those claiming "historical primacy" in a given activity were thought capable of uttering the strongest *njɔm*.

All of these concepts were drawn upon in the rituals that served to install a *fɔn* in order to invest him with enhanced mystical power and authority. The way in which this was done was described by an informant as follows:

The *fɔn* is put in his place by many people so that all should fear his power. They had the custom in the old days that a person couldn't touch the *fɔn*. This was to show that he was not equal with ordinary people. It is only at the time that the *fɔn* is installed that many villagers touch him and rub him with numerous medicines. Afterward they fear that if you touch a person who has been anointed in this way, you will be sick. The medicines are certain leaves from the bush that they collect just for the occasion. It is the *mikum si* who know the special ones to use. The rubbing is done only once, at the time that the *fɔn* is installed. The *fɔn* also drinks from the cups of the *mikum si* and the cups of the other *fɔn*s who attend. This drinking of wine from the cups of all the *mikum si* belonging to different clans gives the *fɔn* the power to say an *njɔm* that will cure a sick person from any descent group in the village. All the old women from different clan sections within the village also smear the *fɔn* with camwood at his installation. Then they say, "You have been rubbed and there is no one to look at you any more and say that you are not *fɔn*. You are above all the people. You will stop all evil. If the people are fighting and you say something, they will stop." The camwood that the women use to rub the *fɔn* comes from all different clans in the village; it is not the *fɔn*'s own. The *mikum si* also come with their own camwood to anoint the *fɔn*.

According to this informant's description, the mystical power of each important descent group leader within the village (as well as the knowledge and power inherent in the old women of the community) was directly transmitted to the *fɔn* during his installation. Some key ritual objects were used to effect this. Most significantly, as the new *fɔn* was rubbed with the camwood of the various *mikum si* and their senior sisters, a link was established between him and the ancestors of all important descent groups in the village. Afterward, the *fɔn* could draw upon their combined knowledge and power in much the same way that individual *mikum si* did within their own groups.

The use of the sacrificial drinking horns of the *mikum si* had similar implications. Since the *izwi* ("spirits," "breath") of all the important patrilineal ancestors of a *kum si* were thought to reside within his hereditary cup, the powers of speech possessed by the successors of all of the village founders were transferred to the *fɔn* as he drank from their vessels. Through this process he rose to a plane above the other senior notables and was endowed with mystical power capable of affecting every villager, regardless of his descent group affiliation.

The consolidation of such great mystical power in the person of the *fɔn* goes a long way toward accounting for the ambivalent emotions that some informants revealed when speaking of him. This power could be used either to benefit the villagers or to harm them. Its positive aspects were referred to by the informant quoted above when he noted that, after his installation, the chief could speak an *njɔm* that would cure a sick person from any descent group in the village. Its negative side is still commonly expressed today in such statements as, "If the *fɔn* looks at a person in an angry way, that man will not live." At the time of my fieldwork, the *fɔn*'s person continued to be regarded as a source of deadly supernatural power. This belief was the basis for disputants swearing on his body (i.e., using it as an oracle), and it also accounted for the strong taboos on touching the *fɔn*, sitting on his chair, or having sexual relations with his wives.

A final noteworthy point about the mystical power of the *fɔn* is that it was, at least in part, consciously and purposefully given to him by the people. Those writing about divine kingship and sacral leadership in Africa have often emphasized the supernatural source of the ruler's power. The case of Meta' village chiefs was somewhat different. Here, the *fɔn* was not viewed as a divinity, and a substantial part of his mystical power was given to him directly by key members of the human community when they performed a very deliberate set of ritual acts designed to transfer their own potency to him.

Leopards as a source of power. Another symbolic underpinning of chiefly power was found in the set of beliefs and rituals surrounding leopards, pythons, and certain other prestigious animals, the class known as *nyam ŋwaʔ* ("noble game"). In most villages the *fɔn* had the sole authority to receive, butcher, and dispose of such creatures. However, since the animal's capture was also a matter of significance for the entire village, the other *mikum si* participated in the rituals of butchering it and received specific shares of the meat.

Of all noble game, the leopard was the most highly regarded. It was seen as the most dangerous species, since it could easily reverse roles and kill the hunter who pursued it. In addition, leopards (and pythons) were credited with certain mystical powers. Some of these animals were believed to be the doubles of distant sorcerers coming to wreak havoc in the village, and the whiskers of a leopard or the bile of a python were thought to be extremely deadly sorcery medicines that only a *fɔn* could legitimately possess.

In general terms, the leopard represented a double-edged force of nature. It was the fiercest of animals and possessed a power that could operate in both natural and mystical ways. Yet this power was also useful to society, since a *fɔn*'s possession of the whiskers of leopards enhanced the mystique of his authority and enabled him to place stronger curses on offenders. In this context, organizing rights over leopards through the system of rules regulating *čam*-able properties can be seen as a means by which society sought to harness an important resource—the physical and supernatural powers of these beasts.

Because the *fɔn* had the exclusive right to receive slain leopards, and because he derived power from these animals in a symbolic way, he seems to have become identified with the leopard in the minds of some Meta'. This emerges in a clear (an unsolicited) fashion in two statements by informants who had been asked to expound freely on the essence of a *fɔn*'s role:

A leopard is important because the people know that it is very wild and only a brave man can shoot it. The whiskers of a leopard are what a *fɔn* wants to get. If he gets one such whisker and touches it while calling your name and speaking of some bad thing that you have done, you will not be alive. The word for chief (*fɔn*) is related to the word for leopard (*ʒfɔn*). This is because a *fɔn* has power like a leopard. If you go to hunt a leopard, it can kill you too. In just the same way, the *fɔn* can kill you or sell you if he wants.

A *fɔn* is like a leopard. You can't catch a leopard with your bare hands; in the same way you can't put your hands on a *fɔn*. The *fɔn* acts like a leopard if a person touches him. The *mikum si* are his claws, and they call the person down and fine him. If a person refused to pay, he would be tied and beaten and have to bribe all of the *mikum si* before they released him.

The rituals and beliefs associated with leopards thus provide a second example of the way in which some of the most vital symbols of mystical potency were manipulated to focus power in the person of the *fɔn*. In the rituals of installation discussed earlier, the community purposefully transferred the power of its collective voice to him, while in the ceremonies surrounding the capture of a leopard, he appropriated the power of the slain beast and in doing so came to be seen as a kind of leopard among men. Moreover, in both instances power was acquired by methods that the community regarded as legitimate.

Attitudes Toward Chiefly Authority

In the preceding pages, we have seen that both economic and ideological factors contributed to a *fɔn*'s authority. However, this was also an authority that the Meta' people viewed with great ambivalence. Though accepting its legitimacy and positive uses, they seem to have feared that the *fɔn* would employ it to escape normal social obligations. This can be seen in two statements from informants who were asked to contrast a good *fɔn* with a bad one:

(A common person speaking)
A bad *fɔn* is one who receives gifts from people and never gives anything in return or doesn't even greet them when they bring some-thing for him. A person is also a bad *fɔn* who tries to get someone's daughter without paying bridewealth; the father of the girl will call him a bad *fɔn*. It is a good *fɔn* who respects the fathers of his wives. It is a good *fɔn* who marries a girl from the village and receives her father well when he comes bringing wine. A good *fɔn* would send out wine for the father of his wife to drink, order his wives to cook a fowl for the man, and come himself to inquire what the trouble is.

(A statement made by a *fɔn*)
A bad *fɔn* is one who agrees to buy people's things and takes them without giving anything. A bad *fɔn* associates with thieves in the village

and goes about beating people for no reason. A good *fɔn* calls the people and feeds them and judges them. He also calls his wives and feeds them and settles disputes in his compound. A good *fɔn* shares the animals he receives with the correct people and rewards the hunter who has killed one. A good *fɔn* likewise feeds the people when they work for him and calls them to his dancing field to speak a curse against thieves in the village. When he does so and the country is peaceful, they call him a good *fɔn*. It is bad if the *fɔn* allows one of his sons to take the wife of a villager. A good *fɔn* would refuse this and drive his son out of the country if necessary.

As these comments indicate, informants were quite concerned about exploitation through misuse of chiefly power. In this context, whether the *fɔn* abused his authority seemed to emerge as the main standard by which his performance was judged, and other possible criteria, such as whether he had *we* ("sense"), were not mentioned.

Further understanding of the ambivalence with which the Meta' viewed chiefly authority can be gained from an examination of the various concepts of "ruling" associated with chieftaincy, since two of these express quite succinctly the fundamental conflict that underlay the role of *fɔn*.[2]

(1) *ɬtumbɨ*. The most common term used to describe a *fɔn* "ruling" or governing his people is *itumbɨ*. The word is usually translated as "pressing," "ruling," or "oppressing" by English-speaking Meta', and its connotations in contexts where it does not refer to the action of a *fɔn* are all quite negative. For example, it might be used to describe an *mban* head who unfairly appropriates his agnates' shares of bridewealth, a tyrannical husband, or an unruly child.

Situations explained by the word *itumbɨ* always involve one person violating the rights of another, often through a dramatic reversal of normal behavior. For example, a child is said to *itumbɨ* his parents if he refuses to fetch water when asked to do so by his mother. The term would be even more appropriate if

---

2. The following analysis of the phrases "*itumbɨ*" and "*gwɜ bɜt*" derives mainly from an extended discussion with my research assistant Fonbah. It therefore represents a departure from the methodology used in the rest of the study in which primary reliance was placed upon the direct testimony of elderly informants. In the present instance this appears justified, since both of the terms considered are basic concepts of Meta' culture, and their meaning is unlikely to have changed since precolonial times.

the mother herself later went to the stream and the child used up all the water she had brought. Similarly, a wife might be said to *itumbi* her husband if she requires him to heat water for her morning bath and then sits idly by while he prepares their breakfast. A husband could *itumbi* his wife by always taking the money she earns and spending it on wine without even informing her. A violation of normal role behavior is thus an important part of the concept *itumbi* as it is applied in everyday situations.

Another important implication of *itumbi* is that the person who is being "ruled" has the power to resist but chooses not to do so. All of the examples mentioned above describe behavior that is considered improper by the Meta', and in each case the person being "ruled" has the capability of doing something about it. A child can be punished by his parents, as can a wife by her husband. Likewise, if a husband mistreats his wife badly, she can leave him or complain to her father. However, the word *itumbi* does not apply where the person being controlled has no choice but to submit. Thus, fathers are not said to "rule" their children even if they mistreat them badly because, relatively speaking, the children are in a powerless position.

Itumbi is also a very painful word for those who are "ruled" in domestic contexts. A husband should never declare openly to his wife that he is "ruling" her, and if she hears others saying it, she will feel unhappy because she is being treated like a slave. Accordingly, *itumbi* is only used to describe relations between kinsmen and acquaintances when those being "ruled" are not present.

Despite all of these negative connotations, *itumbi* is the most common term used to describe the relation between a *fɔn* and his people, and here it may have both positive and negative implications. In modern times, for example, it is said to be "good ruling" if the *fɔn* instructs the people to keep their yards, latrines, and water sources clean in order to prevent disease. Similarly, in precolonial days it was "good ruling" if a *fɔn* exhorted villagers to work hard on their farms so as to prevent famine or if he gave orders that husbands and wives should "obey" each other and remain together. The *fɔn* might issue such instructions at a public gathering like a mortuary celebration, and it would be considered "good ruling" because the people were able to do something for themselves only after hearing from him. It is also considered "good ruling" when the *fɔn* orders his subjects to prepare a large farm plot for his own wives. This means that when important visitors appear, the *fɔn* will be able to feed them without soliciting the people. Acts such as taking tribute can be either good or bad ruling depending on how they are carried out. If a *fɔn* is evenhanded in collecting and sharing wine, this is good ruling. But if he takes it mainly from a single clan section, he is said to be "pressing" that group is an undesirable way.

In political settings, as in domestic ones, *itumbɨ* is a painful word for those being "ruled," and it should not be used in their presence. Although it is an act of "ruling" when the *fɔn* gives orders at a public assembly, those involved do not employ *itumbɨ* to convey what is happening. Instead they might say *wɨ kɨ bɔt* ("he teaches the people"). Only outside observers would speak in terms of "ruling."

One informant stated vividly what might happen if the people being "ruled" by the *fɔn* heard *itumbɨ* applied to them:

When the people go to clear farms for the *fɔn* and they hear someone tell the *fɔn*, "You are really ruling these people," they will feel unhappy and say, "so it was because of 'ruling' (*itumbɨ*) that we did this work!" After this they will not be anxious to do it again. In the early days, if a *fɔn* came out openly and said to the people, "I am ruling you; you cannot escape," they would ignore his orders and not come to do anything at his compound. There might even be fighting between the *fɔn*'s descent group and the villagers. Even the most oppressed clan section would ignore the *fɔn* if he said openly that he was "ruling" them. It would be just as if a modern politician came up, pointed his finger at you, and said, "I am ruling you; you cannot escape." If a person accepts this, it is like saying he is a slave who cannot resist.

The use of the term *itumbɨ* thus affords considerable insight into the position of *fɔn* in Meta' society. It does not connote normal social relations where reciprocal rights and duties are clearly established. Rather, it describes reversals of expected behavior in which one person uses his power to gain an advantage and the other willingly lets him do it, the most extreme example being that of a child who "rules" his parents. Finally, it is not considered a case of *itumbɨ* if the person being "ruled" is incapable of refusing.

In many ways this is an appropriate term with which to characterize relations between a Meta' *fɔn* and his people. Meta' society was egalitarian in many respects. Each person belonged to a descent group, and every such group could resort to essentially the same means of protecting its members' rights. There was also no significant class structure, since even slaves and war captives became agnates within a generation if they were retained. To be sure, most authority was in the hands of successors to hereditary positions, but since this was based mainly on mystical concepts, its usage was somewhat circumscribed. If a person with authority abused it, his own supernatural powers could strike him down.

In this context, the position of *fɔn* was in some ways unnatural and a violation of the normal social order. The *fɔn* stood above the descent system that so structured the lives of ordinary villagers, since, as chief of all the people, his authority extended to every clan section in the place. He also possessed unique mystical powers and economic prerogatives. Yet although the people recognized his power to "rule" (*itumbi*) them, they refused that the word be applied to them openly because they were not slaves. The concept of *itumbi* thus expresses quite clearly some of the complex and ambivalent feelings that the Meta' people had about a *fɔn*.

(2) *Gwɜ bɜt.* Even when speaking of "ruling" (*itumbi*), informants distinguish between that which benefits the people and that which does not. The benevolent side of a *fɔn*'s role is further elaborated by a second Meta' concept. It is often said that the *fɔn* is *gwɜ bɜt* ("over the people"), an expression which, by contrast with *itumbi*, can be revealed even to the people that the *fɔn* is "over." The use of the phrase was described by one Meta' informant as follows:

When you say that a person is *gwɜ bɜt* or *gunɜ bɜt*, it means that he is the senior person in that place. You can say that a *kum si* is "over" the people in his part of the village or that a *fɔn* is "over" the village. Stating either of these things will not make the people who are under these men unhappy. This term causes no anger because everyone has a person who is "over" him. A son has his father, a grown man has his *kum si*, and a *kum si* has his *fɔn*. Also, when people say *wit ɜgunɜ bɜt* ("the man who is over the people") they mean *Ŋwiɜ* who is God over all the people. A person who is *gwɜ bɜt* must help his people with the problems that are too difficult for them. If they refuse to obey him, he must just be patient. If he begins to "press" (*itumbi*) the people or beat them, then they will escape one by one, and he will be left alone. It is just like a modern work gang. The headman shouldn't mark people absent to punish them when they don't work well. If he did this, he might have nobody working for him. It is better if he is patient and teaches his men how to work better. If a father is disobeyed by his wives and children, he may go to his friend and say, "my people don't obey me, and I don't know what I can do." The friend will tell him to be patient and say, "A person who is over people must hold his heart." This means that he must keep silent in his troubles.

This statement expresses an ideal picture of the *fɔn* as a man who is over the people as part of the natural order of things. His prime function should be to help the people with problems that are beyond them. He should not punish their mistakes; rather, he should gently teach them better ways.

Since it is an ideal, the concept of the *fɔn* as being *gwɜ bɜt* only partially expresses the role of a *fɔn* in Meta' society. While some chiefly actions may have conformed to this benevolent and fatherly ideal, *fɔn*s also possessed real power and tended to use it to their own advantage. One must therefore combine the concept of *gwɜ bɜt* (natural power) with *itumbi* (unnatural power) to achieve the fullest understanding of Meta' *fɔn*ship.

Ambivalence and avoidance in the role of fɔn. An examination of the two Meta' concepts of "ruling" underscores the ambivalence with which the Meta' people viewed chiefly authority. Such feelings posed both personal and structural dilemmas. For any individual chief, the problem was that of how to exercise his considerable pragmatic and mystical power without seeming to "rule" (*itumbi*) too directly. For the community as a whole, by contrast, there was the question of how to use the *fɔn*'s authority to achieve desirable social ends without risking oppression.

A partial solution to these problems was found in the institutionalization of a generalized avoidance relationship between *fɔn* and people. This precluded any appearance of oppressive rule but did not call into question the *fɔn*'s mystical or behind-the-scenes power. If he attended a celebration at another person's compound, for example, the *fɔn* was usually seated in a private room from which he might or might not emerge to dance with the people. Frequently, he would remain secluded throughout the festivities and only send a messenger to announce his greetings or give necessary instructions.

The same pattern of behavior was apparent in the *fɔn*'s use of a spokesman at important events. Although he was under an obligation to advise people on how to conduct such activities peacefully and successfully, he was forbidden to speak for himself at large public gatherings. If he wished to address such an assembly, thereby underscoring his message, he was obliged to go with a *kum si* to serve as interpreter. Then when the crowd became silent, the *fɔn* would begin to talk in a low voice, pausing frequently so that the *kum si* could repeat his words more loudly to the people.

The reasons behind the *fɔn*'s use of a spokesman were described by one informant in the following way:

In the early days, if the *fɔn* had an announcement, a *kum si* spoke for him. This was a custom from the earliest times. Since the *fɔn* has people under him, others should speak for him. If a person has a servant, he does not need to do the work of the servant. If the *fɔn* speaks loudly, the people will think that he is drunken. They will be very annoyed and say, "Is he speaking now because he is *fɔn*? If so, could he have become *fɔn* by himself?" The people feel that this is bad because the *fɔn* has taken away the chance of the *kum si* who ought to speak for him and also debased the position of *fɔn*. Also, if the *fɔn* speaks for himself and says something unreasonable, the people will know that the *fɔn* himself has made a mistake and not respect him. But if a *kum si* speaks for the *fɔn*, the people can always think, "The *fɔn* said the correct thing, and it is the *kum si* who corrupted what he said." The people do not like the *fɔn* to order them directly because he has much power. If he says a bad thing about someone, it might happen. If a *fɔn* always spoke to the people directly and abused them, the people would remove him from his post. They would say, "Since the *fɔn* wants to act like a villager and go about abusing people, let him become one. Then he can go about wildly and fight with people. Let a person who can do the correct thing become *fɔn*."

Several interesting themes are interwoven in this complex explanation. Among other things, the *fɔn* is said to use a spokesman because it would be undignified for him to address the public directly, because it helps to preserve the people's faith in his infallibility, and because it prevents accidental unleashings of his mystical power. However, the reason that the informant stresses above all others is that the *fɔn*'s speaking directly to the people would make them feel as if they were being ruled in an oppressive way. The fact that the informant describes "abusing" the people as sufficient grounds for the *fɔn*'s removal from office suggests how seriously this issue was taken in precolonial Meta'.

It should also be noted that the idea that avoidance was the proper relationship between a *fɔn* and his people went beyond mere seating etiquette and the ceremonial use of a spokesman to affect the way in which he carried out some of his basic political functions. When the *mikum si* of a village met in the main hall at the chief's residence, for example, the *fɔn* himself often remained apart. If he wished to affect the discussion, he could summon several of the *mikum si* to hear his points. Later, these men would return to the public meeting and express the views of the *fɔn* without necessarily identifying them as such. Similarly, even though the *fɔn* was in practice heavily involved in settling disputes (see Chapter 8 for details), informants also stated that he should never directly judge cases. His ideal role was described by one informant in the following way:

> In the case of villagers, it is important that they judge themselves and then have the *fɔn* confirm it. It is not that the *fɔn* judges the people and then the people confirm it. This point is very important in distinguishing good and bad ruling. If a *fɔn* is very intelligent and has a good point to make about a case that nobody else is making, he will take one of the villagers aside and tell him. Then the villager will put this point to the people to see if it is a good one and the others won't even know it came from the *fɔn*. This is a very important aspect of Meta' custom.

As this and the previous examples illustrate, the *fɔn*'s avoiding direct interactions with the people was a pervasive theme in Meta' political ideology.

Conclusion

The various leadership roles that have been described in this chapter and the set of relationships among these leaders formed one of the most important dimensions of Meta' village organi-

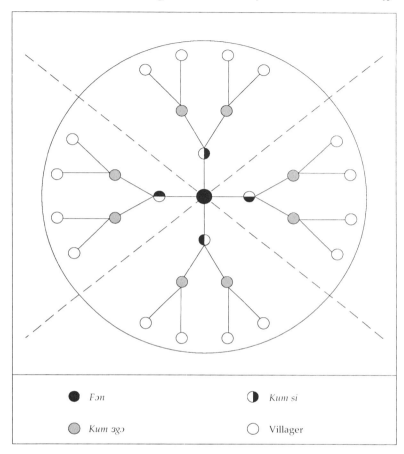

Fig. 4. The network of leadership roles in a Meta' village.

zation. The essentials of this system are illustrated in Figure 4, which shows the outline of the village political hierarchy and the network of communication among villagers and political leaders. As indicated, official relations between the *fɔn* and a *kum ʒgɔ* are mediated by a *kum si*, while those between an ordinary villager and the *fɔn* are channeled through both a *kum ʒgɔ* and a *kum si*. Thus, if a conflict was to be referred to the *fɔn*, the matter should ideally first be brought before the *kum ʒgɔ* under whose jurisdiction the disputants fell and then to the *kum si* with authority over both the *kum ʒgɔ* and the parties. Similarly, a leopard shot by a villager should be taken to the compounds of the appropriate *kum ʒgɔ* and *kum si* before being brought to that of the *fɔn*.

Figure 4 also illustrates, in a simplified way, the descent group organization of the village. Each quarter of the circle (indicated by the dotted lines) represents a distinct clan section under the leadership of a man who is simultaneously the head of that section and a *kum si*. The two roles coincide because, ideally, the clan section head is the descendant of a village founder, whereas the *mikum ʒgɔ* shown in the diagram hold titles that were acquired later by *čam*-ing.

In addition, Figure 4 represents the territorial structure of a Meta' village. Under this system, each *kum si* is the proprietor of a given "side" or area within the village and the person with ritual authority over it.

While Figure 4 clearly illustrates the basic patterns of village organization, it does not indicate some of the complexities and points of variability in Meta' village structure. Thus, the diagram shows each *kum si* as having jurisdiction over two *mikum ʒgɔ* who are also junior segment heads in his clan section. However, as seen in Chapter 5, the lineage segmentation process was the result of many interacting factors. This meant that in some cases there were longer and more complicated chains of mediated authority (e.g., villagers passing through several *mikum ʒgɔ* to reach the *kum si*), while in other instances the route was much shorter (i.e., some villagers reported directly to the *kum si*, since they were members of his own *mban* group). Similarly, although there was a strong tendency for clan sections to be residential units and hence become "sides" of the village under a single *kum si*, there were always exceptions. For example, a *kum ʒgɔ* of a given descent group (A) whose *mban* group had· segmented from that of the *kum si* of A might resettle on land within a "side" of the village occupied by a different descent group (B). In such a case, he would come under the jurisdiction of the *kum si* of B in village affairs but continue to cooperate in matters pertaining to the clan section with the men of A, his agnates. However, in practice this irregular set of circumstances would probably lead to compromises that would further alter the network of relationships among village leaders. If the *kum ʒgɔ* in this example shot a leopard in the area of his new compound, for instance, he would take the slain animal to the *kum si* of group B. Yet, he might also summon his "father" (the *kum si* of A) to view the animal in his compound before doing so.

Keeping such qualifications in mind, Figure 4 does help to make another important point: in the diagram, two important subsystems of Meta' political organization—the system of lineage segmentation and the system of hereditary titles—are shown to intersect. Because all the *mikum ʒgɔ* in the diagram are considered as "sons" of the *mikum si* who have authority over them, we know that at some time in the past each one *čam*-ed to his particular *kum si* in order to receive the rights of *mban* and *sami*, thereby segmenting from the *kum si*'s group. But since the *mikum ʒgɔ* are men whose "names are known" throughout the village, they were also required to *čam* separately to the *fɔn* and the other *mikum si* in order to ratify their statuses. Their present positions thus derive partly from the system of title-taking within the village and partly from the fact that they had emerged as the recognized heads of descent group segments through the normal process of lineage segmentation. In this way two distinct principles of Meta' political organization worked together to establish positions of leadership within the village.

The more exalted positions of *kum si* and *fɔn* likewise derived from the operation of these principles, but here some additional factors were involved. As noted earlier, the rank of *kum si* was distinct from that of *kum ʒgɔ* in that it could not be *čam*-ed. Only those descent group heads who had helped to found the village could qualify for this status, since their having arrived first enabled them to make the strongest possible ritual statements. Meta' concepts of mystical power and of "historical primacy as a source of legitimacy and power" thus provided further criteria to differentiate among classes of local-level leaders, and they gave the *mikum si* a distinct nondescent basis for authority that provided something of a counterweight to the segmentary forces apparent in Figure 4. Finally, as explained earlier, the strongest symbols of mystical power were manipulated to raise the *fɔn* to a pre-eminent position among the *mikum si*, thereby supplying an even more concrete focus for village identity.

SEVEN

Village-Level Rituals and Activities

IN THE preceding chapter, we saw that the unity of the village and the relationships among its leaders were continually being reasserted through the weekly meetings of the *mikum si*, as well as through the occasional *čam*-ing of descent group heads to acquire the status of *kum* and by the payments that successors made to confirm already-established titles. However, the *mikum* of a Meta' village were not simply members of an exclusive club that conferred prestige and perpetuated its existence as a group. They also supervised many important political functions. In this chapter, we shall consider the principal activities over which they presided, including certain village-level rituals, the treatment of noble game, communal hunting, the procedures of *čam*-ing for elite goods and statuses, and the processes through which villages organized themselves for warfare.

Zi Si: An Anti-sorcery Ritual

One of the most important events in a Meta' village was the semi-annual ritual sequence known as *zi si*. The literal meaning of *zi si* is "to prepare a small mound of earth" (as one might do in yam farming for example). In more general terms, the phrase refers to "an action taken to protect something valuable by building up a barrier against hostile forces," and it is sometimes translated even more abstractly by English-speaking Meta' as "blessing the earth."

The explicit purpose of these rites was to seal off the village at its boundaries from a variety of malevolent influences and thereby promote its prosperity and security. Most important, they prevented *bɜd misa* ("sorcerers" or "practitioners of *sa*"), who were believed to reside in Mogamo and more distant groups in the forest to the southwest, from entering the village to steal the fertility of the earth or destroy life and property. Such *bɜd misa* were thought capable of transforming themselves into animal forms, usually pythons, and flying through the air to bring violent storms to the Meta' area. Heavy rains that eroded farm plots or destroyed crops and violent windstorms that demolished compounds were thought to be the work of such animal doubles. (When several houses were laid waste by a small tornado in 1971, villagers claimed to have seen a python flying over the site, and they quickly mounted a party to scour the bush for its hiding place.) In addition to warding off *bɜd misa*, the rites of *zi si* were also thought to protect against ordinary persons who entered the village to harm its members. Thus, thieves, wife abductors, and warriors from other communities were said to be rendered slow and easily caught by the medicines used in *zi si*.

In precolonial times, the rites of *zi si* were performed twice yearly—in the March-April planting period at the end of the dry season and during the early harvest between August and November. The essential phases of the ritual were: (1) the collection of herbs and medicines from the bush by the *mikum si* and other knowledgeable persons. These were taken to the compound of the *fɔn*, where they were sometimes placed in a large heap on the dancing field; (2) the performance of a ritual by the *mikum si* and the *fɔn*, during which they sacrificed a fowl or goat, letting its blood flow over the medicine leaves, poured down libations of palm wine, and spoke an *njɔm* describing the powers that the medicines would assume; and (3) the distribution of the medicines. During this last phase, the various *mikum si* were normally given shares to put at appropriate locations in their own parts of the village. Usually, the medicines were buried beside or across all the paths that entered the village and those that approached small clusters of compounds. This served to seal off the village from *bɜd misa* at every point of access or vulnerability.

In practice, villages varied considerably in their performance of these rites. In one, for example, it was a hereditary group of three specialists rather than the *mikum si* who prepared the medicines ("because their fathers had always done it and they knew the style best"). There were likewise variations in the methods of distribution. The particular form that the ritual of *zi si* took in one village was described by a local *kum si* in the following way:

The medicine is prepared two times a year, around March and again in August. Many people will be present for this, but only the *mikum si* will receive shares of it. When the medicine leaves have been brought they are cut with knives. Then they speak the *njɔm*: "If a woman has left her husband in this village and she walks over these medicines, she will likely return. If a thief walks over the medicine, he will get swollen feet. If a python comes into the village, it will be quickly caught." After the *njɔm* has been spoken, the *fɔn* gives me a fowl to kill, and I cut its throat and let the blood fall over the medicine leaves. All of these things are done at a special spot on the dancing field where the old fathers did it before. I then divide the medicine, giving each *kum si* his own share. The share of the *fɔn* remains down on the ground and he sends a person to collect it later. On returning home each man gives a part of his share to certain *mikum ʒgɔ*. But the medicine is not divided again after this. Each man who has received a part takes it and puts it in the special places that his fathers showed to him. There are about fifteen places where medicine is buried in my side of the village.

An informant from another village gave a somewhat different description:

If the time has come to place medicines in the ground, all the men, women, and children of the village are called by the *mikum si* and ordered to bring the medicine leaves that they know. All of these are placed on the dancing field of the *fɔn*. Then *tɜkɜnɜ* (the village executioner, see p. 169) comes out of the *fɔn*'s compound and strikes the leaves three times with his club. After this the *mikum si* begin to cut the leaves and mix them together. Then the *mikum si* go inside a hut in the *fɔn*'s compound with the leaves and pour wine over them from their hereditary cups. When they have finished this they say, "You who come here with bad, you who come with other medicine to destroy the people, you who come to steal here or to catch a person to sell as a slave, you will meet with us who hold this ground. If a person who changes into a leopard or a python comes, he will become blind and be easily killed by the people of this place." After this *njɔm* has been spoken, each *kum si* takes a share of the medicine and goes to put it at all the junctions on his side of the village.

Performing the rituals of *zi si* was regarded as one of the most important obligations of village leaders in precolonial times, since the kinds of disasters produced by foreign sorcerers (e.g., crop failure and the destruction of compounds by windstorms) jeopardized the very survival of the community. Even in 1970, when the rituals were not being observed regularly in many Meta' villages, women were anxious that their crops might fail and complained about the neglect of the rites. In their view, it was only the mystical power of the village notables that stood between them and potential ruin.

Inquiries about whether the Meta' people themselves were ever the aggressors in invisible warfare through *sa*-like sorcery met with ambiguous responses. Some informants denied that this had ever happened. Others acknowledged that Meta' with the power of transforming themselves into leopards or pythons had existed in the past, but claimed that there had never been any organized rituals through which Meta' villages used this power against other groups. One point that did emerge clearly, however, was that in any Meta' attempt to ensorcel others, the groups attacking them would not have been the targets. Rather than using *sa* against the peoples to the southwest, the Meta' are said to have directed it against groups like Mankon in the northeast by those informants who admit that the invisible power was employed at all.

Ifu: New Elements in Anti-sorcery Rituals

In many Meta' villages during the period under consideration, *zi si* was only one of two sets of rites performed to protect the community from external threats. The second ritual sequence was *ifu* ("medicine"), a cover term for a complex of rights that could be acquired through *čam*-ing by the head of any sizeable clan segment. *Ifu* consisted of several elements: (1) the three dances *ičibi, ɔsimi,* and *ifu*; (2) the knowledge of how to prepare magical herbs and leaves to ward off *sa*; and (3) the dancing disguise known as *ɔtu kwɛm*. Each of these items could be *čam*-ed separately and had its own price in goats, brass rods, and other valuables. Moreover, once acquired, each of them became an hereditary right that was sanctioned by *ndɔn* and transferable to additional groups.

A clan section that had acquired the entire *ifuʔ* complex would normally employ it to carry out an annual cycle of festivities sometime between August and November. This consisted of one day a week of dancing, feasting, and drinking for a period of seven weeks. On the evening before the opening of the cycle, medicines were secretly prepared by the owners of *ifuʔ* (i.e., the principal segment heads of the clan section possessing it) and placed across every path leading into their neighborhood. Then in the morning, all members of the descent group would assemble at the compound of their senior notable to drink palm wine, sing their special songs, and dance in the courtyard. As they sipped their wine, they would declare that they were drinking "medicine" (*ifuʔ*) and thereby incorporating the protection of the substances prepared the night before. Once the ritual cycle had commenced in this way, the drinking and dancing was repeated on the same day for five successive weeks. The *ifuʔ* rituals then climaxed in the seventh week when a goat, provided by the owners of *ifuʔ*, was sacrificed and consumed by all those present. On this occasion, the dancing was also carried from the courtyard to the dancing field, and the masked figure ɜtu kwɛm made its appearance.

Two other noteworthy features of the *ifuʔ* rituals were their strong association with the cultivation of yams and their restrictions on participation by women. Unlike *zi si*, which was thought to promote agriculture in general by protecting the fertility of the village farmlands, the rites of *ifuʔ* were specifically designed to ensure a good yam harvest. Accordingly, participants were prohibited from eating yams until they were consumed in a special ceremonial meal on the final day of *ifuʔ*. The presence of women was also thought to spoil the medicines. They were therefore forbidden to enter the huts where the men were "drinking medicine" or to participate in the dancing. Women were likewise prohibited from doing farm work on the days when the *ifuʔ* rituals were performed, and anyone responsible for a loud noise or disturbance at this time could be fined.

While *ifuʔ* clearly falls within the class of *čam*-able property and was therefore controlled by individual clan sections, it also resembled a society or association in some respects. Men of different descent groups and villages who desired to do so could regularly attend this important ceremony. Such persons were considered "members" (*bɜt ŋga fɛte*) of *ifuʔ* and affiliated themselves with one of three huts in which the men of *ifuʔ* met to drink. Each of these was named after one of the dances of the *ifuʔ* complex (i.e., *ičibi*, *ɜsimi*, and *ifuʔ*), and different houses seem to have represented distinct classes of persons. For example, while *ičibi* was the house of the young men, *ɜsimi* was reserved for senior males with titles. All the members of a given house were required to contribute one large calabash of palm wine on every day that *ifuʔ* met, and in return they received shares of the sacrificial goat. *Ifuʔ* also resembled a voluntary association in that members belonging to different descent groups or villages were entitled to have the dance *ifuʔ* performed at their mortuary celebrations if their kin were willing to provide a goat as the payment for its owners.

Like those of *zɨ si*, the medicines employed in *ifuʔ* were thought to be useful in warding off *sa* ("airborne sorcery"). However, informants disagreed about their potency. While some dismissed *ifuʔ* as the "play of small boys," others said that, since the medicines of both ceremonies were the same, they should have equal effect. The history of the two rituals may shed some light on this question. While most of the descent groups that possessed *ifuʔ* in 1900 are said to have obtained it after reaching Meta' territory, *zɨ si* is invariably described as a custom that the ancestors of the Meta' people brought with them from Tadkon. Also, unlike *ifuʔ*, *zɨ si* was practiced in every Meta' village and drew upon the mystical power of the *fɔn* and the *mikum si*. Given the Meta' belief that the antiquity of a ritual enhances its power and the fact that the *mikum si* were credited with the most commanding mystical force, it seems likely that *zɨ si* was viewed as the more potent form of medicine against *sa*.

The history of *ifuʔ* in the Bome valley provides an illustration of the manner in which the ritual complex was probably introduced elsewhere as well. It was first owned here by the head of a nonchiefly clan section in Njekwa village. In some accounts, his forefathers are said to have brought it with them in their migrations from the forest, while in others he is described as having travelled there to obtain it. For a time, he was the only local possessor of *ifuʔ*. Later, however, the full complex was *čam*-ed from him by several village chiefs and a few additional notables, and one or two nonchiefly clan sections are said to have purchased just part of the complex (e.g., receiving only the dance *ifuʔ*). Finally, another clan section purchased parts of the ritual complex from a group in Ngi shortly before 1900. Through these various processes, *ifuʔ* became widespread in Bome by the beginning of the colonial era. At that time, it was owned by most village chiefs in the valley and by segments of at least five different clans.

Since the objectives of *ifuʔ* and *zi si* were roughly similar and since several descent groups in a village might own *ifuʔ*, coordinating the two rituals was sometimes complex. When a nonchiefly clan section observed the *ifuʔ* cycle, this did not replace the *zi si* rites for the village as a whole. In such a case, even if the medicines to ward off *sa* were equally powerful, they would only protect the neighborhood of the group owning *ifuʔ*. Therefore, *zi si* would still have to be performed twice a year by the village leaders. By contrast, whenever the *fɔn* was an owner of *ifuʔ*, the senior village notables would have a prominent part in the preparation of the medicines, and *ifuʔ* could safely be substituted for *zi si*. However, since *ifuʔ* was performed only once a year, *zi si* would still have to be done at the other appointed time (March or April). Finally, if several descent groups in the same village, including that of the *fɔn*, were owners of *ifuʔ*, there would be potential conflicts of scheduling. In such cases the observances would usually be staggered, with the *fɔn* instructing nonchiefly groups to carry out their rites at slightly different times than his own.

From both the point of view of the Meta' themselves and that of an outsider attempting to analyze their political system, antisorcery rituals can be said to have played a vital role in maintaining the integrity of the village. For the Meta', these rites represented the main bulwark against a number of hostile forces external to their society, while for the anthropologist they can be interpreted as one of the principal means through which village identity was established. By joining to defend themselves against outside attack, Meta' villagers stressed the unity of their group.

The Treatment of Noble Game

The activities surrounding "noble game" (*nyam ŋwaʔ*) provided another important dimension of village organization in precolonial times. This was a relatively large category of animals that included at least two subclasses. Leopards and pythons were the most highly regarded type, while the inferior class was made up of several smaller cats and carnivores, including *imaŋ*, *sɛŋ3*, and *ičɔp*.

Rights to receive any of these animals when they were killed by a hunter, to eat their flesh, or to display their skins could be acquired by two different methods. According to the first, any descent group leader who founded a village in a vacant area might legitimately claim them. Alternatively, a descent group head could acquire rights over noble game by *čam*-ing them from a counterpart who was already a possessor. He did so by purchasing certain symbolic objects such as the stone and knife used for butchering leopards. The fees required in such cases were heavy (e.g., as much as seven goats and a number of brass rods for the "stone of a leopard"). Moreover, rights to noble game were jealously guarded by their possessors and not simply granted to anyone with sufficient wealth.

It should be apparent to the reader that the two principles upon which claims to noble game might be founded were at least potentially in conflict. In a given village, for example, the head of clan section A might be the direct successor of the village founder, while that of section B was the only person who had *čam*-ed the right of noble game. Here there could be two men with legitimate claims to the same leopard. Accordingly, the histories of some villages record a series of struggles over the issue of noble game (see Chapter 9 for examples). However, the two patterns of distribution that informants seem to have regarded as normative were as follows:

1. Cases where the *fɔn* of the village was the sole person possessing rights over both classes of noble game, and

2. Cases where the *fɔn* had rights over leopards and pythons, while certain of the *mikum si* were entitled to keep the less important species.

The second pattern might be the result of the *fɔn*'s having usurped a founder's claim to the highest class of noble game, while allowing him to retain the lesser types. Or such a pattern could come about if the *fɔn* at first controlled all kinds of noble game and later allowed one of his *mikum si* to *čam* rights to the inferior varieties.

When trying to comprehend the rules governing noble game in precolonial Meta' society, it is always important to remember that these were thought of as rights to receive specific animals from within particular territories. Thus, when a *kum si* was said to have *čam*-ed rights over the second class of noble game, as in the example above, he had *čam*-ed the right to receive such animals only when they were killed within the area that he controlled as a *kum si*. Similar animals taken in any other part of the village would continue to be presented to the *fɔn*.

A good illustration of this point is provided by the case of a *kum si* in one Meta' village. In the earliest times, his predecessors are said to have lacked rights over noble game, since the local *fɔn* retained all of these. However, shortly before 1900, his clan section had grown quite large, and the *fɔn* granted him a tract of hunting land where he might found an independent community. Since he was to become *fɔn* of the new village, he was allowed to *čam* rights to receive all types of noble game that were taken there. However, the situation became complicated when enemy pressure prevented him from resettling, and, at the time of my research in 1970, he still occupied his place in the parent village. In this context the *kum si*'s rights over noble game were as follows: If a leopard was shot in his new village site, he would present a small share of the meat to the *fɔn* of his original village while dividing the rest among the men of his own clan section. He would also be allowed to retain the leopard skin. If one of the lesser forms of noble game was taken in the same location, the *kum si* would keep it for himself. On the other hand, if a leopard or any other type of noble game was killed within the "side" of the original village that the *kum si* and his people still occupied, he would present it to the *fɔn* and receive only a foreleg in return. Finally, if such animals were shot in any other part of that community, the *kum si* in question would be given no meat. This last arrangement is somewhat unusual, since all the *mikum si* of a village normally shared in noble game.

This *kum si* explained it by saying, "One should not consume things like noble game in two places. If they have given me a place of my own where I can receive such things, why should I continue to consume them in the place of the *fɔn*?"

Procedures for the Disposal of Noble Game

When important noble game was killed, the hunter's first task was to transport it to the appropriate political leaders. This was seen to be in his self-interest, since such mystically potent animals were thought to be dangerous to handle. Moreover, rights to noble game were sanctioned by *ndɔn*, so that any usurper of them risked a serious curse from the *njɔm* of the legitimate political leaders. Such offenders were believed likely to die from a swollen belly.

After being killed, the leopard or other noble game was taken from the compound of one political leader to another in a way that reflected the political structure of the village. Normally, this meant that it would be brought directly to the compounds of the *kum ʒgɔ* and *kum si* controlling the area in which it had been shot, who, together with the hunter and other onlookers, supervised the carrying of the animal to the residence of the *fɔn*. Their arrival there was marked by great celebration and the firing of Dane guns. Custom also required the *fɔn* to reward the successful hunter with a gift of gunpowder and instruct him to repeat the deed at a later time.

At the *fɔn*'s compound, the leopard was usually placed on the *ti ʒfɔn* (the tall upright "stone of a leopard"). The *mikum si* of the village were then summoned, and one of them, acting for the *fɔn*, skinned and butchered the animal with a special knife. Each *kum si* then received a specific portion as his hereditary share. The leopard skin itself, an emblem of chieftaincy, was reserved for the *fɔn*. However, he might reward a *kum si* with a belt that had been cut from it. Meanwhile, the ordinary men of the village continued their dancing and celebration.

Unfortunately, it is not possible to present a detailed case history of the capture of a leopard or python in precolonial times. However, one *kum si*'s description of the killing of a python in his village in 1971 illustrates some important features of the "traditional" ceremonies:

The python (*jɔ ɜkɔp*) was killed by a hunter at a distant farm owned by the *fɔn* early in the morning. The man who shot it belonged to the clan section of the *fɔn*. When he killed the snake he summoned the veterinary officer to transport it to the village in his car, since it would have taken several men to carry it. The snake arrived at the compound of the *fɔn* at about 11 a.m., but there was no important ceremony until the *mikum si* had been called. In the meantime the veterinary officer was given some wine as the person who had carried the snake. The hunter was also given some medicine, since it is believed that the breath of python is poisonous; if one breathes on a man while he is trying to shoot it, he will become ill. When the *mikum si* had come, two of them who had the right to do so skinned the animal and divided the meat in pieces. Each of these men kept a knife for noble game that his forefathers had *čam*-ed at his compound. Another man, a "brother" of the *fɔn* who was old and knew the custom well, decided which person should receive what share of the meat. All of the *mikum si* received a portion, as did several important visitors from other villages. These were important men who used to summon the *fɔn* when they had killed noble game in their own areas. The person who shot the python should also be blessed, perhaps by rubbing him with camwood, and given double the amount of gunpowder he used to kill the snake. (The informant did not see this part of the rituals). They reward the hunter because there is great danger involved in hunting a python. If he received no reward, the next time he saw one he might just let it escape. The men who butchered the snake also removed the bile (*bu nyam*) and disposed of it in a latrine. Two West Cameroon police were present as witnesses for this. The bile was treated in this fashion because it is a deadly poison. If the leaders did not dispose of it in this way, people would always avoid them. If it was thought that they still had the bile, people might refuse to eat at their compounds and they would always fear that they might be poisoned if they had a small quarrel with one of the men who had it. In the night, all of the people danced *ičibi* as a sign of gladness while the snake lay on the ground. This was just the same fashion as when they used to return from war and put the enemy's head down on the dancing field of the *fɔn* and dance *nguʔu*. Each man also brought palm wine and they drank throughout the night.[1]

1. The extreme care taken to dispose of the snake's bile in this case is noteworthy in that it contrasts with other informants' statements that chiefs could retain such medicines (see Chapter 6). This could reflect either changes in Meta' custom since precolonial times or perhaps the ambivalence and ambiguity concerning chiefly power that was discussed earlier.

The Symbolism of Noble Game

The ultimate meaning of the elaborate ceremonies associated with noble game seems to have depended on Meta' beliefs about *sa* ("airborne sorcery") and other forms of supernatural power. As noted earlier, leopards and pythons were seen as animals with special mystical powers and were also believed to be the doubles of distant *bɜd misa* coming to wreak havoc. They thus stood for a force that could be extremely dangerous to the village, but also one with potentially positive applications (i.e., the *fɔn* derived power from his identification with the leopard and used it for legitimate purposes of social control). In this context, the ritualization of the capture of noble game and the presence of a complex set of rules governing rights in these animals represented an organized means through which society sought to harness their power. This in turn enhanced the prestige of the *fɔn* and the *mikum si* and helped to maintain the authority structure of the village.

Finally, it should be noted that the capture of a leopard or a python represented the victorious climax of a chain of events set in motion with the rituals of *zɨ si*. In *zɨ si*, it will be recalled, the villagers prepared medicines to ward off *bɜd misa* who had transformed themselves into leopards or pythons and to render them easily caught. Thus, when one of these animals was actually killed by a villager, it was proof of the triumph of the community and the mystical powers of its leaders over the hostile forces of *sa*. In this context, the enthusiasm with which the village celebrated such deeds is quite understandable.

Communal Hunting

In precolonial times, collective hunting was one of the most important village-level activities, since meat was highly prized, and since large numbers of animals could be killed when many hunters cooperated. Hunts were undertaken once a year during the November-through-April dry season when it was possible to flush out animals by burning the tall elephant grass that covered many plains and hillsides in the Meta' area. The date of the hunt, which was determined by the descent group owning the hunting territory, would be toward the end of the dry season when tracts surrounding the hunting bush had already been burned over to clear them for farming. By this time, many animals would have sought refuge in the unburnt bush.

Even though it was not supervised by the *mikum si*, communal hunting was still thought of as a village activity, since it involved the participation of most male villagers. In addition, it was ideally the *fɔn* and his clan section who owned the hunt. Some informants even denied that anyone but a *fɔn* could have a hunt, but this was clearly not the case, since in several villages there were hunts organized by nonchiefly groups.

The rights of a *fɔn* over a hunting territory were often traced to the foundation of the village, when his predecessor was said to have set aside a large hunting tract. In addition to controlling the land itself, the chiefly descent group normally possessed a hunting shrine and a set of hunting rituals that had been passed down from their forefathers. Both items were essential to the success of the hunt.

The activities involved in a communal hunt typically began with certain rituals that were conducted by the principal segment heads of the chiefly clan section at the *ji ʒgwʒm* or "hunting shrine."[2] They included the sacrifice of a fowl, the pouring of libations of palm wine over the stones of the shrine, and the addressing of an *njɔm* to the spirits of the descent group's founders in order to secure their assistance in making the hunt succeed. The character of these rites was described in detail by an informant who was a brother of the *fɔn* in his village and who customarily took charge:

The rituals last for only one day. I call four big men in my clan section and tell each person to bring a small calabash of palm wine. I myself bring a fowl. Before going to the *ji ʒgwʒm* we meet in the *mban* at the chief's compound and pour some wine on the ground. We may drink one calabash of wine before going to the *ji ʒgwʒm*. The *fɔn* himself does not come to the sacrifice. He will just stay in the house. Since he is a *fɔn*, he wouldn't want to go to the bush to the site of the *ji ʒgwʒm*. But

2. Such shrines were usually stones marking the graves of certain forefathers who had left instructions for their descendants to seek their blessings before undertaking a hunt.

he meets us when we come to the *mban*. When we reach the *ji ʒgwʒm* I clear the grass that has grown over it, and the others help. Then I take camwood from my bag and place it on the stone. It is camwood that I keep for the *fɔn*. After this I call the name of the person buried at the *ji ʒgwʒm* and throw some wine on the camwood. The other people repeat these actions after me. I myself use the cup of the father who is buried at the *ji ʒgwʒm* when I pour my wine down. The neck of the fowl is cut after the camwood on the stone has been soaked with wine, and the blood of the fowl pours over the stone. This is done to show how animals will be killed at the hunt. After this we smear the camwood that is mixed with the fowl's blood over the stone. This camwood is meant to "open the eyes" of the dead person and wake him up so that he will see the ritual. The person buried there will know he is to wake up, because he will recognize the camwood, which is the same one that he originally gave to his sons. When the father himself died, he spat upon this very camwood. So when we rub this camwood on his burial stone, we wake him up and show him that we are going to hunt. After all of these things are done, we go back to the *fɔn*'s compound. We take a small bit of the camwood from the first *ji ʒgwʒm* and rub it on another at the *fɔn*'s place. This camwood has been mixed with the fowl's blood. We do this to show that we are feeding the second *ji ʒgwʒm* too. After this we go into the *mban* of the *fɔn* and cook the fowl. Then I divide the fowl in equal shares, giving some to the *fɔn* and some to all of the other people who went with me to the *ji ʒgwʒm*. After we finish eating we agree on a day when the hunt will take place. When we drink wine in the *mban* after eating, we all throw some into the *ʒghʒm* ("libation hole") and say that animals should die. It is the power of the dead fathers that makes the hunt succeed. This power is transferred through their spit on the camwood. The people will know that this power is working when they see many animals being shot at the hunt.

After rituals such as these had been carried out, the *fɔn* would inform the *mikum si* that the hunt was to take place within several days. Each *kum si* then took the opportunity to conduct similar rites at his own *ji ʒgwʒm* to ensure the success of his people in the coming hunt. Finally, on the evening before the hunt, several hereditary specialists would broadcast news about it on the talking drums.

In the morning a large crowd of hunters, including many from nearby villages, would assemble in the bush to receive instructions from the hunt owners. Certain men who claimed "burning the hunt" as their hereditary specialty would set fire to the grass, while the rest waited for animals to flee into previously burned-over areas where they could easily be shot. The entire catch was then carried to the compound of the *fɔn* for distribution. Very small animals such as cane rats could be kept by individual hunters, but anything larger was divided under the supervision of the hunt owners. The hindquarters of any large animals went to them, while the remaining parts were retained by the hunters themselves. Some of the hunt owners' portion would also be shared with persons who had established claims and those whom the *fɔn* wished to honor. Thus, the hunt announcers usually received the hindquarters of one large animal, as did the men with the job of firing the bush. The *mikum si* of the *fɔn*'s own village and visitors who possessed hunts of their own might also be given something. The *fɔn*'s claim to the hindquarters of game pertained only to animals killed at a communal hunt during the dry season. Those taken by individuals at other times were the exclusive property of the hunter and his kin.

Activities Associated with *Čam*-able Property

The concept of *čam* has already been discussed rather fully, and we have seen how it provided the basis for certain leadership roles within the village (e.g., *kum ʒgɔ*). The discussion here will be limited to a description of the actual process of *čam*-ing and a consideration of several additional types of *čam*-able property that helped to define the structure of a Meta' village.

The *sami* ("dancing field"), upon which the status of *kum ʒgɔ* appears to have depended, was one of the most important *čam*-able properties whose distribution was controlled on the village level. The process through which a new *sami* was acquired showed some variation from village to village. However, the following informant's description of the procedures followed in his village conveys many of the essentials:

When a person receives his *sami* he is also called *kum*. In order to become a *kum* in the old days, a man had to have many people under him (i.e., be the head of a sizable descent group). The man who wants *sami* must inform the *fɔn* and also the people of his own clan section. He tells his brothers to wait for people who will be coming from the compound of the *fɔn* on a certain day. Then he sends one goat to the *fɔn* and keeps another ready to be killed on the day that has been set. He also sends a bush knife, a hip of plantains, and an old hoe to the *fɔn*. Then he takes the stalk of the plantain that he cut and plants it on the downhill side of his new dancing field. He does this to prevent the new dancing field from eroding and washing away, but they also use plantains for this because it will make everything on the new *samɨ* soft and cool (*bɔtɨ*) like the plantain stem itself. The knife is sent to the *fɔn* to show that it is the one with which the plantains were cut, and the old hoe is sent to represent the one that was used to clear the new field. On the day when the new *samɨ* is to be opened, the *fɔn* comes with several *mɨkum si* and they sacrifice the second goat on the *samɨ*. Then the big men who have come to open the field divide the goat among themselves. The man who is receiving the new *samɨ* may also give a separate goat to the people of his own clan section. He does this on some later day so that they will come and see that the *fɔn* has opened his dancing field. After all these things have been done the man will be known as a *kum* in the village. He will be able to go to the *fɔn's* compound and drink wine with the other *mɨkum*, but he will not be able to have his own special stool kept there or share goats that are presented to the other *mɨkum*. In order to receive these rights he will have to *čam* another goat called the *gwɨ ʒčwi* ("goat of the sun"). This goat is sacrificed on the new *kum's samɨ* by the important *mɨkum* of the village. After this he will be called *kum ʒčwi* ("kum of the sun"), and he will receive a share of any goat that is given to the *mɨkum* in a "daylight matter" (*ʒnu ʒziʒ*).[3]

As this account indicates, the main feature of the process by which a man acquired *samɨ* was the presentation of one or more goats to the *fɔn* and *mɨkum si* of the village and the sacrifice of one of these on the dancing field. These ceremonies served as a public announcement of the new *samɨ* holder's status and were also intended to prevent him from suffering *ndɔn* from any malicious talk that his new prerogatives were unjustified. As the account also illustrates, the status of *kum* was intimately associated with having a *samɨ*. Although some informants claimed that a man could *čam* for a *samɨ* without simultaneously purchasing

3. The term "*kum ʒčwi*" was encountered in some other villages, but it was not generally used as here to refer to a *kum ʒgɔ* who had purchased rights to a share of "village beef." An *ʒnu ʒziʒ* or "daylight matter" was a public occurrence of some import that should be referred to the village leaders (e.g., an inter-clan fight). Such matters were seen as more open than, for example, life and death decisions made by the *mɨkum si*.

the title of *kum*, these two honors were usually acquired together, and no one could become a *kum* without first having obtained the right of *sami*.

Two other types of *čam*-able property whose distribution was controlled on the village level were the right of using *mbɛŋ* ("plaited raffia mats") to fence off one's courtyard and the right of having two doors in a single hut (i.e., both a front and rear door). As with *sami*, these entitlements appear to have been controlled by every Meta' *fɔn*, and it was forbidden for a villager to *čam* them from outsiders.

Although such broad distribution and thorough incorporation into the political system would seem to argue for the antiquity of these customs, oral traditions concerning their introduction to Meta' society are unfortunately incomplete. While one informant claimed that the right of two doors was first acquired when a particular descent group leader traveled outside the Meta' area to *čam* it, others asserted that the Meta' had brought it with them from Tadkon, their legendary place of origin in the southwest. Concerning the right of *mbɛŋ*, the traditions are somewhat more precise. A number of informants asserted that this had first been obtained by a single clan section that *čam*-ed it from the ancestors of people now living near Santa sometime after the Meta' had reached their present territory.

The principal difference between the rights to *mbɛŋ* and two doors and the right of *sami* seems to have been that the first two were controlled by the *fɔn* and his agnates, whereas the allocation of *sami* was controlled by the *fɔn* and the *mikum si*. Around 1900, the rights of *mbɛŋ* and two doors were acquired in the following way: for a substantial payment (informants' estimates ranged from two to seven goats) the *fɔn* might be persuaded to bestow one of these honors upon any descent group leader within the village. As with other types of *čam*-able property, having *mbɛŋ* or two doors then became the hereditary prerogative of that particular segment head, and he could grant it, for a lesser fee, to any junior agnate who also lived within the village. In the case of such secondary transactions, the *fɔn* was not involved and received no payment. However, a segment head who had obtained *mbɛŋ* or two doors in the manner described above would not be permitted to transfer it to members of other clans within the village, since this would violate the prerogative of his chief, nor could he grant these privileges to members of his own clan in other villages, because this would infringe the rights of neighboring *fɔn*s. Finally, when any *fɔn* granted someone in his own village the right of *mbɛŋ* or two doors, he did so in consultation with the principal segment heads of his own clan section and shared with them any valuables.

Mbɛŋ and the right of two doors were mainly important as prestige items. Having both a front and a rear door befit a big man, because his servants could enter the rear door with food and wine without being observed by guests. Similarly, the raffia mats known as *mbɛŋ* could be used to enclose part of his courtyard so that important visitors could sit there secluded during public ceremonies. Of course neither of these rights was as significant as *sami* in defining the political status of individuals. Yet the procedures through which they were acquired did emphasize the centralization of the village as a political unit and the unique position of the *fɔn*. As we have seen, their allocation was carried out entirely within the village and controlled by the chiefly descent group.

Warfare

Mobilization for warfare (*ibit*) is the last village-level activity to be discussed in this chapter. Warfare contrasted with fighting (*ʒčɔp*) in that villages rather than descent group segments were the units of alignment. Moreover, guns and spears could be used, and opponents (even fellow Meta') could be slain without any risk of mystical danger. Finally, the causes of warfare were also distinct. Those most frequently mentioned were: (1) the arbitrary enslavement of persons from other villages, (2) attempts by one community to appropriate farms or hunting land belonging to another, and (3) affronts to the honor of villages or their political leaders.

The smallest wars were those fought between two villages. However, larger alliances did come into play, and in some instances, many villages from different Meta' valleys joined in fighting neighboring peoples such as Mankon and Bafut. The group that mobilized in any given case depended on the size and composition of the aggressor force and the issues at stake.

Since all wars were actually matters of intervillage relations, the more detailed discussion of modes of alliance and the causes of war will be left until Chapters 10 and 11. Here, I only wish to describe the way in which a single village organized itself. In this context, two factors made warfare a village activity. First, each such group had its own independent society of war scouts (*mɜgwe*), and second, all wars were said to be fought under the auspices of the *fɔn*.

The institution of a war scout society appears to have been long established in Meta' society, since several informants portrayed it as a custom of the earliest forefathers and none was able to state the time of its introduction. Affiliation with the *mɜgwe* was not hereditary, new members being chosen secretly by those already belonging. Moreover, no payments were necessary in order to join. Usually, a candidate would not know that he was being considered until he was suddenly "captured" by his fellow scouts at some celebration and presented to the public. Men were recruited in their twenties and retained membership for life. There was also no fixed number of *mɜgwe*, although the village complements that were checked ranged from eight to twelve men. As a group, the *mɜgwe* appear to have been drawn from every clan in the village, including that of the *fɔn*. However, *mikum* were usually not members, since the pranks in which *mɜgwe* sometimes engaged were beneath their dignity. The leader of the *mɜgwe*, the *mba'* *mɜgwe* or "father of the *mɜgwe*," was chosen by his peers; he hosted occasional meetings and conveyed messages from the *fɔn*.

The activities of the *mɜgwe* were twofold. They played an important role in warfare, as well as participating in certain ceremonies. In wartime, their task was to scout the enemy to prevent unexpected raids upon the village. For example, when an attack was anticipated the *mɜgwe* would go out the night before to cover all routes of approach. If they located the enemy, they would fire their guns to indicate that their presence had been detected. This usually halted any advance until morning and meant that the fighting would not take place in the village itself.

In general, the *mɔgwe* behaved in a fashion contrary to that of other village warriors. During the day, while the main forces fought, they were usually sent to scout for small enemy groups that attempted flanking movements. Then when the combat was over, they remained on the battleground to ensure that the opposing forces did not regroup for a raid upon the village.

The *mɔgwe* also participated in certain village-level celebrations. During some annual festivals (e.g., *mɛndɛrɛ*), as well as the mortuary rites of important political leaders, they appeared dressed in rags and fur caps. On such occasions, their role was to reverse normal behavior and provide entertainment for the public. For example, they might dance in grotesque ways to mock the more serious performers, make strange noises and grunts, or waylay food that was intended for the *fɔn*. In return for their efforts, the *mɔgwe* received a share of meat and palm wine.

The techniques for mobilizing a village in precolonial times were relatively simple. Normally, only the *fɔn* was entitled to summon the warriors. He did so by having an elephant-tusk trumpet blown or by using the talking drums. Several informants described this as one of the *fɔn*'s most important prerogatives and a crucial test of his support. If he had been steadily losing favor, villagers might fail to turn out when he gave the alarm. On those occasions when a threat arose suddenly, warriors were usually informed of the enemy's location on the talking drums. They then took their weapons and rushed toward the spot, assembling at some point near the battleground to receive instructions from the *fɔn* and the *mɔgwe*. The fighting itself appears to have been mainly a series of skirmishes and ambushes, and, according to most informants, there was never hand-to-hand combat involving large groups of men.

The *fɔn* himself did not participate in the battle, but might observe from a nearby hill. When it was over, he was expected to provide a feast for the returning warriors and a large quantity of palm wine. After any victory, there would be celebration on his *sami*, with the dance of warriors (*nguʔu*) being performed in a circle around the heads of slain enemies. Head-taking was seen as a glorious deed, since only a very brave man would risk being caught in this act by the comrades of a slain warrior. In some villages the skulls of enemies were also kept on the *fɔn*'s *sami* and displayed during certain dances.

By contrast with other village-level activities (e.g., the antisorcery rituals of *zi si* and hunting), warfare was not highly ritualized. This was partly because there was often little time to devote to rites before a battle. However, in a few villages, the *fɔn* and the *mikum si* are said to have conducted brief rituals to ensure the safety of their warriors, and in the Medig valley area there were more elaborate ceremonies that involved intervillage cooperation.

In precolonial times, the participation of all males in warfare was not mandatory. Cowards were generally allowed to remain at home, since there was no way of transforming them into effective fighters. People were also afraid to force others to go to war, because they might then bear responsibility for their deaths and thereby risk *ndɔn*. However, it is said that a man who refused to fight would always feel shame when he was drinking in the company of others.

Conclusion

A point has now been reached where it is possible to give a more precise answer to a question raised at the beginning of Chapter 6: "What was a village in precolonial Meta' society?" From the Meta' point of view, the village seems to have been a social group that was united under a single set of leaders (the *fɔn* and *mikum si*) and whose members regularly cooperated in important political activities. These included: (1) the antisorcery rites of *zi si*; (2) the treatment of "noble game;" (3) communal hunting; (4) the transfer of *čam*-able properties such as *sami* ("dancing field"), *mbɛŋ* ("plaited raffia mats"), and the right of "two doors"; (5) mobilization for warfare; and (6) the resolution of certain conflicts. From the point of view of the Meta' people, a village can thus be defined economically as "the group that was organized to perform *zi si*, prosecute wars, regulate the right of *sami*, and so forth." Such a definition pinpoints the distinctive characteristics of a precolonial Meta' village in a most unambiguous way.

EIGHT

Ideal and Real in Village-Level Conflict Management

I SHALL NOW present an in-depth analysis of village-level conflict and resolution in precolonial Meta'. Using an approach that differs from previous chapters, I will intersperse data pertaining to ideal and real behavior and, wherever possible, analyze the informants' generalizations in relation to actual case histories that they were able to remember. I take this approach chiefly because the ethnohistorical study of conflict, in contrast to research on leadership roles or village-level rituals, lends itself particularly well to this approach. In the area of disputing, unlike the others mentioned, informants are likely to recall (or to have been informed of) actual sequences of behavior involving specific individuals and groups. This results from the fact that disputes frequently lead to decisive reallocations of rights and duties that may in turn become sources of continuing controversy for descendants of the original parties.[1] Moreover, since conflicts often arise from tensions that are inherent in the social system, the analysis of cases in relation to statements of how things ideally worked is frequently the best means of laying bare such disharmonies.

In seeking to comprehend village-level conflict management in a precolonial African society, two distinct perspectives are

---

1. That it is often impossible to determine the validity of conflicting claims in memory cases such as these does not pose an insurmountable problem for analysis, since our primary objective here is the general anthropological one of clarifying what sorts of things could happen within the Meta' system of conflict and law rather than the historical task of ascertaining the exact outcome of each case discussed.

available. On the one hand, we may ask how order and authority were maintained within the village. Following Service (1975: 13), this can be termed the perspective of "reinforcement." On the other hand, we may question how ordinary citizens utilized various legal and nonlegal institutions in conducting and resolving their conflicts. This is the "disputing" perspective (Nader and Todd 1978). In the present chapter, the conflict-management system of the precolonial Meta' village will be examined from both points of view as the basis for a comprehensive model.

Reinforcement

In the typical Meta' village, order was reinforced primarily through the initiatives of the local notables. Sometimes this involved their own direct measures, but frequently they acted though special anonymous agents, persons whose authoritative actions were legitimized by their possession of certain *čam*-able properties and similar rights. While in most instances these belonged to specific clan sections, they were also incorporated into the regulatory apparatus of the village. The principal properties with legal functions included: *nju mɜnaŋ* ("the masked herald"), *tɜkɜnɜ* ("the village executioner"), and *kwɛʔifɔ* (a chiefly dance complex that had come to symbolize authority in some villages).

Each of these was composed of a unique configuration of elements and subject to a distinct combination of public and private control. *Nju mɜnaŋ*, for example, consisted of (1) *njuŋɜ*, a rough hood of raffia cloth used as a disguise or dancing costume, (2) *mɜnaŋ*, the rhythm to which the person wearing *njuŋɜ* would dance, and (3) the tall skin-covered drums on which the rhythm *mɜnaŋ* was customarily played. This complex resembled in some respects the *ifuʔ* dancing and medicine cycle described in the previous chapter. Like *ifuʔ*, it was a *čam*-able property controlled by certain descent group segments and used at the mortuary celebrations of their members and affines. It was also a highly prestigious dancing society with which men of other descent groups might affiliate. However, *nju mɜnaŋ* differed from the *ifuʔ* cycle in being possessed only by the clan sections of village chiefs. Moreover, it was owned by the lineage of the *fɔn* in every precolonial Meta' village, while *ifuʔ* was less widespread. Because it was used in two types of activities, *nju mɜnaŋ* was normally under the jurisdiction of two separate groups of leaders. During the dancing at mortuary celebrations it was controlled by the *fɔn* and his agnates, while as an enforcer of authority it came under the direction of the *fɔn* and *mikum si*.

Tɜkɜnɜ ("the village executioner") was another disguise used for regulatory purposes. It differed from *nju mɜnaŋ* primarily in the gravity of the missions that it undertook. In addition to dispatching certain incorrigible offenders, *tɜkɜnɜ* exhumed and disposed of the corpses of witches (*izik*) whose spirits troubled the living. It also took part in important rituals such as *zi si* to underscore the authority of the village leaders. Except when en route to execute a victim, *tɜkɜnɜ* was announced by a man playing the *mikakaŋ* ("double-flanged bell").

The actual use of *tɜkɜnɜ* required the assent of two different groups. Although the village authorities possessed the sole authority to direct *tɜkɜnɜ* to impose coercive sanctions, a particular clan section within the village held the hereditary right to carry out their assignments. The members of the latter group clearly occupied a unique role. Whereas no ordinary Meta' could kill another without risking terrible *ndɔn*, they were free from such danger when acting upon legitimate instructions. Like *nju mɜnaŋ*, *tɜkɜnɜ* was a well-established institution. Said to have been brought by the Meta' founders from Tadkon, it was present in every village by 1900. However, *Tɜkɜnɜ* differed somewhat from *nju mɜnaŋ* (and *kwɛ'ifɔ*) in that it was not transferred by *čam*-ing during immediate precolonial times.

The role of *kwɛ'ifɔ* in the village-level legal system is perhaps the most difficult to define. This complex, which was often employed at mortuary celebrations, consisted of a special dance rhythm and a set of musical instruments on which to play it, in this case seven or eight double-flanged bells. While it resembled *nju mɜnaŋ* in being restricted to chiefly descent groups, it differed in that it was possessed by only some village heads. Moreover, most of these are said to have acquired it from other Meta' or Bamenda groups within the two generations before 1900. In this context, *kwɛ'ifɔ* lacked clearly defined legal functions like those of *nju mɜnaŋ* and *tɜkɜnɜ*. Nonetheless, informants did refer to the *mikum si* meeting in their regulatory capacity as *kwɛ'ifɔ* and associate this term with the village-level legal system. This was probably due to several factors. First, these informants may have been making an analogy with larger Grassfields chiefdoms where an institution known as *kwɛʔifɔ* was indeed the main regulatory group. Second, when *kwɛʔifɔ* was used for mortuary celebrations it was often merged with the agent of justice *nju mɜnaŋ*, since in some villages both were owned by the descent group of the *fɔn*. Thus, if a masked figure appeared with *kwɛʔifɔ* at a funeral, it was always *nju mɜnaŋ*. Finally, the *mikakaŋ* or double-flanged bell that was the characteristic instrument of *kwɛʔifɔ* throughout the Grassfields was used by the Meta' to announce the coming of both the *nju mɜnaŋ* masker and *tɜkɜnɜ*. Perhaps the best way in which to view the Meta' *kwɜʔifɔ* is therefore to describe it as a recently imported complex of property that was becoming associated with regulatory institutions in some villages but that by itself represented no substantial change in the village-level legal system.

Having described the several agents of reinforcement, we may now consider how the village leaders exercised their power through them as well as by other means. Often they did so by employing these figures to communicate with the public or enforce key rules of behavior. For example, they could send either *nju mɜnaŋ* or an unmasked crier through the village at evening time to the accompaniment of a double-flanged bell. This might be done to announce a day that had been set aside for work on the chief's farms or to convey other important news. On such occasions, several factors underscored the point that information was coming from a powerful source of authority, including the mysteriousness of the unseen crier's voice and the fact that women were prohibited from watching him. The vigor of legal authority was similarly impressed upon the public in numerous other situations. Occasionally, a man wearing the *nju mɜnaŋ* disguise would appear in the marketplace to announce that special medicines would catch anyone who stole from vendors or attempted to kidnap them. Or *nju mɜnaŋ* would be used to place injunctions within the village. Such signs, usually oil palm fronds or branches of the broad-leafed shrub *mbin*, indicated that the *fɔn* and the *mikum si* forbade any person to pass or enter on pain of a heavy fine. Warnings of this type could be placed on farm plots that were under litigation, at the entrances to compounds of disobedient villagers, or on the roads leading out of the village in order to enforce public attendance at crucial activities.

When injunctions imposed by the village leaders were disobeyed, stronger actions would be taken. If, for example, some women did farmwork on a forbidden day, the *nju mɜnaŋ* mask could be sent to disperse them. They were certain to flee, since they were believed to develop filaria if they looked at the masker closely. After *nju mɜnaŋ* had routed the women, he removed the hoes and other things they had left behind and took them to the *fɔn*'s compound, where they might later be ransomed. Men who disobeyed orders promulgated through *nju mɜnaŋ* were likewise fined.

As these examples illustrate, *nju mɜnaŋ* was not only important for its specific uses within the village-level regulatory system; it also provided a highly visible symbol of the local notables' legitimate power. This emerged clearly in the enthusiasm with which informants described villagers fleeing from the masked figure and enumerated the penalties that anyone scorning its authority would incur. *Nju mɜnaŋ* was an appropriate mask to use for regulatory purposes, since even when it appeared for dancing, it acted wildly, swinging two bush knives in the air and threatening to slash bystanders.

That an anonymous masked figure served as the primary public symbol of village-level authority was also highly significant in terms of Meta' political ideology. As noted in Chapter 6, the Meta' had a strong ambivalence about authority and were very averse to its direct use. In this context it could be argued that having *nju mɜnaŋ* announce the orders of the village notables fulfilled the same purpose as the avoidance behavior that was customary between a *fɔn* and his people: it allowed for the public expression of authority, yet, at the same time, dissociated it from any particular person or group.

In addition to enforcing rules of conduct through maskers such as *nju mɜnaŋ*, the village leaders also helped to control violence. Whenever interlineage fighting erupted, for example, they dispatched an agent to place a stalk of the sacred plant *kiŋ* (*Dracaena sanderiana*?) or a raffia palm frond (*ʒzaŋ*) in the midst of the fray. Or if a notable himself was on hand, he intervened directly. Such actions were believed to enhance the potential for mystical danger posed by the conflict, and they served as a warning to the disputants. The Meta' believed that a killing was likely if the fighting continued, and that this would cause some of the participants to suffer *ndɔn*.

The village leaders also reinforced the social order by using their mystical powers to sanction unknown offenders and to prohibit specific antisocial behaviors. This technique was often used when thievery had become rampant. At such times, the *fɔn* might assemble his notables and people to conduct anti-thievery rituals resembling the elaborate intervillage assemblies of *ikwiri* (see pp. 239–242). After the chief and notables had conferred privately, they would address the assembled villagers on the chief's dancing field, reporting on the problem at hand and announcing plans for action. They then performed ritual acts designed to inflict illness, misfortune, and death on any thieves who persisted. While pouring from their sacrificial cups the notables spoke an *njɔm* or curse to this effect. They also simulated the fate of any would-be thieves by holding a fowl above a stone altar and cutting its throat. Then they buried the fowl while all those present hurled handfuls of dirt to the ground. Finally, the people would shout "*ki, ki, ki!,*" a cry that was expected to be taken up by everyone within hearing until the entire population of the valley was shouting in unison. The raising of such a clamor (a custom known as *ifʒča*) was believed to increase the power of the curse by bringing the people's righteous anger forcibly to the attention of God.

As the foregoing description suggests, village-level anti-thievery rites not only were believed to mobilize powerful supernatural forces but were also intended to intimidate potential deviants by focusing intense psychosocial pressures upon them. The mass participation, the violent ritual acts, and the overwhelming public outcry would have given pause to even the most recalcitrant offender. Some sense of the impact of these rites is conveyed by the following account of a recent traditional-style anti-thievery ritual in one Meta' village:

An *ikwiri* [assembly] was recently called by the chief of this village because young men were using bad medicines [birth-control potions] and stealing goats, chickens, and palm wine from the bush. They gathered around a stone altar [*ji*] while the chief and two *mikum si* said, "You who buy bad medicines or who steal goats and chickens, this will be your head!" As they uttered each phrase, the notables threw some wine down at the very spot. Then everyone began to grab earth and hurl it down. Since the entire village was present, it was assumed that the culprits would be watching and begin to fear for their lives. It was also expected that thieves from other villages would hear about the prohibition that had been established.

Village leaders could also attempt to halt antisocial behavior by establishing a supernaturally sanctioned prohibition (*čɜp*) against certain offenses. Such a "law" was put into operation in one village of the Zang valley during precolonial times because its chief did not wish disputes over divorce and the abduction of women to undermine his people's solidarity in the face of hostility from outside groups. Violators of the prohibition were believed likely to become ill, and could only absolve themselves by paying a fine, consisting of palm wine and a goat, to the village notables. A similar prohibition is said to have been established by two neighboring villages in the Medig valley area. In this case the ritual "legislation" was occasioned by a fight in which the men of both places supported their chiefs after the son of one had eloped with a daughter-in-law of the other.

The slave trade likewise posed a serious threat to orderly relations within the typical Meta' village. During precolonial times, people were sold into slavery under several circumstances. Sometimes a clan section seized a hostage and sold him to recover a debt (see below), and there was also arbitrary kidnapping for profit. In such situations, the dangers of uncontrolled slave trafficking were reduced by the fact that only a few recognized lineages could sell slaves outside the society. In addition to having the capital, experience, and contacts, the members of these groups possessed magical ropes that were believed to render slaves docile and tractable.[2] The Meta' also regulated slave transactions by requiring that local chiefs be notified whenever sales to nonvillagers occurred. This was typi-

2. The Meta' resembled other Bamenda societies both in restricting the right to deal in slaves and in the fact that this prerogative was symbolized by a special rope (which was not actually used to bind the slaves). At the same time, Meta' differed in that its slave dealers did not derive political power from control of the trade like their counterparts in Mankon and Bafut. They were just agents. There were also some contradictions in the informants' accounts concerning why slave dealing was an exclusive specialty. While some claimed that the dealers were simply more experienced in the trade, others believed that slave trading was an *ndɔn*-protected occupation.

cally done, early on the day of the sale, when the slave traders left a length of cloth (which constituted part of their proceeds) at the entrance of the chief's compound. This gesture at once acknowledged the local leaders' ultimate authority in the matter and guaranteed to the public that no villager could arbitrarily be sold. According to some informants, the act also signified that the slave sellers would later return secretly to share more of their profits with the chief.

A final way in which the leaders of a Meta' village reinforced the sociopolitical order was by employing extreme coercive sanctions, such as execution or enslavement, against those who flaunted their authority. Informants mentioned two forms that such repudiations of authority might take: village men could commit adultery with the wives of the *fɔn* or they might openly defy legitimate orders from the village notables and chief (e.g., by refusing to participate in community work or to provide the customary palm-wine tribute). For such misdeeds, offenders were liable to be killed by *tɜkɜnɜ* or sold into slavery. Nonetheless, it appears that decision-making usually proceeded slowly in these cases, with the offender being provided numerous opportunities to redeem himself by paying fines and accepting his guilt. One possible sequence is outlined in an informant's description of a hypothetical case:

If a man failed to come for work at the farms of the *fɔn* on the appointed day, the *mikum* would discuss the case when they met to drink wine and then send someone to the offender's compound. He would take a green branch of the plant called *mbɨn* and place it in the entrance to the man's hut at about chest height. After this had been done, the offender could not enter his compound until the branch had been removed. If *mbɨn* was placed at only one hut, it was meant just for the man of the compound. However, if it was put at the main entrance of the compound, all the people who lived there were forbidden to enter. When such a sign had been placed, the offender had to go to see the *fɔn* right away, and the *fɔn* would tell him the amount of the fine to pay. In a case like this, it might be between one and five goats along with a calabash of palm wine. After hearing from the *fɔn*, the man would take the goats and tether them at the entrance to his compound so that the *mikum* could send someone to bring them to the *fɔn*. Then the man himself would go to present the wine to the *fɔn*. After all this had been done, the *mikum* would send a man to remove the *mbɨn* that had been placed in the offender's compound. If a person refused to obey the injunction sign and entered his house in a case like this, he would have to pay a larger fine, perhaps ten goats. If he resisted even this, the village leaders would say, "This man believes that he is beyond *kwɛʔifɔ*" [i.e., that he doesn't need to obey the village-level regulatory authorities], and let the matter rest for a while. Then at some later time they would send someone to kill him while he was in the bush and throw his body in the river. Afterward, nobody would ask about the missing man because they would know that he was "beyond *kwɛʔifɔ*."

The preceding examples illustrate how the leaders of a precolonial Meta' village used their powers to reinforce the social order. Although it is impossible to assess their capacity for autonomous action precisely from memory data alone, it is worth noting that their authoritative interventions fell into two broad classes. In general, they were able to act decisively only when offenders had breached highly specific rules of conduct or when there was an overwhelming consensus on the need for coercive force. It thus seems that, while the *fɔn* and his notables did have substantial authority, it was also circumscribed and subject to the popular will.

Disputing

Examining Meta village affairs from the perspective of disputing, rather than that of reinforcement, entails the description of an exceedingly complex system. In the precolonial Meta' village, conflict was expressed and resolved in many alternative ways, including violent self-help, negotiation, arbitration, adjudication, the reliance upon coercive authority, and ritual conflict resolution. Here, I shall describe these processes in the context of five different kinds of cases: (1) interlineage conflicts involving contested rights, (2) conflicts over witchcraft, (3) cases of theft, (4) homicides, and (5) disputes involving the abuse of authority.

Interlineage Conflicts Involving Contested Rights

This rubric joins together a very wide variety of disputes including conflicts over land, *čam*-able properties, marriageable women, and the reimbursement of bridewealth following divorce. In certain of these instances, the aggrieved party had an exceedingly low-risk strategy at his disposal. This was simply to exercise patience in the hope that mystical forces would sooner or later punish the offender. As noted previously, rights over *čam*-able properties were believed to be sanctioned by *ndɔn*, and the same was true of all legitimate claims to land. Accordingly, when a person was known to have usurped such properties, a diviner was likely to identify any illness or misfortune in his household as a manifestation of *ndɔn*. The offender might then seek to alleviate his suffering by relinquishing the property in question, and in some instances he also paid a fine to the legitimate owner. His primary objective was to end the latter's verbal complaints (since these were seen as the most immediate cause of his *ndɔn*) and ideally to elicit a statement that absolved him of further blame. Although waiting for *ndɔn* to affect an offender was clearly a slow and uncertain means of achieving redress, it was at least potentially effective. After several members of a land-appropriating lineage had died, for example, their surviving brothers might be strongly inclined to follow a diviner's advice to quit the plot in question. According to such ritual experts, some land disputes are still resolved in this fashion, even though redress can now be sought through the local-level courts.

A more direct method of mobilizing mystical forces to resolve interlineage disputes was for the parties to employ formal oath-taking procedures. This was very common in cases over land and *čam*-able properties as well as in those involving debts. Conflicts such as these were taken to the village chief or to one of several famous oathing sites known as *ɜsum* (see pp. 232–233). In the former instance one disputant would swear upon the chief's feet or upon the life of a fowl. Then if the oath-taker (or the fowl) died within a set period—usually several months to a year—he was deemed to have perjured himself. By custom, only one party was permitted to swear in a given case. If he suffered no adverse effects within the time allowed, the oath-taker had validated his claim to the property in question, and his opponent was required to pay a fine. It was further believed that any person making a false oath would succumb to a dreaded disease known as *mɔro*, whose victims normally died with swollen bellies and feet. *Mɔro* was thought likely to spread to the agnates and dependents of the perjurer unless he was buried by ritual experts with the hereditary power to remove the pollution associated with his death.

Numerous testimonies indicate that oath-taking was a favored means of dispute settlement in precolonial times. They also suggest that its effectiveness may have rested upon its ability to intimidate the guilty. Informants emphasized that potential perjurers would have had second thoughts when confronted by the prospect of swearing upon a mystically powerful object or while traveling to a celebrated oathing site in a distant village. In addition, disputants were often pressured by relatives who feared being affected by *ndɔn* arising from their false statements. For these reasons the informants often became enthusiastic when recounting the efficacy of oathing procedures in precolonial Meta' legal process.

Yet another means of resolving interlineage disputes was mediation by the chief and village notables. When a man's wife had absconded, for example, he could make payments to these leaders to induce them to consider the case. Since conflicts of this kind were considered private matters, the notables had no authority to enforce their decision. However, where the parties were willing it could prove a useful approach. Usually, the notables received secret payments from both sides, with each hoping to have the decisive influence.

Thus far, the discussion has focused on nonviolent strategies of resolving conflict. However, two other common techniques were for the members of an aggrieved group to seize a hostage or to start a fight. Whereas fighting was often the preferred strategy in disputes over land, *čam*-able properties, divorces, debts, and adultery, hostage-taking was employed mainly when there had been a long-term default on a substantial debt. This often stemmed from a woman's having absconded from her husband, with or without her father's consent. When it proved impossible in such a situation to secure either a refund of bridewealth or the return of the runaway wife, it was considered legitimate for the aggrieved husband's lineage to seize a hostage from the debtor group. Although such captives could be taken even within one's village, this normally required prior consultation with both the debtor's lineage and the village notables. By contrast, as the distance between the debtor and creditor groups increased, a wider latitude was exercised, so that any person from the clan or village of the debtor might be seized in his stead. The lineage of such a hapless victim might then attempt to take a hostage from the actual debtor group, in order to exchange him for their own agnate. Finally, hostage-taking sometimes led to fighting between the lineages and/or villages involved. When this occurred, the case became a public matter, to be judged formally by the notables of the village in which the conflict had broken out. At this point they were accorded the authority to render a binding decision in the matter. The pattern is illustrated in the following precolonial case, remembered from his childhood by a Meta' informant. (As with previous case history material, pseudonyms for both individuals and groups are employed.)

CASE ONE

A fight once broke out in Guzaŋ village when Fɔngyɛn, a man of the nearby village of Bat, came with ten men of his own lineage attempting to capture his father-in-law Tati as a hostage. He did this because his wife had absconded. As it happened, Fɔngyɛn's party arrived just when a mortuary celebration was occurring at Tati's compound. By stealth, Fongyen's raiders managed to seize a kinsman of Tati who had strayed from the crowd. However, the man quickly gave out the alarm cry of his clan, and many people ran to his rescue. Then everyone fought with walking sticks and bush knives. Since the defenders, who included both Tati's clansmen and his village mates, were more numerous, they managed to free the hostage and to drive off the attackers. Afterward, the woman over whom they had fought remained in her father's village. But on a later day, the notables sat down to consider the case. The judges included the leaders of Guzaŋ village, along with certain notables sent by the chief of Bat. They were given palm wine by the disputants. After hearing the details of the dispute, they fined Fɔngyɛn's group two bundles of salt for having started the fight. Then they anointed the woman with camwood as a sign of blessing and sent her back to live with her original husband. This finished the case. Afterward, the judges retained the fines for themselves.

As the foregoing account illustrates, violent confrontation was not only a method of self-help but also a means of transferring interlineage conflicts to the village-level legal system. Once fighting had erupted, the parties, even if one came from a different community, had no choice but to submit their dispute to the judgment of the local leaders.

Interlineage fights seem to have involved relatively little actual violence and only small numbers of men. Each side usually assembled less than twenty supporters, although it could be more if one or the other had mobilized as a village unit. This might happen, as in the case cited above, when a group of outside raiders suddenly appeared, intent upon seizing a hostage. However, even then the use of guns and spears was strictly prohibited. At most, the opponents would employ walking sticks to beat one another, and if the fighting resulted in any deaths, they were considered cases of homicide (ʒbɛne).

The resolution process in cases of fighting typically involved two distinct steps. First, the village leaders intervened to halt the violence itself. Then they judged the dispute in order to achieve a permanent resolution. The fighting was usually stopped when the village leaders sent a representative to separate the combatants by planting a stick trimmed with branches of the sacred, peace-giving plant *kiŋ* between the antagonists. This act was believed to enhance the potential for mystical danger inherent in the fight, and it served as a warning to the disputants. The Meta' believed that a person was likely to be killed if the violence continued, and that this would cause some of the participants to suffer *ndɔn*.

Once the fighting had halted, the village leaders prepared to judge the case. This was sometimes done on the spot, but more commonly the parties assembled on the following day at the compound of the chief in whose village the conflict had occurred. Here, they listened to each side's testimony while consuming palm wine provided by the disputants. In the end the notables gave a judgment, perhaps stating the amount of bridewealth to be refunded or ordering one party to surrender a particular plot of farmland. They also imposed fines, which were called *fingwan rič̌ɔp* ("the salt of the fight"), on those who had broken the peace of the village. These could consist of either bundles of salt or goats and fowl, and they were shared among the notables who had helped to judge. Usually, each party gave something, since right was rarely believed to be on one side only in the case of a fight. However, when a runaway wife was returned, the husband sometimes paid the entire amount, since he was once again beholden to his wife's father.

In general, the village leaders are said to have been in a good position to impose their authority in cases of fighting. If the parties were unwilling to settle, the notables, in the words of one informant, "simply kept judging the case." These conceptions of authority made fighting an effective summons technique. Frequently, a long-denied creditor took advantage of his debtor's presence at a mortuary celebration to start a fight, thereby ensuring a hearing of his case. It is, of course, impossible to assess the effectiveness of the conflict-resolution procedures just described solely on the basis of memory data. However, the evidence does suggest that we are dealing here with actual conflict-resolution procedures and not merely idealized scenarios. Only three of the twelve cases of precolonial fighting that were collected were said to have been settled in a manner other than that outlined above. Moreover, several cases illustrate the fact that village leaders were able to deal with outbreaks of fighting even when some or all of the participants resided in other villages. Two examples will be summarized here. The first conflict occurred during the childhood of the informant who gave it and involved members of his own lineage. In it, groups from villages located in two different valleys began to fight at a mortuary celebration in a third village, because of the failure of one side to refund bridewealth after a divorce. The fight was then stopped and judged on the spot by the chief of the third village. The second case entailed fighting over a farm plot between the members of lineages from two different villages. However, the violence was soon halted, and the dispute was judged on the spot by a notable from one of the communities. This example contrasts with the first one in both its relative informality of procedure and the lack of involvement of the village chief. The informant here witnessed the case as a youth and claims to have supported his own side.

CASE TWO

The daughter of Fɔnji of Zam village was married to Ayɔ, the chief of Njindɨk village in the next valley. After a time, Fɔnji decided to call his daughter back so that he might arrange for her to marry a son of Tanyi, chief of the neighboring village of Gunɔbɛŋ. However, this led to problems: although Tanyi had paid the appropriate bridewealth to Fɔnji, the latter had never made a refund to Ayɔ. In his conversations with Ayɔ, Fɔnji always claimed that this was because he himself had received nothing from the new husband. After this situation had persisted for some time, Fɔnji died. When the day of his mortuary celebration was announced, Tanyi made plans to participate as a son-in-law is required to do. However, Ayɔ decided that he too would attend the affair in order to see if Tanyi appeared. [Since a son-in-law's lineage is expected to assist in mourning for his wife's father, this would give some indication of whether Tanyi had been fulfilling his affinal obligations, including the payment of bridewealth.] When Ayɔ arrived at Fɔnji's compound, he saw that Tanyi's group was indeed present. Then a fight broke out between his party and that of Tanyi. During the melee, the participants used walking sticks, and the masked dancers removed their costumes so that they could also join in. After a while, the chief of Zam village ran into the midst of the crowd with a branch of *kiŋ*. This stopped the violence. Then he began to inquire into the matter. Ayɔ was adamant that he had never received a refund from Fɔnji, whereas Fɔnji's son admitted that his father had received bridewealth from Tanyi. On hearing this, the chief told Fɔnji's successor to pay Ayɔ the amount owed him. It was also agreed that Tanyi would pay additional bridewealth to Fɔnji's heir, so that the latter would be able to reimburse Ayɔ. This finished the case.

CASE THREE

A fight over boundaries occurred here in the days before the people were taken to Bali. A man from the neighboring village of Mbo attempted to clear a farm plot on land that belonged to us. The area in question had some oil palms as well as a few stands of raffia. People from the two sides met at the farm boundary and began to argue. This led to fighting, and, after a time, those on the side that was losing started to cry out. Then more men from the lineages of the principals began to join in, and people of other groups came to see what was happening. There were no more than eight men fighting on each side. After several hours, a *kum si* from the other village came with a stalk of *kiŋ* and stopped the fight. He acted on his own initiative because he was a good man and a friend to both sides. When he had separated the combatants, those present began to discuss the case, and they settled the matter right there and then. Each side also had to provide some palm wine, which was consumed while the matter was discussed.

A final option for disputants in interlineage conflicts involving jural rights was to perform an act of symbolic aggression directed at the other party. This tactic was usually employed in cases of divorce or debt and was normally a measure of last resort. The most common acts of symbolic aggression included throwing a spear into an opponent's roof, slashing a plantain stalk in his yard, and committing suicide by hanging one's self from a tree in his compound. All of these behaviors were believed to carry the threat of *ndɔn* to the person who was their target. They were therefore performed to bring pressure to bear on an intractable fellow disputant or in some cases to obtain revenge. When a man slashed a plantain stalk in his debtor's compound, he was conveying a dire message to the man: "If I had not cut the plantain, I might have killed you instead." But in addition to serving as a warning, such an act was thought to create a severe state of *ndɔn* in the compound where it had occurred. The severed plantain stalk (or spear in the roof or man hanging from the tree) was a highly visible reminder that the offender and all other residents of the compound were likely to suffer *ndɔn* if preventive measure were not taken.

The purpose of many disputants in committing acts of symbolic aggression was to set in motion a complex but effective process of ritual conflict resolution. For one thing, such actions ensured intervention by the local political authorities. Just as in cases of interlineage fighting, performing an act of symbolic aggression transformed a private matter into a public one, and legitimized the imposition of fines by the village leaders. In discussing this aspect, some informants drew an analogy with the present-day court system, characterizing the act of symbolic aggression as a kind of "summons" through which a deserted husband or other hapless creditor could ensure a proper hearing of his case.

A second important aspect of the resolution process was the intervention of an appropriate ritual specialist. Should such an expert fail to be summoned, it was believed that people in the compound where the act of symbolic aggression had occurred would surely begin to sicken and die. It was the role of this specialist to remove the tangible evidence of the symbolic attack (e.g., the slashed plantain stalk or the spear), thereby withdrawing the threat of *ndɔn* as well. For this work he received one or more goats along with other valuables and palm wine, and, according to informants, he often used his monopoly on a particular type of mystical power to extract ever-increasing payments from those threatened by *ndɔn*. Sometimes, even the basis for determining fees facilitated this. When a spear had been thrown into the roof, for example, part of the specialist's payment consisted of one brass rod for every rung of the ladder that he climbed to retrieve the weapon, and some specialists are said to have used ladders with very closely spaced rungs in order to receive the highest possible fees.

In most accounts, the combined intervention of the village authorities and a ritual specialist was portrayed as leading to a just settlement of the dispute that underlay the symbolic attack. Normally, the person who had been its target bore the major burden of paying fines and ritual specialist's fees. Since acts of symbolic aggression were not performed lightly, he was most likely to be at fault. Furthermore, he was usually the party with the strongest motivation for removing *ndɔn* from his compound. It was only if a runaway wife returned so that the erstwhile disputants became in-laws once again, or if the act of symbolic aggression had been completely unjustified, that the attacker himself was sanctioned.

Some sense of the various situations in which acts of symbolic aggression were performed and of the possible resolution procedures is conveyed by the following three cases, recalled by informants from precolonial times. The first two involved conflicts over the return of runaway wives. In both of them a deserted husband (and/or his group) directed an act of symbolic aggression at his father-in-law, which then led to ritual treatment and adjudication of the underlying dispute. However, the two cases also differed in certain respects. Whereas in the first dispute the person who was the object of the symbolic assault bore all the costs of settlement, in the second, these were paid by the members of the attacking group. Still, in both instances the woman over whom the dispute arose was returned to her husband. The third case illustrates the possible outcome in a situation where a disputant resorted to an act of symbolic aggression without just cause. Here, the aggressor himself was fined heavily and made to pay the ritual specialist's fees for removal of pollution from his opponent's compound.

CASE FOUR

A woman ran away from the compound of her husband and took refuge at her father's place. The husband went to his father-in-law to claim his wife, but the latter asked, "Why have you come with empty hands?" The son-in-law replied that he had already paid a full bridewealth and complained that he had been without anyone to cook his food for several days. Still, the father-in-law did not release his daughter. At this point the younger man cut down two plantain stalks in his father-in-law's compound. The latter then ran to the village chief in order to report what had happened. The chief first sent for two notables who dealt with matters of this kind. Then he proceeded with the two to the compound of the father-in-law. The father-in-law gave each of the notables 20 brass bracelets and presented a large goat to the *fɔn*. He also provided a fowl that the two notables swung over his threshold in order to remove the *ndɔn*. They then rubbed his daughter with camwood and handed her over to her husband while keeping the fowl for themselves. This settled the case completely.[3]

CASE FIVE

A woman from Kwe village in the next valley had married a man from here. But after a while her fathers called her home so that she could remarry to a man from her own place. To prevent this, some twenty men from my lineage traveled to the compound of the woman's father ready to fight with their walking sticks. Finding that the residents had fled, they decided to destroy some things. First they ruined all the medicines that the compound head had stored in twenty large pots. They put *ʒčat* (a leaf) in each pot, removed it, and then took the pot outside in order to smash it. Next, they cut down all of the plantains that were standing in the compound, and finally they left. After this attack, the woman's relatives decided to send her back to her first husband. Sometime later, my fathers traveled once again to Kwe in order to settle the matter. The chief of that village was present along with certain of his *mikum si*. Our side paid these big men a goat and some palm wine because of the damage that had been done, but the woman's brothers only had to provide palm wine. Finally, they poured a libation on the ground in order the settle the case.

CASE SIX

Anji used to make belts from dwarf cow pelts in order to sell them. He customarily bought his pelts from Tandi, who in turn got them from Mankon town. But Anji was not the only customer of Tandi. One day Tandi refused to sell any pelts to Anji because the price he offered was too low. After they had argued, Anji returned to his own compound, took out his spear, and went right back to the place of Tandi. Then he threw his spear into Tandi's roof. Once Tandi had informed the village of Anji's action, many people gathered at his (Tandi's) compound. Both chiefs of this village and all the important notables were present along with many relatives and friends of Tandi. Tandi provided them with palm wine to drink while they discussed the case. Finally, they decided

3. Case collected by J. P. Warnier, June 12, 1973.

that Anji was in the wrong and fined him three goats. Two of these were given to the village chiefs while the third was killed and the meat shared among all the important men present. Then they called for a ritual specialist to remove the spear from the roof. Once again, Anji had to bear the cost: a fowl for the specialist to pass over the hole that the spear had made and four brass rods (one for each rung on the ladder that the specialist climbed to retrieve the spear). Finally, Anji was sent away and told to take his trouble with him back to his own compound. It appears that the *ndɔn* did follow Anji, because only a few months later one of his brothers accidentally shot and killed a dancer during a mortuary celebration. Anji might have avoided this if rituals to remove the *ndɔn* had been performed in his own compound as well as at the place of Tandi.[4]

Witchcraft

In precolonial Meta' society, witchcraft (*izik*) was seen as the work of spiteful persons who afflicted others with illness and death. This was normally thought to happen only between those kinsmen who shared jural relations or claims upon one another's property. For example, the members of a minimal lineage could bewitch each other as could a mother's brother his sister's son. Such persons were believed likely to resort to witchcraft when dissatisfied with their shares of an inheritance or the allocation of bridewealth. In these situations the complaints of the slighted person were thought to load down the other party with *ndɔn*. Conceived of in this fashion, an assault through witchcraft differed little from the sequence of events in which one person caused *ndɔn* to affect another who had violated his rights. What transformed such actions into witchcraft was primarily difference in motive and degree. In precolonial Meta', witches were persons who made excessive use of their powers of speech. Typically, they were male elders who misused these powers to kill their junior kin.

When a conflict involving witchcraft accusations first arose, the kinship group usually attempted to control its deviant member's behavior through informal pressures. After having been named as a witch by several diviners, for example, he might be confronted and asked to swear to his innocence. Dramatic anti-

4. This case, which occurred right in the informant's compound, was collected by J. P. Warnier, October 22, 1973.

witchcraft rites were also sometimes performed during funerals in order to retaliate against guilty lineage mates. The pattern is illustrated in the following informant's account:

> When a child has been killed by witchcraft, the father may obtain seven seeds of *fisɔ*. Then while calling out the names of his brothers, he places these one by one in the mouth of his dead child. After this he announces a certain period of time and cuts the throat of a fowl. This will cause the witch to follow the child into the grave within the time stated.

Whenever such measures failed and a man had been implicated in the deaths of several relatives, his kin might turn to the village-level authorities in order to arrange for his execution or sale into slavery.

As may be surmised, witchcraft cases posed a unique challenge to the Meta' legal system. In contrast to the various interlineage disputes just discussed, these conflicts invariably involved closely related persons. The village authorities thus needed to help resolve a crisis among kin rather than to head off a collision between two opposed groups. By custom, action could be taken in cases of this sort only after very complex and broadly based consultations. Two characteristics of this decision-making process are especially noteworthy. First, it is striking how greatly mystical beliefs influenced executions in Meta' society. Not only was there much concern with warding off supernatural dangers, but everyone relied upon the mystical powers of the village leaders to ensure that the outcome of the legal action would be just. A second noteworthy feature of decision-making was the compartmentalization and secrecy involved. According to most informants, there was never a single meeting at which all interested parties conferred. Instead, the matter usually seems to have been carried from group to group, with the result that the identity of all participants was often known for certain only by the village chief. Typically, the acquiescence of each person or group was formally expressed by the giving or receiving of payments that served to commit it to the decision. Some of this secrecy is of course understandable, as a precaution to avoid alerting the potential victim of an execution. However, it is also fair to say that an air of mystery surrounded the entire decision-making process. Even today, when executions are merely history, knowledgeable informants are not eager to reveal the identities of those village-level notables whose predecessors would have decided capital cases in the past.

Consideration of a witchcraft case usually began when a request for the execution of the witch was secretly brought to the chief of the offender's village. Typically, this was done by his close agnates, since these were his most likely victims, although such a request could also come from the lineage of his sister's son. In either instance, the petitioners were obliged to make substantial payments (*čam*) to the chief before their request could be considered. The amounts involved varied, but sometimes as many as seven goats were given, together with other valuables and palm wine. Whenever the witch's agnates were not the complainants, the chief was also required to gain their unanimous approval. According to several informants, failure to observe this would likely have provoked these kin to attack the executioners or the village leaders. A final group that had to be consulted included those *mikum si* whose forefathers had first settled the village. Such men were believed capable of making the strongest ritual statements concerning the traditional appropriateness, and hence legitimacy, of any executions. They were therefore in a good position to curse either the victim's agnates or the village chief if they proceeded independently with the elimination of an offender.

When they met to deliberate, the notables received a lesser share of the valuables that the original complainants had presented to the chief. The overall distribution of payments, which seems to have varied from village to village, was described as follows by one Meta' informant:

First, those wishing the death of a witch make payments of many goats and brass rods to the village chief. Both the brothers of the witch and the kinsmen of his victim contribute to these fees. Any lineage mate of the witch who agrees to his execution must give a goat. Most of these animals are kept by the chief. However, the senior village notables are provided with one goat to feast upon, along with ten brass rods each. For their part, the executioners are given a goat when they meet to plan the deed. Finally, one beast is sent to the compound of X, the ancestor from whose place the forefather of our village chief long ago migrated. As the source of the chiefly clan, the successor of X is able to perform rituals that will prevent *ndɔn* from affecting anyone involved in the case.

In those instances where the notables also decided against the offender, they sometimes took steps to transform the execution itself into a supernatural test. They did so by making a ritual statement in which they asked that the execution should miscarry if by some chance the victim was innocent. The general content of such a statement is suggested by the following testimony from a Meta' informant:

When they decide to kill an offender, the notables first tie knots in two small bundles of the grass called *čiŋ*. They then hold one of the bundles while they speak a ritual statement: "If you really killed another person by your witchcraft, may the executioner kill you too!" After this, the first bundle is placed under one of the hearthstones in the chief's sacrificial hut. Next, the notables take the other bundle of grass in hand and say, "If you did not kill anyone, then may the executioner miss you altogether!" Finally, they throw the second bundle out the door of the hut.

Once the notables had accepted the fact that a witch was to be eliminated, there followed secret consultations with *təkənə*, the local executioner. In most places this costume was worn only by the members of a special lineage, often a group of stranger-settlers with a distinct minority representation in the village. Such persons made desirable executioners because the absence of kin ties between them and their victim was thought to minimize the mystical dangers associated with shedding the blood of a fellow Meta'. They were also believed to have acquired, through the long-term practice of their specialty, an immunity to suffering *ndɔn* from killing officially designated victims. However, in some cases, prior intermarriage with the kin group of the potential victim rendered even these outsiders liable to supernatural sanctions. Hence agreements were sometimes made whereby executioners in different localities acted on each other's behalf. This pattern is illustrated by the following precolonial case, provided by an elderly informant:

CASE SEVEN

In one instance, *təkənə* from a different village was asked by the authorities here to kill a person. This was done in order to prevent *ndɔn* from affecting the parties if any marriages took place between the families of the executioner and the victim. The man who was killed had been bewitching his lineage mates and openly predicting that they would die from certain diseases. When this did occur several times, it was decided to execute the witch. In order to get him to the village where *tɜkɜnɜ* waited, his brothers used a ruse. They asked him to accompany them to visit a diviner so that they might discover why a certain member of the lineage had recently died. After all were assembled in the diviner's hut, the brothers of the witch, pretending that they had to relieve themselves, began to drift out one by one. Finally, finding himself alone, the witch also attempted to leave. However, some men from the other village prevented him. They told the man, "It is you that the diviner finds guilty of killing by witchcraft!" Then *tɜkɜnɜ*, who had been hiding outside in the plantain bushes, came in to kill the offender.

After receiving a goat from the village chief, the men of the executioner lineage made their plans. On the day of the execution, *tɜkɜnɜ*, dressed in a hood of raffia cloth and carrying a large raffia bag and soot-blackened club, attempted to surprise the victim and either kill or subdue him. As noted earlier, when the ambush failed, it was taken as evidence of the innocence of the accused. In such a case, according to one knowledgeable informant, the burden of moral responsibility shifted to *tɜkɜnɜ*, and the executioner himself became liable to suffer *ndɔn* from having wished to kill a fellow Meta'. He was then required to make substantial payments to the village notables, in order to čam or "pay for" the eyes with which he had looked upon his intended victim. Once this was done, the notables made a ritual statement absolving the failed executioner of any guilt.

When the ambush by *tɜkɜnɜ* was successful, on the other hand, the executioner returned from it to the open accompaniment of a double-flanged bell, which symbolized the regulatory authority of the chief and the village notables. If the victim had been killed, his corpse was cast into the bush, whereas if he had merely been captured, he was sold by a slave dealer, with the proceeds going to the village authorities.

Finally, there were, in at least some cases, additional post-execution payments that the agnates of the victim made to the chief and notables. Various informants suggested different reasons for these. While some stated that they were given to pay for the removal of the victim's body, others said that they were intended to dissociate the living kinsmen from the evil qualities of their dead brother, or to absolve the victim's kin from any *ndɔn* for having had a hand in his death. In view of this diversity of accounts, it may well be that there was variation from village to village in the customs surrounding these post-execution payments.

The foregoing description hopefully conveys something of the intricacy of the decision-making process that preceded the use of ultimate coercive sanctions in precolonial Meta'. Both the pains that were taken to consult the widest range of interested parties and the participants' concerns about mystical danger are noteworthy. Underlying these preoccupations were some very real problems posed by violence and bloodshed within a society like Meta'. Where patrilineages were the primary sources of political and economic support, it was clearly risky to employ coercive sanctions upon the members of one's own group. Since this contradicted the solidarity of the descent unit, it was necessary to involve outsiders, such as the village leaders. However, this in turn meant ceding a dangerous amount of authority to the members of other descent groups. A partial answer to these dilemmas was found in the complex set of procedures outlined above. However, as several informants made clear, there was always the possibility that the decision-making process could break down in interlineage violence.

Such an evaluation of the tensions underlying the use of ultimate coercive authority is supported by the following account of a precolonial execution that led to fighting. In this case, which occurred before the informant's birth, the relatives of a man bewitched by his mother's father took matters into their own hands and killed the suspect. Yet even though their action was approved by the chief of a neighboring village (a leader who was aspiring to the status of paramount in the area), it resulted in uncontrolled violence and the forcible expulsion of the avenging group from its own community. In view of the ideal decision-making process outlined above, such an outcome seems almost predictable. In virtually no respect did those taking action in this case follow the prescribed procedures.[5]

5. See Chapter 11 for further discussion of this case and its implications for the organization of the wider Meta' polity.

CASE EIGHT

A, a man from village X, once captured a stranger in the outlying farm area in order to sell him as a slave. When he heard about this, B, the chief of village Y who was also the father of A's mother, asked A to give him the captive. "If you shoot an animal, don't you give me part of the meat?" he asked. But A refused him, saying that he had already sold the captive and shared the proceeds with Fonnyen (the pretender to paramountcy in this area). Soon A fell ill and was informed by a diviner that B had bewitched him. He told his brothers that if he died from this, they should kill B. Then A died. Afterward, his brothers informed Fonnyen that B had killed A through witchcraft and received his permission to kill him. They had a woman lure him into the bush for a liaison so that they could attack him. When the brothers of B saw that he had been slain, they decided to take revenge. So they joined with fellow clansmen of B from neighboring villages and raided the place of A. They destroyed the oil palms and plantains, burned the houses, and took all of the livestock. The lineage of A then fled to another village and remained there for two years. After this they were able to return, since Fonnyen had himself been involved in the decision to kill B. The latter said that the case should be forgotten, and this was done.

Theft

In discussing precolonial conflict resolution, elderly Meta' informants portrayed theft (*idzi*) as a special kind of offense that was condemned with the greatest vigor by public opinion. This may have been because it threatened both the kinship order and the economic system. Goats seem to have been the primary target of thieves, since they were of relatively high value, readily transportable, and easily convertible into other forms of wealth. However, since goats were also the major component of bridewealth payments, their loss threatened the vital interests of every household and lineage. The men of these groups would be unable to marry or beget children, and the groups themselves could not prosper, if they lost their livestock.

Another unusual quality of theft under precolonial Meta' law was the thoroughgoing secularization of its prosecution. In contrast to many delicts, theft was not believed to pose mystical dangers to the perpetrator. It was therefore sanctioned by the most coercive methods. In the view of at least some informants, thieves who were surprised in the act could justifiably be killed on the spot. Even when this did not happen, their captors were entitled to sell them into slavery or to hold them for ransom.

The treatment of thieves also involved the liberal use of corporal punishment. Ordinarily, physical sanctions were not employed upon adults because of the possibility of violent retaliation by their agnates. However, the act of theft seems to have removed such fears of reprisal. Both thieves caught in the act and those merely suspected were often held captive at the compound of the village chief with their feet secured in cumbersome wooden stocks. There they were painfully bound and mercilessly beaten. Such harsh treatment typically continued until a confession and fine were extracted or the thief was ransomed by his lineage.

The fines imposed on thieves were in most cases quite substantial and always far more than the value of the goods stolen. For example, if one goat had been taken, seven might be demanded. When the thief had been caught red-handed, these fines were shared by the intended victim and his agnatic and maternal kin, with only a small portion being sent to the chief of the village in which the offense had occurred. On the other hand, when a suspected thief was tortured into confession at the chief's compound, the village head and notables usually received whatever he and his kin group gave. In either event, when payment was not quickly forthcoming, it was taken as a declaration by the thief's agnates that they were not averse to their brother's sale into slavery. At this point, the captors were free to dispose of him, retaining the proceeds in lieu of a fine. It thus appears that, just as with incorrigible witches, habitual thieves were sold into slavery only with the assent of their agnatic kin. Whether or not this was given seems to have depended at least in part on the scope of their operations. According to some informants, the kin of a captured thief would be most likely to support him if he had restricted his exploits to distant places and most inclined to condemn him if he had stolen from them or from fellow villagers.

The foregoing comprises the ideal system for dealing with thieves under precolonial Meta' law. While remembered cases tend to confirm the fact that procedures such as these were actually employed, they also demonstrate that interlineage violence often lurked just beneath the surface. Three such conflicts, which were witnessed by the informants as children, will be presented here. In the first, the men of two lineages began to fight when those from one taunted the others, whose brother they had previously caught in the act of theft and sold into slavery. In the second case, an attempt by the members of one village to apprehend a thief in a neighboring community led to a scuffle. Only then was the conflict adjudicated by notables from the two villages. The final case records the fate of a habitual thief who was sold into slavery by the authorities of his own village. This account illustrates that, despite the strong public condemnation of thievery, the decision to dispose of a notorious offender was still difficult.

CASE NINE

A fight once broke out between members of the Bɔnji and Bɔzam lineages, each resident in a different village, at a mortuary dance in yet another place. Ndičik, a Bɔzam man, had previously been caught in the corral of a Bɔnji man, trying to steal a goat. Ndičik's agnates had originally acquiesced to his being sold, since he had been caught in the act of theft. However, when the two groups later met at a dance, a Bɔnji man boastfully displayed the razor that he had taken from Ndičik. This enraged Ndičik's lineage mates and a fight erupted. Several people were injured, although none were killed. After a while, members of the host village rushed in to stop the fight and sent the two hostile parties on their way. This finished the matter. The Bɔzam men made no further attempt at retaliation, because they recognized that the sale of their brother had been legitimate. Even the brother of a thief will not take his side. Ndičik's brothers had fought only because of the arrogant public behavior of the Bɔnji men.

CASE TEN

A son of the chief of village X was suspected of stealing a goat in village Y. So one morning people from Y came to his compound and seized him. Then his wife began to cry out, attracting men from his own village, and soon the people of both places were fighting [i.e., there were representatives of many descent groups, not just one lineage per side]. The violence was halted when the chiefs of the two villages persuaded their people to end it. They then appointed two *mikum* from each village to discuss the matter and settle the dispute. When the judges found that the man from X had actually stolen, they asked him to pay a fine of seven goats. Three of these were presented to the person he had robbed, and two additional goats were given to the notables from each side. The village chief received one of these animals while another was killed, with the meat being divided among the notables of his village. This finished the matter.

CASE ELEVEN

During my childhood, several men were sold away from the village as slaves. One was a man from the chiefly lineage itself. He had taken about fifteen goats from various owners before it was finally decided to sell him. Many attempts to discourage his thievery had been made. Once, they had brought him to the chief's compound to be tied and beaten and made him pay heavy fines. On the last occasion before he was sold, the notables had even permitted the thief's compound to be razed. They warned the man at this time that if he stole again he would be sold into slavery. However, several months later he again began to steal. People suspected that he was taking stolen goats to sell at distant markets, so some decided to follow him, and they caught him in the act. After this, the man was seized by *tɜkɜnɜ* and sold.

Homicide

The killing of a fellow Meta' in any context save warfare was termed *ɜbɛne*. This term applied whether or not the killer and victim belonged to the same descent group and regardless of the accidental or intentional character of the slaying. The motives for homicide appear to have been diverse. The close agnates of one man are said to have dispatched his mother's brother after the man declared in his dying statement that the mother's brother had bewitched him. In another instance, a man's own lineage mates are reported to have slain him because they wished to gain control of the property that he held in trust. In yet another case, homicide resulted from a quarrel in which the victim refused to repay several brass rods to the murderer. Accidental killings happened most frequently during mortuary celebrations when men were drinking heavily and firing their Dane guns in the air.

There was an abhorrence of murderers in Meta' culture. Since all Meta' were seen as brothers, any person who had killed a fellow citizen was an aberration. Such persons were forbidden to cut their hair for six months to a year as a sign of their wildness and disgrace.

Murderers also had to cope with mystical danger. Any homicide, deliberate or accidental, was believed to threaten the killer himself, his agnates, and even unrelated parties with *ndɔn*. Like the acts of symbolic aggression mentioned earlier, all homicides were thought to create severe states of polluting *ndɔn* in the places where they occurred. This was a type of mystical danger that might affect anyone in the immediate locality. In addition, homicide was viewed as a moral violation of an extreme sort, one that could cause a personal *ndɔn* affliction for the killer. He was seen as "carrying" (*bɛʔɛ*) on his head a heavy load of *ndɔn* of the sort that could easily spread to his agnates as well. Perhaps partly for these reasons, homicide does not seem to have been a common offense in precolonial Meta'. Few informants who were born before the German occupation could recall more than one instance, and half of the cases that were collected were accidental killings. This infrequency of homicide may also reflect the absence of any pattern of revenge killing or feuding in Meta'.

The sequence of events in a typical homicide case, reconstructed from many informants' statements, was as follows: On learning of a killing, all the people of the surrounding area were overcome by violent feelings of horror and rushed to the compound of the slayer. The group that assembled there included not only members of the victim's clan section but also those of many others. Such mobs were capable of beating murderers to death. However, since their reaction was anticipated, the perpetrator usually hid in the bush until their anger had passed. Failing to find the killer at his compound, the mob would then proceed to destroy it, smashing in the sides of his huts, cutting down his plantain stalks, uprooting crops, and carrying off movable property. This stereotyped destruction of the murderer's compound was referred to as *nayi* in precolonial times, although it later came to be described as *ɔkwatɨ* (a Bali loan word).

After the outburst at the killer's compound had subsided, procedures designed to remove any *ndɔn* associated with the killing began. The owners of the compound where the killing had taken place were forced to hire a ritual specialist to remove the corpse with a bamboo litter, since this was the only way of dissociating themselves from mystical danger. So great was the peril thought to be that the owners were usually willing to pay considerable fees, including a goat and other valuables. Similarly, the head of each compound through which the litter bearers passed had to present them a fowl in order to "buy their footsteps away from his place." If anyone refused, they simply abandoned the corpse with the load of *ndɔn* that it represented and left the reluctant householder to deal with the problem as he saw fit.

On the day following the destruction of his compound, the killer himself began a long process of atonement. As a first step, he was obliged to make heavy payments (*čam*) to secure the cooperation of the leaders of the village in which the homicide had occurred. Since they were responsible for the lives of their people and, as a group, capable of speaking the strongest *njɔm* in their place, it was necessary that they declare the matter of homicide to be finished. Once they had done so, it was thought unlikely that the talk of anyone else would cause the killer to suffer *ndɔn*.

The payments to the local leaders seem to have been handled differently from village to village. In one community, for example, it is said that two notables were sent with large sacks for the agnates of the murderer to fill with fowl and brass rods, while the killer himself delivered a number of goats to the *fɔn* and *mikum si*. Elsewhere it was claimed that any murderer would have had to pay at least seven goats to the local leaders. Yet in no village were the chief and notables said to have shared such prestations with the kin of the victim. In fact, the only payments that could be construed as compensation came much later, if a woman of the clan section of the victim married a man belonging to the killer's own. In such cases, the bridegroom was required to pay an additional goat, so that the "fathers" of his bride would speak an *njɔm* to the effect that no *ndɔn* from the previous homicide should afflict the newly married couple.

In addition to atoning in the above-mentioned ways, murderers were obliged to seek the aid of a single ritual specialist, the chief of Zang Tabi village, who handled the final cleansing of such offenders for Meta' society as a whole. The role of this expert will be discussed in Chapter 10, and here it is necessary to mention only that his payments were even higher than those received by the local leaders. The most noteworthy part of his fee was a slave that the murderer gave to replace the person he had killed. Since it usually took some months for his agnates to accumulate enough wealth to purchase this slave, the killer's period of disgrace was often protracted.

As is apparent from the foregoing description, the resolution of homicide differed markedly from that of most other disputes. In homicide cases a complex process of ritual resolution simply overwhelmed the offender and his kin group with fears of mystical danger and demands for costly fees. At the same time, a conventionalized outlet was provided for the anger of the descent group that had lost a member. The strength of the retaliatory urge that was thus deflected is seen in the following precolonial case:

CASE TWELVE

A man was once killed by his own lineage mates in this village. They killed him because they wanted to install another in his place, thereby gaining control of his property. This was not a killing by witchcraft or an execution that had the chief's approval. The men simply plotted against their brother and speared him. When the people of his mother's lineage heard about what had happened, they themselves went to attack the murderers. They were assisted in this by their sons-in-law. Finally, the chief of the village sent someone bearing a bamboo pole and his fly whisk to stop the fighting. Then the important notables of the village sat down to discuss the case. The victim's brothers had to *čam* ("pay fines"), while the principal instigator gave more than 1,000 brass rods and let his hair grow very long. This finished the matter.

The above case is also of interest for two additional reasons. First, it shows how a victim's maternal lineage could assume the role of vengeance group when he was betrayed by his own agnatic kin, and second, its resolution process differs somewhat from the ideal one described earlier. Most significantly, the case is not said to have been taken to the ultimate homicide specialist in Zang Tabi village. Now this might indicate that there was wide procedural variation in the settlement of precolonial homicides. However, it could also be that the informant's account was to some extent colored by contemporary political considerations. Since his village chief was an archrival of the chief of Zang Tabi at the time of the interview, he may have wished to avoid any statement that would enhance the latter's prestige. Such an interpretation is in fact supported by the testimony of an informant from Zang Tabi itself, who independently mentioned the same case and described it as having been handled by ritual specialists in his village.

Disputes Involving the Abuse of Authority

Although the misuse of authority by the village chief and notables was a potentially serious source of conflict in precolonial
times, informants were able to provide little concrete data about
such cases. According to one, any chief who berated his subjects
or assaulted them physically would sooner or later be rejected.
In his imagination, the people would simply inform the chief
that they no longer respected him as their *fɔn*, rather than committing regicide or expelling him from the village. Other informants envisioned conflicts as most likely to arise in situations
where the chief had abused his position for reasons of personal
gain—for example, if he failed to share meat to which his notables were entitled. Additional possible offenses included the
chief's attempting to marry his subjects' daughters with only
partial payments of bridewealth, his accepting presents without
making any return, and his harboring thieves. As is apparent,
all these conflicts between *fɔn* and people turned upon nonre-
ciprocity and the betrayal of trust.

As for redress, the informants emphasized that offended parties would only employ very indirect means of obtaining it. According to some, simply waiting for the chief to experience *ndɔn*
for having violated his subjects' rights was the usual procedure.
Under such circumstances, a chief might ultimately make resti-
tution on his own initiative. Another common tactic was to
await a situation in which the chief required one's assistance and
then withhold it. For example, the *mikum si* of a village might
boycott important rituals or meetings when summoned by the
chief. The strategies of subordinates thus involved using subtle
and indirect pressures to appeal to the chief's self-interest in
maintaining cooperative relations. A concrete idea of how such
approaches might work is conveyed in the following hypothetical case given by a Meta' *kum si*:

If the chief tried to seize my hunting ground, I would ask, "Was your
father also hunting in this place?" Later the chief would begin to suffer
ndɔn. Then he would call his *mikum* to inform them that he had been
having troublesome dreams. He would acknowledge that these might
be caused by people who believed that he had been seizing the property of others but deny that he had done so. Although he is the chief,

everything is really the people's own. After this the *mikum* would bless (*fa*) the chief and say that he should dream no more.

Conclusion

To complete this analysis of precolonial Meta' law, let us return to the fundamental questions posed at the outset of the chapter: (1) how was public order reinforced within the typical Meta' village, and (2) what patterns can be discerned in Meta' processes of disputing? Regarding reinforcement, it is clear that precolonial village leaders had many means of dealing with threats to both the peace of the community and their own authority: masked figures could be used to announce their orders and to place injunctions, other agents could be called upon to quell disturbances, elaborate rituals could be conducted to intimidate unknown offenders, and *tɜkɜnɜ* (the village executioner) could be used to dispatch incorrigible witches and thieves. It is also noteworthy that these mechanisms of village-level reinforcement were broadly expressive of the popular will. Though acephalous in its political organization, Meta' was nonetheless characterized by a strong "law and order" consciousness that emphasized the importance of property rights and the maintenance of public order. This is evident in many kinds of conflict-management behavior, ranging from the coercive techniques that were used upon habitual offenders, to the dramatic rituals that were performed at public assemblies to curse unknown culprits, to the zest with which captive thieves were beaten, to the widespread enthusiasm for subjecting litigants to mystically sanctioned oaths.

At the same time, however, careful circumscription of authority was also a striking feature of the Meta' legal system. Although the village notables did possess some legitimate powers, their exercise of these was constrained. For one thing, the fact that patrilineages remained the fundamental support groups restricted their freedom of action. Moreover, as shown earlier, the use of ultimate coercive force required that all interested parties be painstakingly consulted.

Turning to disputing, we have seen that the Meta' system of conflict resolution was characterized by its extreme flexibility, as well as by the multiplicity of alternatives that it provided to disputants. In a conflict over the refund of bridewealth, to take just one example, the choice was very wide. The creditor was free to employ self-help by seizing a hostage, to negotiate, to seek mediation by the village leaders, to start a fight leading to adjudication by the village notables, or to commit an act of symbolic aggression that would in turn prompt both adjudication and rituals of purification. What option (or sequence of measures) he chose was influenced by many factors, including the personalities of the disputants, their ability to marshal support for a violent confrontation, and the risks and costs involved in each approach. Clearly the village-level legal system did not confine dispute settlement to narrow routine channels.

It is also evident that, despite the numerous nonviolent forms of dispute management that were available, the backing of a strong descent group remained the final guarantee of one's legal rights in precolonial Meta'. This comes through clearly in the numerous case histories of interlineage fighting that occurred when more peaceful approaches to conflict resolution had broken down.

A final conclusion relates to the rather ambivalent role of the chief himself in conflict management. On the one hand, the *fɔn*'s pivotal position made him an ideal mediator of interlineage disputes. Moreover, his enhanced mystical powers enabled him to initiate vigorous action in rituals to reinforce the public order, and, in sudden disturbances, the chief might even intervene personally as a peacemaker. However, as we have also seen, Meta' political ideology required that the chief tread very lightly. He had always to maintain the appearance of an indirect relationship between himself and the people, and whenever he authorized the employment of coercive sanctions, to make certain that he was supported by the broadest possible consensus. Thus, while the Meta' village chief had a significant role in dispute settlement, and while some things might have been difficult without his coordination, he was also rarely capable of strong independent action.

Female farmers

Market-bound women in the Medig valley

Funam market in the Bome valley

Palm-oil sellers at
Funam market

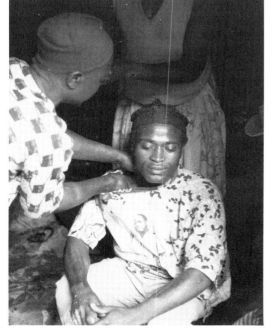

Applying camwood to
a successor's chest

An elderly Meta' village head, Chief Aje of Njimetu village

Buffalo-horn drinking cups (undecorated horn is in the precolonial style)

A chiefly compound with *mbɛŋ* ("plaited raffia mats")

Tзkзnз, the village executioner

Food and palm wine displayed at a mortuary celebration (note photo of the deceased)

Dancers at a mortuary celebration

A funeral masquerade

Preparing for an interview

NINE

Process and Variation in Village Organization

In the three previous chapters, various aspects of Meta' village organization have been discussed, but with the exception of some actual disputes analyzed in Chapter 8, the data have all pertained to the informants' idealized model. One unresolved problem is that of determining the extent to which ideology really influenced behavior. Was process in local groups simply a realization of the norms of village-level activities as outlined above? Or did behavior diverge radically from these ideals? Although these questions are extremely difficult to judge for a political system that was defunct for over 65 years at the time of my fieldwork, certain kinds of evidence can still be adduced. In this chapter, I will describe the actual organization of several precolonial villages (whose names have been changed to protect their modern-day residents) and examine discrepancies with the ideal model of village structure. As we shall see, some important insights into village-level political processes can be gained from such an exercise.

Njindik Village

Njindik had an estimated population of 400 persons residing in some 60 households in 1900.[1] There were seven distinct clan

---

1. The population estimates given in this chapter are based on a method of reconstructing the size of localized descent group segments in 1900. According to numerous informants, the size of the *mban* group or minimal lineage segment was restricted to a fairly narrow range of variation and was on average about five households. Ethnographic investigations in 1970 tended to bear these assertions out. Therefore, the size of larger descent group segments was estimated

sections represented in the village, but the heads of only six of these were accorded the status of senior village notable (*kum si*). One of the latter was also recognized as the *fɔn* or chief. Although these facts might seem to suggest that, at least in terms of leadership structure, Njindɨk conformed to the ideal model of village organization, this was not the case. Interestingly, the first hint of this came not from the informants' discussions of precolonial times but from observation of their collective behavior in 1970. My initial approach to the Njindɨk elders was at their modern "village council" meeting, nowadays a weekly event in most Meta' communities. I had planned merely to introduce myself and obtain a brief official version of the local history, since previous experience made me expect that nothing controversial would be revealed in this kind of public encounter. I was therefore surprised when one of the notables rather than the *fɔn* came to dominate the discussion. Most of my questions were referred to him, and his account of village history strongly favored his own forefathers. Since nobody seemed to object to this slanting of the testimony, it could only be assumed that the notable had solid public backing. But such a turn of events contrasted sharply with the course of similar inquiries in other Meta' villages. While their chiefs had often asked the older notables to answer me, they had always seemed to retain firm control over the situation, and the resulting accounts of precolonial village organization had almost invariably stressed the role of the *fɔn*. I consequently left my first session in Njindɨk somewhat puzzled. It was only after further information had been obtained in private that I realized that the peculiarities of my initial encounter were rooted in the precolonial history of the place. Njindɨk, it turned out, had had a dual system of leadership in which the *fɔn* was primarily a figurehead, while effective power rested with one senior village notable who had the backing of most of his fellows. This dualism had been important in 1900, and it remained a vital factor after 65 years of colonial and independent regimes.

---

by asking informants in each segment how many *mban* subdivisions had existed within their groups just before the people of the Bome and Zang valleys went to Bali. Village populations were obtained by adding the totals for all descent group segments in a village.

Njindɨk's divided system of leadership seems to have resulted from the late arrival of the *fɔn*'s descent group, for its members had come as refugees more than a generation after the village was founded. Prior to the appearance of Njirɜbaʔ, the first *fɔn*, there had been no one of that status in Njindɨk, and the five original notables had governed the community. As direct successors of Njindɨk's first settlers they had great mystical powers over its land and people. They were capable of speaking the strongest ritual statement concerning the place, and they had conducted most village-level activities independently, under the leadership of one Tɛče. Symbolically, however, these notables were still the inferiors of Njirɜbaʔ, who had already achieved the status of *fɔn* while in his previous village. In 1900, his successor was the only villager who could be addressed as *fɔn*, possess chiefly regalia and properties, or project the aura of chiefly mystical powers. Yet despite his clear superiority of rank, Njirɜbaʔ had been unable to establish exclusive control over many important activities. The antisorcery rites of *zɨ si*, for example, were performed annually at both his compound and that of Tɛče. Moreover, while Njirɜbaʔs rituals involved only the members of his own clan section, Tɛče's were treated as a village affair.

Other typical village-level functions were organized similarly. Thus, anyone of nonchiefly descent who wanted a dancing field had to make payments to Tɛče and his four fellow notables. Likewise, interlineage fighting was judged by the original notables at the compound of Tɛče. However, these arrangements do not seem to have extended to capital decisions, since if anyone was to be killed or sold in precolonial times, the matter was considered by Njirɜbaʔ and Tɛče in private consultation. It may have been that Njirɜbaʔ was included in such decisions because his mystical powers of *fɔn*ship made it less likely that the planners would suffer misfortune (*ndɔn*) from having condemned a village-mate.

The situation with regard to communal hunting was also complex, since two groups of Njindɨk villagers controlled their own tracts. While the agnates of Njirɜbaʔ carried out separate prehunt rituals and retained all the game from their own bush, the hunt of Mɨnangɔ (another of the original notables) involved wider cooperation. Not only were collective rites observed prior to it at Tɛče's hunting shrine, but he and the three other original notables were customarily given the hindquarters of one large animal. The only connection between Njirɜbaʔ and Mɨnangɔ in all of these activities was that each normally sent the other one hindquarters out of respect.

Informants in Njindɨk were unable to agree about how rights over "noble game" had been organized in precolonial times. Some said that leopards and pythons killed in any part of the village were taken to Njirɜbaʔ, while Tɛče might retain lesser animals if they were slain within the territory of his own clan section. Others contradicted this, saying that all noble game, except animals killed in the hunting territory of Njirɜbaʔ, would be butchered at Tɛče's compound and shared by the village's original notables. These two versions were actually the conflicting claims of Njirɜbaʔ and the notables, which, even up to 1970, remained unresolved. Tɛče and his fellows could, as original settlers, put forward strong claims to noble game, while Njirɜbaʔ could justifiably assert that he was the only villager who had acquired the rank of *fɔn* and purchased the rights over noble game in an orthodox fashion.

This brief description of Njindɨk in 1900 indicates that it diverged in several ways from the ideal model. It was a village subdivided into two semi-autonomous sides, each of which performed many typical local-level functions on its own. Yet interestingly, no informant claimed that Njindɨk had been two separate communities in precolonial times. In part, this was because Njirɜbaʔ and his people had settled on what was already village land when their residential sites were given to them by Tɛče. But Njindɨk may also have been considered a single village, since its people had willingly recognized Njirɜbaʔ as "their *fɔn*" upon his arrival, there having been no one else who had already attained this rank. Finally, both factions did cooperate in some village-level affairs. This is clearest in the case of executions of villagers, where the final decision could only be made by Njirɜbaʔ and Tɛče in joint consultation.

One may well ask why Tɛče had not become a chief himself before or after the arrival of Njirɜbaʔ, since he had established a position of *de facto* village leadership (his supporters comprised two-thirds of the population), and he had substantial control over many village-level activities. However, Tɛče' did not belong to one of the two Meta' clans that had largely monopolized the position of *fɔn* and were reluctant for others to purchase it. Furthermore, Njirɜbaʔ, according to some informants, had allied himself with neighboring chiefs who did not wish to undermine his legitimacy by granting a *fɔn*ship to Tɛče. Finally, Tɛče's own clan was among the lowest in rank, and in many villages the members of such groups were unable to acquire properties like plaited raffia mats and two doors, much less the status of *fɔn*. In this context, Njirɜbaʔ remained as the *fɔn*, but his position was insecure.

The case of Njirɜbaʔ and Tɛče helps to clarify the nature of chiefship in precolonial Meta' society. When speaking of the role of *fɔn* in general terms, Meta' informants describe it as a combination of attributes—rights over properties (such as noble game, cowries, and finely-carved stools); effective village leadership; and the possession of special mystical powers. However, in practice, these aspects of chieftaincy were separable. When Meta' informants speak of a person "purchasing" (*čam*-ing) the position of *fɔn*, they are thus referring to the acquisition of rank only. This might later lead to actual village headship but it need not.

Mbo Village

The community to be considered next presents analytical difficulties beyond those of Njindɨk. On the one hand, Mbo resembled a "village," since its members performed some typical local-level activities under the direction of one set of leaders. On the other hand, it was unusual for its many aspirants to *fɔn*ship and for the complex way in which communal activities were controlled. It is thus unclear whether to treat Mbo as one village or several separate units. As will be seen, the case of Mbo stretches the ideal definition of a "village" almost to the limits of its usefulness.

One of the best ways to approach an understanding of precolonial Mbo is to disregard, for the moment, all claims that it was a single community and to describe it as two villages, each with an internal complexity comparable to that of Njindik. This was the tack that the British colonial administration had taken, apparently unable to face the possibility of one village with four or five chiefs. It also made sense in that there was a definite line of cleavage between two sides of Mbo, oriented toward different senior chiefs. In this analysis, the same approach will be adopted for convenience of exposition. First, the organization of each side of Mbo will be described, and then the ways in which they cooperated will be discussed. During the British period, one-half of Mbo came to be called Gunɔbɛŋ, while the other continued to style itself as Mbo. Here, they shall be designated as "Gunɔbɛŋ" and "Small Mbo," respectively, and the term "Greater Mbo" will refer to the larger combined group.

Small Mbo

In 1900 this was a community with an estimated population of 650 persons, living in some 100 households, who belonged to five different clans. The leadership picture was complex in that there was both a senior chief (Ndabik) and a junior man (Atesaŋ) who, though ranking as a fɔn, could not conduct many village-level activities independently. The genesis of this divided fɔnship was described by one informant as follows:

Atesaŋ originally separated from the descent group of his "father" Chief Ndabik. Atesaŋ had delivered many sons, and some of these had gotten their own rights of *mban* and dancing fields, so Atesaŋ moved with his people to a different side of the village. The place was called Nyɛn. At the time of this move, Atesaŋ was not a fɔn. Then Chief Ndabik died, leaving a young child as his successor. While the successor was growing, Atesaŋ came to sit on the stool of Chief Ndabik as trustee (*wit ni wɛr ɔtɔn*). When the true successor of Chief Ndabik had grown, he said that he was ready to take the chair of his father. Atesaŋ accepted this, but added that the people should consider what to do with him after they installed the successor of Chief Ndabik, since they had previously been clapping to him and answering him with "*ngi*" [both forms of honorific behavior used when addressing a fɔn]. The people of the village then said to Atesaŋ, "Since you left the chair of Chief Ndabik peacefully, go to your own compound and be fɔn there. Then we will clap our hands to you and say 'ngi.' From now on you two chiefs will rule as brothers, and, if one of you says something, there will be no need for the other to speak." [Q. What did they give Atesaŋ when they made him a chief?] They gave him long upright stones to put on his dancing field and *ndik* [a drum platform]. They also gave Atesaŋ the right of using cowries and a private cup from which nobody else could drink, as well as a chair that nobody else could sit upon and the right of keeping less important noble game like *imaŋ*. These were the only things given to Atesaŋ when he became *fɔn*. [Q. Did Atesaŋ acquire the right of keeping leopards killed in his part of the village?] No. If he was getting big and wanted this right, he would have had to purchase it from Chief Ndabik and the other big men in the village who helped Ndabik to butcher leopards. Atesaŋ would get this right by first giving seven goats and some brass rods to pay for the stone on which leopards are butchered. Then he would give another castrated goat to purchase the knife with which noble game is cut.

This account of how Atesaŋ became a *fɔn* illustrates one process by which new chieftaincies were established in precolonial times. A member of the chiefly clan in any village might be allowed to purchase the rank of *fɔn* by *čam*-ing for certain prestige goods and rights. In the case of Atesaŋ, the fact that he was stepping down as the "trustee" also seems to have been a consideration, although this was not a precondition for such a rise to chiefship. More important, according to informants, was the candidate's heading a large descent group segment, and while the size of the original Atesaŋ's clan section is unknown, some three generations later in 1900 it included about twenty compounds.

After Atesaŋ's ascent to *fɔn*ship, Ndabik continued to be the senior chief of the entire village, while Atesaŋ's authority was limited to his own section of Nyɛn. There he presided over both his agnates and the members of three nonchiefly clan sections that were headed by lesser village notables.

The way in which most village-level functions were structured reflected Small Mbo's divided leadership. Although the antisorcery rites of *zi si* were performed only at the compound of Ndabik, with Atesaŋ participating as "one of his notables," both chiefs used their own *ifuʔ* medicines to conduct similar rituals during August. On such occasions, the people of each would attend the ceremonies of the other as guests.

As noted by the informant quoted earlier, rights over noble game still largely belonged to Ndabik in Small Mbo. Thus, any leopard or python killed in the village would be butchered at his compound, with Atesaŋ receiving an honorable share of meat. On the other hand, Atesaŋ and his own notables in Nyɛn were allowed to retain any lesser forms of noble game that were killed there.

During hunting season Small Mbo also operated as a single unit, since only Ndabɨk possessed a hunting ground. Before any communal hunt, rituals were performed by several *mban* heads in the clan section of Ndabɨk. Then the village notables were allowed to conduct similar rites in their own descent groups. After the hunt had taken place, the owner's share of game was given to Chief Ndabɨk and his agnates, while Atesaŋ shared the hindquarters of one large animal with the other notables.

Informants in Small Mbo were not in complete agreement about how the rights to dancing fields, plaited raffia mats, and two doors were acquired in 1900. Some said that anybody who wanted these would have to make payments to Ndabɨk, and that Atesaŋ, as one of his notables, would receive only a lesser share. However, others suggested that Atesaŋ might be able to grant some or all of these rights to an appropriate person in Nyɛn.

The precolonial legal system in Small Mbo also showed complexities. Both Ndabɨk and Atesaŋ possessed the regulatory masker *nju mɜnaŋ*, while Atesaŋ alone had the dance *kwɛʔifɔ*. The *nju mɜnaŋ* masks of the two chiefs are said to have operated strictly on their own "sides" of the village, making announcements and placing injunctions. Yet while Atesaŋ and his notables could resolve less difficult disputes that took place in Nyɛn, all serious cases (e.g., homicide and interlineage fighting) were taken to the compound of Ndabɨk, where Atesaŋ attended as one of the notables. Finally, as regards warfare, Small Mbo seems to have formed a single unit, since it had just one group of *mɜgwe* ("war scouts") drawn from all parts of the village.

A brief survey of the organization of Small Mbo has shown that, like Njindɨk, it diverged from the ideal Meta' village in having had a dual system of leadership. Yet it differed from Njindɨk in some respects. In 1900 the latter village was divided into two factions—the descendants of the original settlers versus the chief, Njirɜbaʔ, and his agnates. By contrast, the duality of authority in Small Mbo resulted from two persons having attained the rank of *fɔn*. Moreover, whereas in Njindɨk the members of each faction performed many of the same village-level activities independently, Small Mbo had a fairly unified village structure. Its organizational pattern might aptly be described as that of "a village within a village." Most crucial activities were carried out at the compound of Chief Ndabɨk, with Atesaŋ assisting as "one of his notables." However, Atesaŋ was also able to observe some less important ceremonies at his compound in Nyɛn with his own "small notables." Nyɛn was thus a microcosm of Small Mbo as a whole.

The process by which Atesaŋ attained the rank of *fɔn* appears to have been fairly common in precolonial times, as similar cases were reported in other Meta' villages. In fact, it seems likely that this was a part of the normal lineage-segmentation process in chiefly clan sections. A man who had become the head of a sizable segment was allowed to purchase some but not all of the properties associated with chiefship. This act was interpreted by many informants as his first step toward going off to found a new community, since he could not hope to exercise full chiefly powers while still in his parent village without challenging the original *fɔn*. Therefore, he would wish to settle elsewhere with his people.

That Small Mbo showed greater unity than Njindɨk was partly due to the tie of clanship between Atesaŋ and Ndabɨk. As the informant quoted earlier reported, their relationship was ideally one of brotherhood. They were supposed to cooperate in all things and to "speak as one." This theme of amity between chiefs belonging to the same descent group is one that occurs in the history of many Meta' villages, and it should not be dismissed as merely an ideal. The cases indicate that some such cooperative relationships did endure, although others ended abruptly in conflicts that caused the elimination of one of the chiefs.

In the case of Small Mbo, it appears that the political shrewdness of the first Atesaŋ was also a factor that enabled his arrangement with Ndabɨk to persist over three generations. The original Atesaŋ is said to have had much "cleverness" or "sense" (*we*). Informants cite his having acquired so many chiefly properties, including the mortuary dance *kwɛʔifɔ* that Ndabɨk himself lacked, as proof of this. They likewise recount how he enlisted the support of Tabi, a chief who was aspiring to the status of senior Meta' *fɔn*, and claim that this was one of the main reasons that he was allowed to purchase the rank of *fɔn* in the first place.[2]

Gunɜbɛŋ

Gunɜbɛŋ was the other half of "Greater Mbo." Its organization resembled that of Small Mbo and Njindɨk but was somewhat more elaborate in that there were four rather than two aspirants to *fɔn*ship. The most serious contenders were Fɔmɨndam, the senior chief (whose clan affiliation was different from that of Chiefs Ndabɨk and Atesaŋ in Small Mbo), and Azoŋɜ, the main representative of the original settlers. In 1900 Gunɜbɛŋ had an estimated population of 700 persons residing in some 100 households. It was thus about the same size as Small Mbo. Of the five clans that were represented, that of Fɔmɨndam was the most sizable, with almost two-thirds of the village population, while Azoŋɜ's had but a fifth.

Before the coming of Fɔmɨndam, Azoŋɜ is said to have been the senior notable in Gunɜbɛŋ. As the first settler in the area, he could speak the strongest ritual statement concerning it, and it is claimed that in the earliest days villagers were bringing him noble game and "fallen" animals (i.e., ones that were found dead). They also submitted their disputes to him. But Azoŋɜ was still addressed by the people as *tita* ("father") rather than *fɔn*.

The arrival of Fɔmɨndam and his large descent group, five or six generations before 1900, seems to have eclipsed the role of Azoŋɜ. Among other things, he lost his rights to the highest forms of noble game and control over many village-level activities. However, his status as original settler remained important, and by British colonial times, his successor was reasserting claims to village leadership by purchasing new rights to noble game from a chief in the next valley.

The other aspirants to chiefship, Čiganjɛʔ and Awaʔmbaŋ, were the heads of sizable sections within Chief Fɔmɨndam's

2. A pseudonym is not used for Chief Tabi here, since he figures in later discussions of intervillage politics (see Chapter 11), and it would have been impossible to conceal his identity.

clan, and shortly before 1900 they had purchased the right to use cowries. Since these were major insignia of chieftaincy, they were thereby taking the first steps toward their own *fɔn*ships. Yet they lacked rights to even the lesser forms of noble game and could not perform village-level activities on their own. Their chieftaincies thus appear to have been mainly a matter of rank, although in one respect they did have an impact on village affairs. Ordinarily, as "sons of the palace" (i.e., members of Fɔmindam's descent group) Čiganjɛʔ and Awaʔmbaŋ would have been excluded from meetings of the senior village notables, but having become chieflets, they were accepted as members of the group.

The situation in Gunɔbɛŋ in 1900 thus seems to have been a more elaborate version of those seen in Njindik and Small Mbo. In this context, most village-level activities were carried out at the compound of Fɔmindam, where Azoŋɔ participated as a senior village notable. The antisorcery rites of *zi si*, for example, were performed there, with Azoŋɔ receiving a share of medicines to distribute among his people. However, hunting and the control of noble game favored Azoŋɔ more. As his descent group was the only one to organize a hunt, the owner's share of game went to its members alone. Moreover, since he had retained the right to receive lesser species of noble game, Gunɔbɛŋ was split into two zones for the purpose of allocating such animals.

There was disagreement among the informants about the way in which properties such as dancing fields and the right of two doors were acquired in precolonial Gunɔbɛŋ. According to some, Azoŋɔ and Fɔmindam would each direct such transfers within their respective territories. Others (who were mainly supporters of Fɔmindam) claimed that, while Azoŋɔ would take no part in transactions concerning these rights on Fɔmindam's side of the village, the latter would accompany Azoŋɔ when he gave them out within his own zone and would receive a share of the valuables. Whatever the case, both versions underscore the point that Azoŋɔ played a significant role in granting these properties.

Fɔmindam appears to have had somewhat stronger control over conflict management. Although Azoŋɔ, like Atesaŋ, could resolve less serious disputes among his own people, he was required to refer cases like homicide and interlineage fighting to the Notables who met at Fɔmɨndam's residence. Furthermore, no informant mentioned Azoŋ3 as having had the regulatory mask *nju mɜnaŋ*, and decisions to kill or sell villagers were considered in secret at the compound of Fɔmɨndam. Only Azoŋ3, Fɔmɨndam, and another notable normally took part in the sessions, Čɨganjɛʔ and Awaʔmbaŋ being excluded as "sons of the palace." Finally, in times of war the people of Gunɜbɛŋ organized as a single unit. There was but one group of war scouts, drawn from all parts of the village, and no history of warfare between its two sides.

The organization of village-level activities in Gunɜbɛŋ, like that of Njindɨk and Small Mbo, thus reflects a divided pattern of leadership. There were two factions, and the leader of each advanced some village-wide claims. In Gunɜbɛŋ, as in Njindɨk, the division of the community was based on a distinction between a group of original settlers and the chiefly clan. However, Gunɜbɛŋ differed in that the positions of these two factions were reversed. In Gunɜbɛŋ, the latecoming Chief Fɔmɨndam had emerged as the dominant leader, whereas in Njindɨk *Fɔn* Njirɜbaʔ was mainly a figurehead. This difference may have been partly due to the fact that Fɔmɨndam headed a large clan section that included two-thirds of the village population, while Njirɜbaʔs descent group constituted only a third.

One may well ask why Azoŋ3 did not purchase the right to retain the highest forms of noble game earlier and thus reestablish his claim to chieftaincy; he is said to have done so only in colonial times, when the people of Fɔmɨndam had already been in the village for generations. The influence of Fɔmɨndam's sizable descent group may partly explain this. However, the rank of Azoŋ3's clan was probably also a factor. He belonged to the same prestigeless group as Tɛče in Njindɨk, so that members of the main chiefly clans would not have wished to provide him with properties symbolizing *fɔn*ship. Had they done so, Azoŋ3 could have easily transferred them to clansmen like Tɛče. This would have reduced the monopoly of the original chiefly clans on the position of *fɔn* and, over time, undermined their power in many villages.

In view of these facts, the way in which Azoŋ3 finally acquired senior rights to noble game is highly significant. According to several informants, he purchased them from Tabi, the same chief who had encouraged the candidacy of Atesaŋ in Small Mbo and who had played a similar role in several other cases. As mentioned earlier, Tabi had for some time been attempting to establish himself in the previously nonexistent role of senior Meta' *fɔn*, and it seems likely that supporting the claims of minor candidates for chieftaincy, such as Atesaŋ and Azoŋ3, was part of his strategy. By granting them properties associated with *fɔn*ship, he established his own right to settle chieftaincy disputes in other villages as well as gaining a group of loyal supporters in intervillage politics.

Finally, a useful comparison can be drawn between Gunɜbɛŋ and Small Mbo, since it resembled the latter more than Njindɨk in the degree of cooperation shown by its major leaders. Azoŋ3 and Fɔmɨndam collaborated in many village activities in a manner similar to that of Atesaŋ and Ndabɨk in Small Mbo, and Azoŋ3, like Atesaŋ, appears to have accepted his junior status for the sake of performing these harmoniously. By contrast, the people of Njindɨk were divided into rival camps that displayed little ability to cooperate. There was the same basis for a conflict between original settlers and the chiefly clan in Gunɜbɛŋ as in Njindɨk, but the overt manifestation of it was less intense.

Greater Mbo

The precolonial political organization of both sides of "Greater Mbo" has now been described. It remains only to consider why some informants claimed that Small Mbo and Gunɜbɛŋ had been a single village in 1900. As has been shown, each half of Greater Mbo had an organizational complexity comparable to that of Njindɨk. However, if both of these groups are considered a single village, they comprised a unit several times larger and more complex than Njindɨk. As a combined group, Greater Mbo had a population of about 1,300 under two senior chiefs, two junior leaders, and two other descent group heads who possessed the rank of *fɔn* without having a chieflike role.

The primary reason that informants gave for considering Greater Mbo one community was that the people of Small Mbo and Gunɔbɛŋ had collaborated in certain village activities. For example, the leaders of these groups are said to have cooperated in bringing about the resolution of some disputes. After a serious fight between clan sections had happened in either place, for example, it is said that the notables of both Fɔmindam and Ndabɨk might meet to consider the case and share any fines. Moreover, some informants claimed that after a killing in either Small Mbo or Gunɔbɛŋ, Atesaŋ and a notable from Fɔmindam's side would jointly collect fowl and brass rods from the compound where the incident had occurred, on behalf of both sets of village authorities. It also appears that the leaders of Small Mbo and Gunɔbɛŋ cooperated in arranging for the execution of villagers. While the notables of each place decided about such matters independently, they normally requested their counterparts to provide the executioner, in order to avoid being affected by misfortune (*ndɔn*) brought on by their involvement in the case. Finally, the leaders of Small Mbo and Gunɔbɛŋ are said to have cooperated to an extent in the division of noble game. Although both Fɔmindam and Ndabɨk retained leopards and other noble beasts when these were killed within their territories, they also customarily reserved a share of the meat for each other.

It is difficult to assess the importance of these forms of cooperation among the leaders of Greater Mbo. One informant tried to explain the relationship between Fɔmindam and Ndabɨk by saying that "they were drinking their wine from one cup." This phrase suggests not only secular collaboration, but also that they could use each other's sacrificial drinking horns and that each could speak a ritual statement on behalf of the other. This in turn implies that their inherited mystical powers were merged, and that their cooperative arrangement was of a strongly traditional character. However, some informants differed on this point and described the association of the two leaders as merely voluntary. The answer to the question of whether Greater Mbo was really one village or two may appear to depend on the resolution of this conflict in testimonies, but to say this is to attribute more rigidity to the concept of "village" than it had in the minds of the Meta'. The organization of Greater Mbo can be quite reasonably described by saying that, for the purpose of some village-level functions, it was a single unit, while, for other activities, it operated as two or three separate groups.

Bat Village

By now the reader may have begun to wonder whether any Meta' community corresponded to the rather centralized model of village organization presented in Chapters 6 and 7. Although many villages diverged from this ideal by having more complex patterns of internal organization, some did approximate it fairly closely. Bat was one such village.

In 1900, Bat had an estimated population of 450. There were members of three clans residing in the village, with that of the *fɔn* divided into five sections that freely intermarried. Bat was unlike the villages thus far discussed in that it lacked any rivals for the *fɔn*ship. Moreover, its leader did not belong to one of the main Meta' chiefly clans. In fact, the chief of Bat was its only *fɔn*. Besides the chief, there was a group of five senior village notables, at least some of whom held their positions by virtue of being the successors of original settlers of the village, rather than because of the size of their groups. Four of the notables belonged to segments of the chiefly clan, while the remaining two were affiliated with another descent group.

As in the ideal Meta' village described in Chapter 7, all important village-level activities in Bat appear to have been carried out by the *fɔn*, Asaʔɜnje, and his senior village notables. The anti-sorcery rites of *zi si*, for example, were performed by them at the compound of Asaʔɜnje, and all serious conflict matters, such as public fighting between clan sections and decisions to execute villagers, were considered by the same group of men.

The allocation of properties such as dancing fields was said to be under the control of Asaʔɜnje and the notables as well, so that anyone wishing to have his own would have to apply to them. However, Bat differed from the ideal Meta' village in that a person acquiring a new field would make payments only to Chief Asaʔɜnje and the notable controlling the area in which he resided, rather than to the senior village notables as a group. Asaʔɜnje is also said to have received a share of the fee of any ritual specialist, such as the one charged with removing *ndɔn* in cases of plantain slashing. In these respects, Bat contrasted with most other Meta' villages, where the *fɔn* had no comparable claims.

The organization of hunting in Bat appears to have been somewhat more complex than in the ideal Meta' village. Two local clan sections—that of the *fɔn* and one of the nonchiefly groups—possessed hunting territories. Each of these performed its pre-hunting rituals separately and received the hunt owner's share of game, although the village as a whole normally participated in the actual hunting at both places.

As for rights over noble game, with one small exception all such animals that were killed in any part of Bat were taken to the *fɔn*. This applied to both the residential area and the outlying farmlands and hunting tracts that belonged to village members. However, any such beast that was killed in a small part of the village where a neighboring chief had once resided was taken to that *fɔn* in his new village.

This brief summary of village-level activities in Bat demonstrates that in 1900 the community conformed closely to the ideal model of village organization. It had a unified political system under a single *fɔn* and a set of senior village notables. It was also a multifunctional group that carried out village-level activities as a cooperative unit, and it appears to have lacked strongly developed factions like those of Njindɨk and Gunɔbɛŋ.

However, there are some indications that Bat may have tended farther toward a centralized system than the ideal model of village organization itself. Chief Asaʔɜnje's sharing the ritual specialists' fees provides some evidence of this, as does his almost exclusive control over the allocation of dancing fields. One informant also claimed that, upon his arrival, Asaʔɜnje's ancestor had usurped rights over noble game from the one nonchiefly clan section that had possessed a hunting territory. Thus, it may have been that Asaʔɜnje, whose clansmen made up three-fourths of the village, had consolidated his authority beyond what was envisioned in the ideal model of Meta' village organization. Even though he did not belong to one of the principal chiefly clans, having such a large descent group concentrated in one village would have facilitated this.

Process in Village-Level Politics

The several case histories presented in this chapter illustrate the considerable variability that characterized precolonial Meta' village organization. Some communities, like Njindik and Mbo, diverged radically from the ideal model, while others, like Bat, conformed to it closely. The main difference between the ideal village and groups like the former two was that they had less centralized and more complicated ways of organizing the typical village-level activities. This resulted partly from the Meta' tendency to regard the village as more a series of discrete activities and leadership roles than as a general model of social organization. Certainly, as seen in the case histories provided by Meta' informants, political actors seem to have been more interested in exercising given types of leadership, carrying out specific activities, and controlling various *čam*-able properties than in translating some abstract conception of what a village should be onto reality.

This emphasis on the specific had one very important implication for the Meta' system of village organization: it meant that the distributions of rights over particular leadership roles, politically significant properties, and village-level activities could vary independently. Although the ideal model of village organization suggests that most of these rights would be under the control of a single *fɔn* and group of notables, in reality they were often held by the heads of different descent groups and subdivided in various ways. Thus, in Njindik there was dual organization within what was considered one village—two factions, based on lines of descent group cleavage, performed many of the same village-level activities independently.

The same emphasis on specific rights could also lead, as in Greater Mbo, to a complicated pattern of cross-cutting and overlapping activity groups in which it was difficult to decide which units should be termed "villages." At its lowest organizational levels, Mbo possessed minor leaders, such as Azoŋ3 and Atesaŋ, who had independent claims to chieftaincy but who assumed the role of senior village notable in most local affairs. On a slightly higher plane, two senior chiefs, Fɔmindam and

Ndabik, controlled the majority of typical village-level activities within their respective territories, as the ideal model of village organization suggests that they should. However, in the broadest contexts, these two chiefs cooperated to carry out certain functions and shared some of their prerogatives in the process. The resultant organizational pattern is most aptly described as one of "a village within a village within a village," and, as noted previously, it is equally arbitrary to say that Mbo was one village, two, or four.

In view of such diversity in the organization of actual Meta' communities, it would appear that the "village" could be most accurately defined by saying that it was simply a focusing in the distribution of rights over leadership roles, properties, and activities at some point in the overall political field. Such a definition would cover both groups that conformed to the ideal model and those with more diffuse and complicated structures. The informants' own statements that villages were places under their own *fɔn*s that carried out their activities independently may have been attempts to make a similar point. However, phrasing the matter in this way tends to conceal the high degree of variability that was present in Meta' village organization.

In much of the case material presented here, two processes characteristic of Meta' village politics have been apparent:

1. the sequence of lineage segmentation and making payments by which new leaders within a chiefly clan section achieved the rank of *fɔn*, and

2. the emergence of different types of village organization through competition between the head of a village's chiefly clan and the leader of its "original settlers."

These were not routine processes with invariably the same outcome. In some cases (e.g., those of Čiganjɛʔ and Awaʔmbaŋ in Gunɔbɛŋ), the new chieftaincies were purely matters of rank, while in other instances (e.g., that of Atesaŋ in Small Mbo), cadets of the chiefly clan section managed to establish themselves as important chieflets within their parent villages. In still other situations, such men went even further by displacing the original chiefs of their home communities (case histories showing this were collected, although none have been presented here).

In a similar fashion, competition between the original settlers and the chiefly clan within a village did not always lead to the same result. In Njindɨk, for example, Tɛče, who was the leader of the original settlers, had remained the effective village leader, even though he was not recognized as a *fɔn*. In Gunɔbɛŋ, by contrast, the late-coming *Fɔn* Fɔmɨndam emerged as the dominant power, and Azoŋɔ, the head of the original settlers, had to accept a subordinate role. Also, as mentioned earlier, the factional conflicts in Gunɔbɛŋ and Njindɨk varied considerably in intensity. Njindɨk remained a fragile union of two openly hostile factions, while in Gunɔbɛŋ the rival leaders had smoothed over some of their differences and expressed more unity for the sake of achieving common goals.

In any given case, the outcome of both processes mentioned above depended on various leaders' access to political resources and their abilities in strategy and planning. The greatest single resource was the support of a large group of agnates. Numerous Meta' informants identified this as the key factor determining success in contests for village leadership, and the case material presented in this chapter seems to bear them out. In Bat, Chief Asaʔɔnje's having achieved the status of *fɔn* when no member of his clan had previously done so may be explained partly by the fact that his clansmen comprised three-fourths of the villagers. Similarly, Fɔmɨndam's position as a senior chief in Gunɔbɛŋ was reinforced by the fact that his agnates made up two-thirds of the population, while those of his rival, Azoŋɔ, represented less than a fifth. In the case of Njindɨk, Tɛče's own descent group was not large, but he was the leader of a coalition of small clan sections that represented two-thirds of the village population and had aligned itself against Njirɔbaʔ. Finally, in Small Mbo, where Atesaŋ and Ndabɨk were fairly evenly matched with descent groups of about twenty households each, it could be argued that this factor was partly responsible for the persistence of their cooperative arrangement.

However, a large descent group was not the only resource that was important in village-level political competition. As has been seen in the case of Atesaŋ, having "sense" (*we*) was an asset that sometimes tipped the balance when a leader's position was under attack. This may have often been the deciding factor in cases like that of Small Mbo, where the size of the rival leaders' descent groups was comparable.

Belonging to one of the main chiefly clans was also an important resource in village-level political competition. A man like Atesaŋ could acquire the rank of *fɔn* with relative ease, since it was expected that some segment heads in descent groups like his would become chiefs as part of the normal process of lineage segmentation and also because his being *fɔn* did not threaten the monopoly of the dominant chiefly groups. This in turn legitimized his status as a contender for actual village leadership. By contrast, belonging to a low-ranked descent group was a definite liability. This is seen in the cases of men like Tɛče and Azoŋ3, who had little hope of being recognized as *fɔn*s even after they became *de facto* leaders of their villages.

A variety of strategies was also possible in village-level political competition. Contenders from low-ranked descent groups, for example, often sought to counterbalance the power of the *fɔn* by making alliances with chiefs outside the village. This is shown in the case of Azoŋ3, who re-established his rights to noble game by purchasing them from a powerful *fɔn* in another valley. A similar approach is apparent in the history of a low-ranking clan section in a village that has not been discussed here. In the earliest times, its members found themselves oppressed by the chiefly clan in their village. To remedy this, they moved to a neighboring community and shifted their allegiance to its *fɔn*. However, when they found their treatment little different, they returned to their original site, and, at the same time, began to take part in some village-level activities at the compound of a third neighboring *fɔn* who was himself in great need of supporters. Subsequently, the members of this lowly clan section maintained themselves by playing their original village chief and the third *fɔn* against each other, a strategy that they have maintained into modern times.

Two of the most common themes in precolonial case histories are arrangements where different chiefs cooperate "as brothers" and sudden encounters in which one rival for village leadership "consumes" (*jig3*) another. Examples of the brotherhood motif are found in the accommodation between Ndabɨk and Atesaŋ and in that of the chiefs of Greater Mbo, who "drank from a single cup." As the cases illustrate, it was not only when rival leaders were of the same clan that these arrangements occurred, and some such alliances were mutually beneficial, especially where the rivals for leadership were fairly evenly matched.

The precolonial case histories that were collected contain an almost equal number of instances where the ethic of brotherly cooperation between leaders was maintained as cases in which it broke down. Frequently, in situations of the latter type, the contenders are said to have resorted to violence.[3] In one case reported from a Meta' village, the successful rival for chieftaincy is said to have used *tɜkɜnɜ* to execute his opponent. This was apparently an open violation of the rules governing the employment of this executioner-masker, since the victim had not committed an offense. However, the brothers of the slain village leader, fearful for their own lives, let the matter rest.

A survey of several precolonial village histories thus seems to indicate that there were strong elements of both regularity and variability (or should we say regular variability?) in Meta' political behavior. Some almost stereotyped processes can be found in the case material, such as the one by which new chiefs were created within the chiefly clan section and the ever-present conflict between original settlers and members of the chiefly group. It has likewise been possible to identify the more important resources and strategies used in village-level political competition, as well as the liabilities under which certain groups suffered. And finally, we have noted recurrent themes in the development of village organization—e.g., cooperative arrangements in which two chiefs acted as "brothers" versus confrontations in which one rival "consumed" the other. Yet it must also be stressed that these regularities merely reflected certain traditions and constraints within which village-level political competition was carried out. The outcome of this process was by no means either determined or predictable.

---

3. That no examples of the latter type appear in this chapter is partly an accident of the villages that were chosen for presentation and partly a result of the informants' dislike of revealing such conflicts. It seems possible that there had been violent episodes in Bat, and informants from Gunɜbɛŋ also hinted at this.

TEN

Political Organization in the Intervillage Sphere

IN THIS chapter, I shall present an ideal model of the wider Meta' polity, based upon the general statements of knowledge-able informants, in order to contextualize the case histories of intervillage conflict to be analyzed in Chapter 11. Despite its lack of strongly centralized authority, Meta' society was noteworthy for the wide-ranging political integration that it was able to achieve. In immediate precolonial times, there existed an extensive polity that covered approximately 335 square kilometers and had a population of roughly 20,000. These people occupied some 30 villages scattered about in three different valleys.[1]

Of the fact that the Meta' villages did constitute a political community, there can be little doubt. However, since the polity was based upon a variety of principles, its organizational pattern is not easily defined. Here, I shall approach the task by taking inventory of the different modes of relationship and describing the situations in which they came into play.

Informants' Conceptions of the Meta' Polity

As seen most clearly in the customs surrounding blood guilt, Meta' political unity depended more than anything else upon

1. The number of villages in precolonial Meta' cannot be known with certainty. As we have just seen in Chapter 9, the boundaries of such communities were sometimes ambiguous, and it requires a detailed inquiry into the local history before each case can be clarified. Since this kind of in-depth investigation was not carried out in all three of the main Meta' valleys, it is impossible to be confident in stating the total number of villages that existed in precolonial times.

the concepts of brotherhood and shared patrilineal descent. When asked why a murderer would suffer *ndɔn* for killing a fellow Meta', informants usually replied that this was because the Meta' were "brothers" (*bɔrangɔp*) or "people of one clan" (*bɜt nga nibi mɔʔ*). If pressed further, some would add that all were descended from two men, Tɜmbɜŋjɔ and Tɜɣɜnič̌a, who were themselves sons of one father. Putative common descent was likewise used to explain why villages in different valleys assisted each other in wars against outsiders and why many restrictions were placed on the conduct of intrapolity warfare.

However, despite such apparent consensus regarding pan-Meta' brotherhood, certain facts suggest that this belief was more an expression of political ideology than one of historical fact. It became the basis for action only in certain limited contexts and was generally ignored in discussions of other aspects of Meta' sociopolitical organization. For example, many informants cited the *absence* of common patrilineal descent as the reason why members of different Meta' clans could freely intermarry without suffering *ndɔn*. Furthermore, as noted in Chapter 4, the picture of precolonial Meta' society that emerges from an investigation of individual clan histories and migration legends is one of fifteen or so unrelated descent groups, co-resident in a single polity. While a few of these did claim remote patrilineal ties, most asserted that they were not so linked. Thus the principle that all Meta' were "brothers" was applied very selectively. Although it served to organize some relationships in the wider society, it was largely irrelevant in others.

Patrilineal Descent and Internal Polity Organization

Turning from the informants' conceptions of the Meta' polity as a whole to its specific organization, patrilineal descent once again plays a central role. Most significantly, the notion of common descent provided the basis for a society-wide network of clan relationships that cross-cut the affiliations of localized clan sections to particular villages. Such ties of clanship were of both practical and moral significance. Given Meta' rules about property, even distant clanfellows were linked by residual interests in each others' estates. Moreover, the beliefs that all members of the same clan bore a moral responsibility toward one another, and that loyalty among agnatic kin was sanctioned by *ndɔn*, laid the foundations for cooperation between even widely separated clan sections. Since Meta' descent groups usually had segments in different villages and valleys, precolonial travelers often relied upon agnates in the areas they visited to provide hospitality and protection.

There was also considerable cooperation in formal descent group activities among scattered clan segments. For example, the leaders of many related clan sections might participate in the rites done to settle a serious intralineage conflict, since the *ndɔn* caused by such incidents potentially threatened them all. Similarly, all the sections of a clan that were resident in a single valley might send representatives to attend each others' major mortuary celebrations and rituals done to resolve incest. In chiefly descent groups, such ties of ceremonial cooperation sometimes extended much further. Among the Bɔnjɔ, for example, chiefs in the Bome and Zang valleys regularly participated in the installation rites for their counterparts.[2] Ties of clan affiliation thus ramified throughout Meta' society, creating cooperative relationships among clanfellows living in different areas and establishing lines of cleavage between them and the members of other groups.

A second way in which clanship became important in the organization of the wider society was by defining relationships among villages in terms of the clan affiliations of their respective chiefs. This influenced both alliance formation in intervillage warfare (see pp. 252–253, 260–261) and nonviolent political competition in the intervillage sphere. Since the great majority of chiefs belonged to just two clans (Bɔnjɔ and Mindik), their descent links provided another society-wide framework for the structuring of political relations. In the most generalized conceptualization of this system, all villages having Bɔnjɔ heads were opposed to those with Mindik chiefs, while on a lower structural level, the major subdivisions of each chiefly clan be-

2. In the present chapter the actual names of descent groups and villages are employed rather than pseudonyms. It would be impossible to discuss the Meta' system of intervillage organization in a meaningful way without using such names.

came the basis for alliances and oppositions between specific villages. Among the Mɨndɨk, for example, there were a number of semi-autonomous segments that claimed descent from different sons of Tзɣзniča, the legendary founder of the clan. While the leaders of these segments are said to have been each others' strongest rivals in many contexts, they sometimes also united as sons of Tзɣзniča to oppose outsiders. This was likely, for instance, in intrapolity warfare.

In situations like this, where the network of chiefly clan affiliations became the basis of political relationships within the wider polity, villages were the primary units for organizing support. The members of the several nonchiefly clans in each village would temporarily disregard their own agnatic links to the outside and adopt the clan ties of their chiefs as the basis for relating to people of other villages. Men of such nonchiefly groups would naturally try to avoid harming their clanfellows if they found themselves face-to-face during an intervillage war, but they were obliged to unite with their village mates against all outsiders, including these agnates. Any failing to do so would be regarded as traitors by their co-villagers and very likely deprived of their rights in the place.

The twin principles of grouping by descent (*nibi*) and territory (*bεŋ*) thus combined to produce a complex system of political alignments for Meta' society as a whole. While the notion of territory grouped people into villages, that of descent laid the foundation for a comprehensive set of relationships among such units. For the members of nonchiefly clans, the use of this dual model did pose some contradictions. However, these were partially offset by the concept of traditional associations between particular chiefly and nonchiefly clans. Some of these groups are said to have always "traveled together" in past migrations and to have thereby developed a kind of "brotherhood" through long-term association. They are also reported to have settled in the same villages at the end of their migrations.

In general, these claims are substantiated by the evidence on precolonial Meta' settlement. In the Bome valley, for instance, where the location of all minimal lineages in 1900 was carefully reconstructed, there was a strong residential association between specific chiefly and commoner groups. In terms of chiefly clan affiliation, the entire valley was roughly divided into two sides. On one side, most village chiefs belonged to the Bɔnjɔ clan, while, on the other, they were Mindik. In addition, the members of particular nonchiefly clans were generally restricted to a single zone. For example, the Bɔrangɔp and Mitiŋ resided in villages with Bɔnjɔ chiefs, while the Mɜnɔŋ, Ʒzwe3zuʔ, and Bogwanik were almost always located on the Mindik side. Despite a few exceptions (i.e., small Bɔrangɔp or Bɔnjɔ lineages in villages with Mindik chiefs and two cases in which the village head belonged to an altogether different clan), the overall pattern was clearly an important factor in the political structure of the Bome valley.

The significance of these residence patterns was that they reduced the potential for conflicting loyalties in a situation where descent and local group ties cross-cut and villages united or opposed each other on the basis of their chiefs' clan affiliations. Thus, if the "Bɔnjɔ villages" united against the "Mindik villages" in Bome, the problem of contradictory clan and village loyalties would face only a few small lineages. Traditional ties between unrelated clans thus reinforced the system of intervillage alliances based on chiefly descent groups.

A final way in which patrilineal descent organization influenced political relations in the intervillage sphere was through the ranking of clans. Each such group had a slightly different position in an overall hierarchy, and the political rights of its members were sometimes affected by this. For example, the most prestigious *čam*-able dances and costumes were difficult for segments of humble clans to acquire. Moreover, the properties that represented village-level political authority, such as the right of noble game, were usually restricted to the highest-ranking groups.

There seem to have been three broad categories in the Meta' hierarchy of descent groups: (1) chiefly clans, (2) ordinary groups that suffered only the inability to acquire chiefship, and (3) groups that were described as *nibi ko* ("oppressed clans"). However, there was considerable vagueness in this schema and disagreement among informants about the assignment of particular clans to each category. Thus, a group that was generally regarded as "oppressed" might count some *de facto* village heads among its members (see the case of Tɛče in Njindik for example, pp. 203–205). In fact, the only aspect of the system upon which all informants concurred was the identity of the highest groups: those clans that possessed village chiefs were invariably listed as being the most prestigious.

Ɨɣi Wit: The Lost Man

In precolonial days, clanship was not the sole basis for cooperative kin-based relations between different Meta' communities. Because of frequent intervillage and intervalley marriages, a diffuse network of affinal and uterine ties pervaded the entire polity. Such relationships provided an additional source of security for travelers, since they could rely upon their nonagnatic kin for protection. Moreover, in those instances where wayfarers were attacked or abducted, unique procedures for assigning moral and financial liability came into play under the institution known as *iɣi wit*. The literal meaning of *iɣi wit* is "the eye of the man." Its primary reference is to cases in which people become "lost" (*nimi*) by disappearing without a trace. Whenever this happened, men who stood in "wife-taking" relationships to the clan section of the missing person and who also lived in the general direction that he had been traveling when last seen incurred a degree of responsibility for his disappearance. The phrase "the eye of the man" was used to describe this situation because the persons held accountable had "watched the lost man go and not seen him return." This meant—from the point of view of the close agnates of the "victim"—that such people might well have had a hand in killing him or selling him as a slave. Such a state of affairs left them quite vulnerable to *ndɔn* brought on by the complaints of the lost man's kin.

These beliefs set the stage for payments by certain men whose wives belonged to the clan section of the missing person. Normally, each son-in-law living in the area concerned was expected to present a fowl to the head of his wife's *mban* group within a few days of the disappearance. Any who failed to comply promptly were obliged to give goats to the leaders of their wives' clan sections instead. The latter then sacrificed the animals and performed rites to absolve their sons-in-law. In their ritual statements, they asserted that those who had given the goats had had no hand in the death or sale of their brother, and that therefore no *ndɔn* from the case should affect their households. This finished the matter for the time being.

However, a case of *iɣi wit* also established a lasting potential for *ndɔn* and permanent indebtedness on the part of "suspect" clan sections.[3] If any man living in the general direction that the lost man had traveled later married a woman from his group, he was required to present an additional goat along with his bridewealth. The leaders of his wife's clan section then sacrificed the animal and performed a ritual to clear their new affine from any *ndɔn* stemming from the previous instance of *iɣi wit*. Such relations of potential indebtedness theoretically lasted forever, and long after the details of the original event had been forgotten, a diviner might still attribute some illness or misfortune to the ancient case of *iɣi wit*. Then another goat would have to be given.

Iɣi wit indebtedness also existed in a variety of other situations. Thus, if a person was "lost" in the area where a daughter's daughter of a man from his own clan section had married, the husband of that woman was obliged to present a goat of *iɣi wit* to her mother's agnates. Moreover, when a man suddenly died while visiting the next village, the husbands of his clan sisters who resided in the area were generally held accountable, and homicides and killings during intrapolity warfare likewise established debt relationships between the groups of the slayer and the victim. During the time of fieldwork, *iɣi wit* debts were still paid, since many people feared that they would suffer *ndɔn* if they ignored the custom. However, the practice was becoming cumbersome in a situation where travel was freer and people often died away from their homes.

The primary significance of the institution of *iɣi wit* appears to have been in that it improved personal security within the Meta' polity. It utilized the widespread network of affinal ties and the fear of *ndɔn* to make the safety of travelers a matter of general public concern, and since in an actual case there would

3. Usually the groups owing and receiving *iɣi wit* payments were clan sections, but their size seems to have varied to some extent from clan to clan and case to case.

probably be several affines who lived in the direction that a lost man had traveled, even a single instance of *iɣi wit* would be likely to establish many long-term debt relationships. Because of *iɣi wit*, no person could disappear from Meta' society without someone being held accountable.

Market Organization

The internal market network was another important facet of the wider Meta' polity. In immediate precolonial times, a complex trading system existed through which several markets served each of the three main Meta' valleys. Various markets, whose approximate locations are shown in Map 3 (see p. 64), were held on different days within the eight-day weekly cycle.[4] The items exchanged included a variety of crops and subsistence products (maize, beans, yams, colocasia, palm oil, palm wine, meat, groundnuts, fowl, and tobacco); handicrafts (clay pots, raffia bags, and blacksmith wares); livestock (goats, pigs, and fowl); and imported goods (brass rods, hoes, salt, and cam-wood). Slaves and luxury items—such as cloth, guns, gunpowder, and carved stools and masks—were rarely if ever traded in the open marketplace. Yet when professional merchants exchanged them privately, their flows still paralleled those of the more mundane goods. Such transactions were often conducted nearby the market and on market day.

Meta' markets and exchange networks served both to circulate goods locally and to transfer products through this society to other groups within the regional system (see Chapter 3 and Dillon 1981). The latter was accomplished by a relay trade. Although Meta' merchants sometimes bypassed nearer markets in order to participate in more distant ones within the polity itself, they generally did not travel farther than the closest markets in neighboring groups. In a similar fashion, traders from other societies were rarely permitted to penetrate beyond those Meta' markets that were close to their home villages.

As one of the most common reasons for travel, marketing was clearly the cause of considerable insecurity in intervillage social

4. See Dillon (1981: 368) for details on the scheduling of precolonial Meta' markets.

relations. Traders faced threats such as kidnapping and robbery, and markets were often held on the outskirts of villages in order to minimize the damages from violent disturbances. Yet since it prompted measures to contain conflict, marketing can also be said to have contributed to security in the wider Meta' polity. As many people routinely traded, social relations became more predictable within this zone. To assure their safety, the marketers relied upon ties of uterine, agnatic, and affinal kinship with members of other villages. Marketing journeys were in fact among the most common occasions on which such kinship-based alliances were activated. By contrast, non-Meta' traders who wished to obtain protection from local hosts would initiate voluntary pacts of friendship, backed by supernaturally sanctioned oaths (Warnier 1985: 84–87).

The leaders of those Meta' villages in which markets were held likewise took active measures to ensure tranquility. For example, they customarily performed special rituals shortly after the inauguration a new market in order to bring their mystical powers to bear on potential violators of the market peace. Typically, the *mikum si* of the village entered the market to bury a dog and some weapons of war while pouring from their sacrificial cups and stating that anyone who subsequently harmed a market-bound person would suffer *ndɔn*. They sometimes also ordered the regulatory masker *tɜkɜnɜ* to strike the ground at each entrance to the market in order to intensify the curse.[5] In a more routine fashion, the chief of a village in which a market was held, normally lent his authority to it by holding court in a hut just outside the marketplace. From this vantage point, he and the other notables could employ their usual techniques to manage any violent altercations that occurred.

Ritual Specialists

Another factor that helped to order relationships in the inter-village sphere was a complex system of hereditary ritual special-

5. Popular legends maintain that human sacrificial victims were buried to establish even more powerful prohibitions at the inauguration of great markets such as the one in Nyen-Medig. However, it was impossible to verify these accounts.

ists. All such practitioners were referred to by the general Meta' term for "specialist " (*wit ɜtu ɜfay'i*), and they provided solutions to a wide variety of problems that affected individuals and groups. For example, certain ritual experts, such as those who dealt with acts of symbolic aggression (see pp. 181–185), participated in the resolution of overt social conflicts. Others handled supernatural dangers deriving from deaths by unnatural causes, and still others operated oath-taking sites. All of these specialists were the hereditary leaders of localized descent units larger than single *mban* groups, since their roles were considered *čam*-able properties and associated with the headship of such segments. However, in other respects the statuses of the experts were quite varied. Some were important village chiefs, others *mikum si*, and still others simply *mikum ɜgɔ*. Moreover, while certain of the specialties conferred considerable prestige upon their practitioners, others were disgraceful and dangerous jobs.

The ways in which particular specialist roles were introduced to Meta' society remain obscure. Most present successors of precolonial experts merely say, "My fathers performed this work from the earliest times." However, it is also possible that the roles had been purchased at some point in the past. This is suggested by the fact that in 1900 all of the specialties were treated as *čam*-able properties so that any clan segment that lacked one could, at least theoretically, acquire it. In practice, however, transfers of the rights to fulfill these roles took place only under unusual circumstances. No specialist, it is said, would have wanted to grant comparable powers to the head of a related clan section residing within his own area of operation, since this would have reduced his opportunities to profit from his role. Nor would he have wished to release the specialty to members of a completely different clan. Thus, rights to ritual specialties were most commonly passed to geographically distant junior segment heads within the donor's own clan. Occasionally, they were also *čam*-ed by a sister's son, but it was preferable to avoid even transactions of this sort, since they might ultimately lead to the specialty being widely distributed within two clans instead of one.

In 1900 several types of ritual specialists were found within Meta': (1) those who dealt with cases of symbolic aggression (e.g., slashing a plantain stalk in your opponent's yard, throwing a spear at his roof, or committing suicide outside his door); (2) those dealing with cases of actual physical aggression (e.g., burning an opponent's house or murdering him); (3) those who coped with the effects of death from unnatural causes (e.g., death by lightning, death by falling from a tree, death with a swollen belly) and death during pregnancy; (4) those who handled threats to the welfare of society as a whole (e.g., the "rumor specialist" described below); and (5) those who operated oath-taking sites or oracles for the purpose of determining which party to a dispute might be lying.

In every instance (except that of the oathing experts) the power of these specialists depended upon their having exclusive jurisdiction over particular kinds of cases within given territories. Persons suffering *ndɔn* from any of the causes mentioned above could receive help only from the specialists in whose zones they resided. Moreover, their monopoly, like the rights to other *čam*-able properties, was itself sanctioned by *ndɔn*. Anyone usurping it could be cursed by the words of the specialist.

The sizes of the specialists' territories varied considerably. Some, like those who removed *ndɔn* in cases of death by lightning and plantain slashing, served only one or two villages. Others, such as those who treated death from a swollen belly and the spreading of malicious rumors, had exclusive territories that encompassed five to ten communities, and as noted in Chapter 8, the ultimate homicide specialist had the entire Meta' polity as his area of operation.

At this point it may be useful to describe the way in which several ritual specialists carried out their particular roles:

ʒsum: This was the name for a kind of oath-taking site operated by three important village chiefs in the Mindik Clan (i.e., Tabi in the Zang valley, Fongu in Bome, and Fonnyen in the Medig valley). The *ʒsum*, which could be consulted for a fee of one or more brass rods, was used to determine the validity of contradictory testimonies in certain kinds of disputes, especially those concerning land and other property. The procedures involved were essentially the same as in the village-level oath-taking sessions described in Chapter 8. However, the *ʒsum* appears to have been exceedingly important as a means of dispute settlement in the precolonial period. It was reputed to have had awesome powers to "seize" (*gwi*) any person who lied to it, and the threat of consulting the shrine was frequently sufficient to prompt the guilty to confess. As noted earlier, the *ɔsum* differed from most of the other specialties in that the notable who possessed it did not have an exclusive area of operation. Since an *ɔsum* was located in each of the three Meta' valleys, people tended to bring their cases to the closest one. But consulting a different *ɔsum* would not be interpreted as a violation of their local specialist's rights. Moreover, there were many less renowned oath-taking sites in each valley. In this context, the importance of the *ɔsum* lay mainly in its prestige and its formidable reputation.

Ɔnibɔ: This was the name of a round stone possessed by the chief of Tuanyang village in the Bome valley, a notable of the Mindam Clan. Like the *ɔsum*, the *ɔnibɔ* could be used for oath-taking, but it was more famous for conferring the power to remove *ndɔn* after a death by *mɔro*.[6] The latter was a dreaded disease that typically caused the feet and belly of the victim to swell until he died (probably a chronic liver disorder, in the opinion of the doctor at nearby Acha Tugi Hospital). The Meta' believed that people became afflicted with *mɔro* for making false oaths on the *ɔsum*, as well as for unauthorized consumption of noble game, and certain other grave offenses. *Mɔro* was regarded as a highly contagious type of *ndɔn* that could quickly wipe out the clan section of its victim if the *ɔnibɔ* specialist was not summoned.

The specialists who handled cases of *mɔro* typically claimed large territories. The Tuanyang chief, for example, served the entire Bome valley, a zone of about ten villages. However, his right to practice in one part of Bome came under attack during the early colonial period. At this time, the local holder of *ɔsum* had attempted a ruse in order to gain *ɔnibɔ* and the right to treat cases of *mɔro* within his own village. In the Zang valley, there were two practitioners who dealt with *mɔro*. One of these belonged to the Mindam clan, while the other was of the Mɛnɔŋ

6. In other valleys, where the comparable specialty was in the hands of various clans, it was referred to by different names.

group, and each had a relatively large zone of operation, including several villages.

ʒnibʒ was regarded as a very dangerous specialty, since the expert who attempted to remove *ndɔn* after a death by *mɔro* might easily be struck down himself. He was accordingly given generous payments, which included a goat, some brass rods, a fowl, and a quantity of palm wine. The people of the compound where the death had occurred normally set these things outside and remained hidden in their huts while the specialist performed his rites. By doing so they hoped to prevent any *ndɔn* from clinging to them or remaining in the place. As the ritual expert departed, local residents sometimes also ran after him and fired their guns in the air at the first stream that he crossed. They then shouted that since the man of ʒnibʒ had taken away all of the *ndɔn*, it should affect them no longer.

Mbaŋ Mʒniʒ: This was a walking stick that empowered its owner to deal with cases involving malicious rumors. One such staff was possessed by a lineage head in Bessi village of the Medig valley, who claimed that entire valley as his exclusive zone. Whenever a dangerous rumor (e.g., a false accusation of witchcraft or theft) came to the attention of the leaders of a Medig village, they summoned this expert. The *mbaŋ mʒniʒ* man then went to the compound of the last person known to have transmitted the story and planted the special walking stick in his doorway. This was believed to threaten the people of this place with *ndɔn*, since responsibility for the rumor had been laid at their feet. It was now necessary for the compound head to pay the specialist one brass rod and identify his own source for the story before the latter would remove his staff and say an *njɔm* to end the potential for *ndɔn*. In this way, the *mbaŋ mʒniʒ* specialist traced the rumor from one person to another back to its originator. Once he had been located, he normally fined the person a stack of brass rods coiled into bracelets "as high as his own walking stick," and this finished the matter.

To grasp the full significance of this account, one must recall that the Meta' regarded speech as an inherently powerful thing. Therefore, when a village was alive with talk about a particular offense, the combined voices of its people were believed to constitute an overwhelming ritual statement (*njɔm*) against the offender. In this context, the *mbaŋ mɜniɜ* specialist provided a method of curtailing the dangerous force of speech and making citizens more careful about passing on unsubstantiated reports.

3bɛne: This was the most famous of all Meta' ritual specialties. It derived its name from the special walking stick carried by its practitioner, the chief of Zang Tabi village. The staff was believed to convey the power to remove *ndɔn* arising from a homicide. As noted earlier, the initial steps in the resolution of such cases were taken by the leaders of the village in which the killing had occurred. Following this, the murderer was obliged to travel to Zang Tabi to present a slave to the *3bɛne* specialist. However, his journey was complicated by the fact that certain intermediaries in each part of Meta' had the job of "showing the road to Zang" to all killers. These escorts had to be compensated for their services, and one could not bypass them without incurring both their anger and that of the *3bɛne* specialist himself. Anyone attempting to do so would ultimately be forced to pay even greater fines.

After the killer had satisfied such middlemen, he traveled to the compound of the *3bɛne* specialist with a goat lashed to one arm and a slave tied to the other. The slave was welcomed by the expert as the symbolic replacement of the murder victim and given a place to settle in his village. The specialist then took the murderer into his sacrificial hut, shaved his head, and performed a ritual designed to "wash" (*so*) all the *ndɔn* from his head. This finished the matter, and the murderer was free to return to society as a normal member. As noted earlier, Chief Tabi of Zang was the only practitioner of the *3bɛne* specialty in Meta'.

In the preceding pages the way in which the Meta' belief in *ndɔn* provided the basis for a society-wide system of hereditary ritual specialists has been explained. The dependence of the public upon these resolution agents raises the question of whether their ritual expertise enabled them to acquire substantial political power in the intervillage sphere. Here, the answer appears to be a qualified no. It is certainly true that some ritual specialties did confer prestige upon their practitioners and allowed them to accumulate wealth. It is also clear that during the colonial period certain village heads based claims to authority over entire valleys or Meta' society as a whole on their possession of ritual specialties like *ɜsum* and *ɜbɛne*. However, careful inquiry with many informants (including the supporters of chiefs claiming seniority on such grounds) indicated that these specialties were not viewed as a means of "ruling" (*itumbi*) the people of other villages in precolonial times. The specialization of *ɜbɛne* perhaps came the closest to this, since the resolution of homicide cases was regarded as one of the most vital legal functions. It was also inextricably bound up with the concept of a Meta' polity. Yet even this renowned specialty remained in the final analysis a service to disputants, and did not provide the basis for an activist legal authority.

Other Modes of Conflict Resolution

To a considerable extent, conflict resolution in the intervillage sphere depended upon ritual specialists such as those just discussed. However, many disputants also found other means of redress. Techniques of self-help were especially important. As the relationship between the parties grew more distant, they naturally hesitated less in seizing hostages in lieu of debts or in starting fights.

The approach to resolving such disputes did not differ dramatically from that seen in intravillage cases. In most instances, settlement was sought through the village-level conflict-resolution mechanisms. In a fashion quite analogous to modern state-level legal systems, a number of specific offenses came under the jurisdiction of the local authorities. Thus, for example, outbreaks of fighting, instances of symbolic aggression, and cases of theft were all handled by the leaders of the village in which they occurred, regardless of where the parties might reside within Meta' territory.[7]

Certain conventions regarding internal warfare also helped to regulate conflict in the intervillage sphere. According to a strict interpretation of Meta' political ideology, intervillage warfare

7. Several of the cases presented in Chapter 8 support such a claim (see Cases 1, 2, 3, and 5). Although the resolution process was not always smooth or automatic, most conflicts were said to have been ultimately resolved in something approximating the ideal fashion. See Chapter 11 for further analysis of actual conflict and resolution patterns in the intervillage arena.

was impossible. It was clearly inconsistent with the concept of pan-Meta' brotherhood as well as with a legal system that defined intrapolity homicide as mystically dangerous fratricide. Yet as several case histories attest (see Cases 14, 15, and 17 below, pp. 250–251, 253–254, 260–262), wars of this kind did occur. Even then, however, the violence could be halted and a resolution achieved through customary procedures.

The difference between internal warfare (*ibit nuʔu nɔp*) and fighting (*ɜčɔp*) was rather clear-cut. In terms of the limitations placed on the expression of violence, internal warfare was a form of conflict intermediate between interlineage fighting and warfare against non-Meta' groups. In internal warfare, the principle of a supernaturally sanctioned moral community was temporarily suspended, and the killing of an enemy became, for the time at least, a legitimate act. However, many tactics used in external warfare were still not permitted: surprise attacks and night raids were not undertaken, and warriors did not attempt to kill women and children, to take heads, or to burn enemy settlements. Moreover, despite its legal permissibility, killing was still regarded as a shameful deed, and there was always uncertainty concerning its potential to cause *ndɔn*.

The actual fighting in internal warfare seems to have been loosely organized. Usually, warriors met along a relatively well-defined battlefront located somewhere between their opposed villages. Then, armed with Dane guns and spears, they dispersed by small groups into the tall grass and bush and attempted to ambush similar parties coming from the other side. Pitched battles are said not to have occurred, and the fighting was usually restricted to the area of the front itself.

The resolution procedures in intervillage warfare resembled those employed to deal with cases of fighting. Combat was customarily halted when representatives of one or both sides ran onto the battlefield and planted a tall bamboo pole trimmed with branches of the sacred plant *kiŋ*. In internal warfare, however, this act was performed by hereditary specialists, several of whom resided in each of the three Meta' valleys. The ritual use of *kiŋ* also differed in that it here served to reestablish the principle of a supernaturally sanctioned moral community after the temporary suspension of that premise. Although killing was not regarded as mystically dangerous in the context of an internal war, the placing of *kiŋ* altered this situation so that, once again, anyone who slew an enemy would suffer *ndɔn*.

In describing the use of *kiŋ*, it should be stressed that this procedure was neither automatic nor infallible. The Meta' were not superstitious beings, paralyzed by their fears of mystical danger, nor were they slaves of custom. Indeed, the placing of *kiŋ* is probably best viewed as an attempt by responsible parties to curtail violence by intimidating the fighters and playing upon their latent fears. One informant described how, upon finding himself ignored, the man bearing *kiŋ* might pretend to be wounded in order to shock the combatants to their senses. On the other hand, the placing of *kiŋ* was also clearly an overture that could, under certain circumstances, be rejected. Another informant revealed that the bearer of *kiŋ* could himself be shot if he came from one side to stop the fighting without seriously intending a discussion of the issues.

When it proved possible to halt the hostilities, the parties could begin to negotiate. By custom, a meeting was held on the battlefield, with each group providing palm wine and appointing several notables or chiefs as its spokesmen. Although there existed no authority capable of imposing a solution, the parties were often motivated to settle out of fear of the killing that further fighting would entail. In addition to the serious threat of supernatural danger posed by bloodshed among "brothers," intrasocietal strife was recognized as creating severe problems for affinal relationships within a compact and densely settled community of intermarrying villages. As one informant put it, the Meta' tried to curtail warfare with neighboring villages "so that they would have somebody to marry from."

Any negotiated settlement of an internal war was customarily sealed by joint sacrifices and the establishment of a magical prohibition (*čɜp*) against breaking the terms of the peace. First, each side provided a goat to be sacrificed on the former battleground. The leaders then addressed a joint statement to Ŋwiɜ, the traditional high God of the Meta', in which they asked that he eradicate the lineage of any man who subsequently crossed over their common boundary in order to wage war. They also prayed that *ndɔn* would "seize" (*gwi*) anyone who recounted the war, since such talk was itself believed to cause *ndɔn* for those who had fought against their "brothers."[8]

Ikwiri: Joining the Voices of the People in One

Ikwiri was another institution that organized relations in the wider Meta' polity. It took its name from the verb *kwiri*, meaning "to gather together." In precolonial times, *ikwiri* was a periodic assembly at which people from many villages met and used the power of their collective voice (*njɔm*) to ward off generalized threats, such as epidemics, famines, and sudden increases in thievery and wife abduction. But the forum could also be used to promulgate new laws backed by supernatural sanctions (e.g., rules prohibiting the men of a given area from taking each others' wives), to place curses on unknown offenders, and as a setting for oath-taking.

There was considerable disagreement among informants concerning the places in which *ikwiri* was held in precolonial times. Some asserted that only five or six village chiefs were entitled to call an *ikwiri*, while others claimed that any *fɔn* could do so. The most likely interpretation is a combination of the two versions. It seems probable that the most effective type of *ikwiri* could be held at only one or two traditionally sanctioned sites in each Meta' valley, but that a lesser form could be observed independently by any village if a problem seemed to be affecting just that place. In the following section, only the larger intervillage assembly (*ikwiri kyɛŋ*) will be described, since this alone was significant to the organization of the wider polity (see Chapter 8 for a description of village-level *ikwiri* rites).

Ikwiri kyɛŋ is said to have been held as the need for it was felt. There appear to have been five or six regular sites, including Ku and 3zi-Funam in the Bome valley, Nyen and Mbemi in the Medig valley, and Zang Tabi and Njah Etuh in the Zang valley. According to some informants, the chiefs of these villages had been instructed to call the people to observe *ikwiri* on their dancing fields by the legendary founders of Meta' society; this then

8. Several informants mentioned an alternative method of establishing a *čɜp*. This entailed burying a living dog, or even a human victim, on the battlefield, along with representative weapons of war. However, the use of the procedure was not reported in any case history.

became their exclusive right. Others claimed that *ikwiri kyɛŋ* was performed in these villages simply because they were among the largest and their chiefs the most powerful. Whatever the case, most are in agreement that *ikwiri kyɛŋ* was held in rotation at all of these places. After each assembly, the location for the next meeting was chosen, and *ikwiri kyɛŋ* would not return to the first site until all of the others had been visited. Although there was no specified interval of time between sessions, some informants estimated that it normally took about two years to complete a full cycle.

Ikwiri kyɛŋ is said to have been attended by five to ten representatives from each of a number of villages, some of whom had inherited the right to speak at *ikwiri* whenever it was called in a given location. Certain meetings of *ikwiri kyɛŋ* appear to have been more widely attended than others. The assemblies at Nyen, for example, are said to have been the most famous and to have drawn people from many villages in all three Meta' valleys. By contrast, the rites at Zang Tabi—a much less centrally located village—were attended mainly by people of the Zang valley.

The activities that were performed at *ikwiri kyɛŋ* are difficult to reconstruct, since the institution was disrupted when the Germans forced many Meta' villages to move to Bali and not resumed upon their return. However, its overall organization appears to have been as follows: Talking drums were beaten throughout the night preceding an *ikwiri* to announce its occurrence and location. Then during the following morning or early afternoon, the leaders of all of the villages in attendance would meet privately behind the *mbɛŋ* ("fence of raffia mats") that screened the courtyard of the host chief. There, they would drink palm wine and discuss the matters to be brought up later at the public session on the dancing ground. During this preliminary meeting, the leaders would attempt to "fix their talk in one" (*tɛk ngam nga mɔʔ*) so that one of them could subsequently speak an *njɔm* ("ritual statement") that had been agreed upon by all. Such unanimity was important, since it was believed to strengthen the public *njɔm*. When the single representative uttered his statement, it was as if all the other leaders were speaking with him.

After reaching agreement on what would be said, the leaders emerged onto the chief's dancing field, where the common people were seated. Then their spokesman delivered the *njɔm* while the others performed appropriate ritual acts. The latter naturally differed according to the problems at hand. In many instances as the ceremonies ended, all those present would join their voices in a common cry (*ifɜča*) that was repeated by everyone within hearing distance. This was seen as an additional means of amplifying the *njɔm* of the leaders, and according to some informants, the shout would be taken up by one village after another until the voices of an entire valley or the whole Meta' population were united in one outcry.

As noted above, the precise character of the rites performed at *ikwiri kyɛŋ* varied with the problems that were addressed. When confronting an epidemic, for example, the leaders spoke an *njɔm* to the effect that the sickness should pass off into the air and be carried away by the breeze. They then "blessed the people" (*fa bɜt*) by swinging a fowl, with its wings flapping, over their heads.[9] According to some informants, the resultant stirring of the air was considered effective in attracting the attention of the god Ŋwiɜ. During the same sort of *ikwiri*, the leaders might walk in single file around the people seated on the dancing field and blow mouthfuls of palm wine, taken from their hereditary drinking horns, over their heads. (The meaning of this ritual act was not explored with informants. However, in other contexts it would be interpreted as a form of blessing that transferred the leaders' hereditary powers of speech directly to the people.) Finally, the fowl that had been used to *fa* the people would be thrown down in their midst and observed by everyone present. It had now become a symbol of the populace itself. If the bird defecated soon after its release, this was taken as a sign that "everything bad had been excreted" and that the epidemic would soon pass. This concluded the rites on the dancing field. Afterward the fowl that had been used would be kept alive by

9. The term *fa bɜt* is difficult to translate. It refers specifically to the act of swinging a fowl in this fashion during a ritual, but in rites like the one described here it takes on a more general meaning of bestowing some goodness on the people present. In other cases, it is done at the conclusion of rituals to end states of *ndɔn* and seems to signify that the problem is really finished.

the host chief as a sign that the country should dwell in peace and no longer be affected by sickness.

In cases where *ikwiri* was called to place a curse on thieves, a fowl also played an important role, but otherwise the rites were quite different. On such occasions, the fowl, now representing the thieves, would be killed on the dancing field and buried there to symbolize the offenders' becoming sick and dying. Everyone would then take dirt in his left hand and throw it down violently in order to cause the death of the thieves. At such times, the *njɔm* took the form of a curse, and parts of it were repeated in unison by all in attendance.

The rites of *ikwiri kyɛŋ* may be interpreted as a method of concentrating the power of speech of the entire polity and bringing it to bear on threats to the general welfare. Given Meta' beliefs about the power of speech, *ikwiri* represented the ultimate *njɔm*: when all Meta' spoke as one, how could the god Ŋwiɜ fail to answer their requests?

Ɨkwiri kyɛŋ was described by many informants as one of the most important features of precolonial Meta' political organization. According to one, it was "the highest court of the early days." Several also claimed that it was a means by which important chiefs tried to "rule" (*itumbɨ*) the people of other villages. This seems quite consistent with what we know of Meta' political ideology. Since the rites of *ikwiri* were thought to unleash the most potent forms of supernatural power, anyone who controlled them even indirectly would have considerable influence in the intervillage sphere. In this respect, *ikwiri* appears to have differed from ritual specialties like *ɜsum* that conferred upon their holders only very limited kinds of authority, and that were not described by informants as means of "ruling" the Meta' people.

Cooperation in External Warfare

A strong tradition of mutual aid in wars against outsiders also served to unify the Meta'. Although no centralized system for military planning encompassed the entire polity, even villages located in different valleys routinely assisted each other when threatened by external warfare. On such occasions, the organization was rather loose and improvisational. Groups of *mɜgwe* ("war scouts") and warriors simply assembled at the battlefront before dispersing in smaller groups to skirmish with the enemy. In ideal terms these wars were said to be waged on behalf of the chief on whose farmland or village territory the fighting occurred. Yet, aside from calling the people to war, providing extra gunpowder, and holding feasts to celebrate victories, host chiefs seem to have offered little leadership to the combatants. Whatever coordination was achieved at the battlefront usually derived from informal consultation among the war scouts of the villages involved.

In addition to securing the common defense, the institutions associated with external warfare also contributed to the integration of the Meta' polity in two other ways. First, the war-scout societies of the various villages in a valley customarily joined in certain ceremonial activities. If the chief of any village held an annual festival, for example, war scouts from other nearby communities would be likely to attend, and the scouts also assisted in the mortuary rites of noted warriors. Second, in at least the Medig area, there seems to have been a pattern of valley-wide cooperation in the rituals that preceded external war. According to several informants there were three long-established sites in the Medig villages of Mbemi, Guneku, and Nyen, where rites to promote success in warfare were conducted in a coordinated fashion. Whenever circumstances permitted, rituals were performed at all three locations before warriors entered battle against groups such as Bafut, and similar rites are said to have been observed annually at the start of the dry season. Accounts differed on whether the latter were part of a cycle or simply performed simultaneously in each village.

Čam-able Property and Intervillage Organization

The distribution of *čam*-able properties among clans and clan sections also lent structure to the wider Meta' polity in precolonial times. In addition to the various ritual specialties already discussed, the uneven distribution among descent groups of "dancing complexes" (i.e., the dances, costumes, instruments, and associated paraphernalia discussed in Chapters 7 and 8) clearly had such an effect. There were many *čam*-able properties of this type, and they varied considerably in prestige. Some were old and highly acclaimed items of Meta' culture, while others had been acquired shortly before 1900. Those that the informants considered most important included *kwɛbit, mɛndɛre, kwɛʔifɔ, ifuʔ, inyɛrɛsɛ,* and *ʒjɔŋ kɔm.* According to oral traditions, the majority of these had been introduced to Meta' society when the leaders of particular clan sections purchased them from neighboring groups. One significance of such *čam*-able properties was that they supplied standards for assessing the prestige of clans and clan sections. As noted earlier, some dancing complexes, like *kwɛʔifɔ,* were held as monopolies by descent groups of chiefly rank. Others were occasionally transferred between clans of intermediate status but generally denied to the members of lesser groups. However, even the lowest-ranked clans had their own dances, instruments, and costumes, and were therefore not completely eliminated from this mode of competition for prestige.

Dancing complexes were used most often during mortuary celebrations. When a person died, the exclusive dance of his clan section was customarily taken to the funeral. The lineages of all his sons-in-law were similarly obliged to perform their own special dances, and groups with which the deceased had voluntarily associated might be asked to come as well. The mortuary celebration of an important man or an old and revered woman thus became a stirring event at which the people of many descent groups and villages competed to offer the most prestigious dances and breathtaking executions.

The excitement produced on such occasions understandably gave rise to tensions, and each clan section typically feared that its masked dancers might be attacked with lethal "medicines" (*ifuʔ*). Performers were accordingly subjected to elaborate protective treatments on the evening before a mortuary celebration was held. However, funerals were also occasions for the people of different clan sections and villages to participate jointly in activities that were highly valued by all. There was usually much feasting, since each party of dancers had to be fed with a goat and given large quantities of palm wine. Moreover, everyone was free to take part in each dance as it was performed. Celebrating a person's career at the time of his death thus provided opportunities for both cooperation and competition, and it was *čam*-able properties that supplied the principal idiom for structuring social relations in this context.[10]

Another way in which the dancing complexes helped to organize relations within the wider society was through annual celebrations. Some dances, such as *kwɛbit* and *mɛndɛre*, were performed each year during the dry season. On such occasions, all the clan sections within a valley that owned a particular complex might agree to hold combined rites, and men of nonproprietor groups were likewise free to attend.

The segments of different clans that owned the same dancing complex could also join together whenever it was being granted to a new group. In such instances, representatives of all of the co-owning clan sections within a valley might meet to witness the *čam*-ing and receive shares of the valuables that were presented. This procedure had the advantage of precluding disputes over whether a clan segment really owned a dance when its members performed it for the first time.

A number of activities associated with *čam*-able dancing complexes thus provided the basis for cooperation among different descent groups and villages. By doing so they established alternative modes of grouping that cross-cut clan and village boundaries and contributed significantly to the integration of the Meta' polity.

One last way in which the system of *čam*-able property helped to structure relations in the intervillage sphere was by restricting some special prerogatives to certain senior chiefs. Here, "noble game" provides the best illustration. Although rights to portions of such animals were most important as the means of defining relations among the notables of a single village, they were sometimes also significant in intervillage politics. Thus certain chiefs claimed leopards killed anywhere within their own valleys. Moreover, Chief Tabi of Zang village asserted his right to the most honorable "chest" (*igɔ*) portion of all leopards slain in Meta'. Now, even though the legitimacy of these claims was rejected by some informants, they do illustrate that, given the

---

10. See Haaf (1977) for further discussion of death rituals in Meta' culture.

Meta' concept of *čam*-able property, it was perfectly logical for rights over noble game to be used as an idiom of paramountcy.

Hunting

A final activity that created linkages between the members of different villages was collective hunting. Since the organization of communal hunts has already been discussed in Chapter 7, the details need not be repeated here. However, it is important to note that this was a highly valued pursuit that provided the context for a good deal of intervillage visiting and cooperation in precolonial times.

An Overview of Meta' Polity Organization

As the foregoing analysis has shown, the wider Meta' polity had a surprisingly elaborate structure. While the greatest organization clearly existed at the village level, a substantial polity encompassing the entire Meta' population had also taken shape. This, it must be emphasized, was a loose and flexible political community. Individuals and groups mobilized in many different ways depending on the situation at hand. In fact, one of the most striking characteristics of the Meta' polity was that it made available so many alternative procedures and modes of relationship. Selective use of these principles allowed Meta' citizens to achieve many important political goals and objectives. Among other things, it enhanced the security of those who wished to travel, it made possible the resolution of many kinds of conflicts in the intervillage sphere, it promoted intervillage alliances in wars against outside groups, and it permitted the performance of rituals that were believed vital to the welfare of the entire polity.

However, even though it was complex, the precolonial Meta' polity remained uncentralized. While some village chiefs such as Tabi may have been accorded a vague seniority, this had certainly not enabled them to control decision-making processes at the societal level. Moreover, the political and economic rights of the nonchiefly clans had been largely preserved.

It is perhaps the ambiguity that pervaded the informants' accounts that provides the best clue to understanding the precolonial Meta' political community. In their testimonies, Meta' was both a polity and it was not. As noted at the outset of this chapter, it was not unusual for informants to assert both pan-Meta' brotherhood and the unique origins of their own patrilineal clans. The contradiction that apparently underlies such testimonies can be resolved only if it is realized that the Meta' polity was ever emergent. Under the appropriate circumstances—e.g., the resolution of a homicide, the need for an *ikwiri*-type assembly, or the necessity of organizing for an external war—a strong and effective polity could rapidly materialize. Yet on other occasions, when a common effort was no longer required, the awareness of membership in a large-scale political system would tend to lapse.

ELEVEN

Conflict and Competition in the Intervillage Arena

WHILE SOME knowledge of the ideal model of polity organization is essential if we are to grasp the assumptions underlying precolonial politics, remembered case histories of conflict and competition can better enable us to reconstruct actual political behavior in the intervillage sphere. This chapter presents two kinds of data that shed light on this topic. First, I shall analyze some routine conflicts involving parties from different villages in order to assess how well the ideal dispute-settlement procedures worked in practice. Then I will review several more detailed case histories of conflict between village chiefs as a means of assessing tendencies toward centralization in the wider polity. Together these data should yield additional insights into the strengths and limitations of precolonial Meta' polity organization.

Routine Intervillage Disputes

Several conflicts in which the principals came from different villages have already been discussed, in Chapter 8 (see Cases 1, 2, 3, 5, 8, 9, and 10). Together with some additional cases to be presented below, they suggest certain generalizations concerning ideal versus real behavior in the wider Meta' polity. Most significantly, they tend to support the informants' claims that this polity functioned as a moral and legal community. Although the parties to these cases resided in different villages and/or valleys, their disputes were still settled by the same procedures employed in intravillage conflicts. This was equally true in cases where absconding wives had caused their husbands to start fights or perform acts of symbolic aggression (see Cases 1, 2, and 5), in disputes involving theft (see Cases 9 and 10), and in conflicts over land (see Case 3). However, the cases also reflect a darker side of life in the precolonial Meta' polity, since many of them record violence as either the intermediate or final stage (see Cases 1, 2, 3, 8, 9, and 10). On balance, the material concerning actual intervillage disputes thus seems to suggest that there was a continuing interplay between the tendency toward violent self-help and collective efforts to reimpose order through customary legal procedures.

The powerful tension between these opposed tendencies is well illustrated by two conflicts of yet another type—cases of violent altercations that were precipitated by attempted kidnappings. We have already seen that random abductions were regarded as a major problem by the Meta' and that many institutions had developed to counter this threat. In addition to the belief in pan-Meta' brotherhood, the doctrines of clan loyalty and *iɣi wit* ("lost man") rendered everyone responsible for at least some travelers under pain of severe supernatural sanctions. There were also rituals to place curses on those who harmed marketers and the complex system through which the notables of every village regulated the slave trade. Given such an array of security measures, it may seem surprising that kidnappings were even attempted. Yet occur they did, and as the following two cases attest, such flagrant violations of a cardinal legal rule often led to the outbreak of violence between groups. In some instances this prompted warfare, while in others simple interlineage fighting was the result.

The first case occurred when members of two distantly related clans tried to abduct a man belonging to a third as he was passing through their village. However, the seizure was thwarted when local clanfellows of the traveler, together with some allies from a fourth group, attacked the kidnappers. This ultimately led to adjudication of the matter by the village authorities and the imposition of fines on everyone involved. The informant witnessed the case as a small child during the immediate precolonial period.

CASE THIRTEEN

The people of Clan A once seized a man who belonged to a section of Clan B in a neighboring village. They had no reason for doing this other than to profit from selling him as a slave. They captured him as he was passing through this village. However, when the clansmen of the victim who were living here saw what was happening, they attacked the captors. Soon the fighting became general, with some members of Clan C assisting the men of B and people from Clan D helping the other side.[1] They used walking sticks and as many as fifteen or twenty people fought on each side. During the scuffle, the man who had been captured made good his escape. On seeing this, the men of A demanded to know why the members of B had rescued the person they had wanted to sell. The men of B countered by asking why the men of A had seized their brother. After several hours, a notable ran in the midst of the fighters to place a stalk of *kiŋ* and this halted the violence. The next morning all concerned went to the compound of the chief in order to drink palm wine and settle the conflict. The case was judged by the *mikum si*, who fined each side two bundles of salt. The men of A had to pay, because they had tried to capture the traveler, and the men of B were fined for coming to his aid. This finished the matter.

The second case of kidnapping differs from the first in that it led to warfare between two villages. The informant who described it claimed that this was because the abduction was seen as a wholly unwarranted act. In his view, an otherwise similar case involving only the seizure of a debt hostage would have just resulted in an interlineage fight. In any event, the war broke out when a woman was taken from her bush farm by men from a village in the next valley. After a time, the violence was halted, and rituals were performed to reestablish peace. This case illustrates both the serious threat posed by kidnapping and how the combination of violent retaliation and ritual resolution could be an effective response to such attacks. It occurred during the

1. The alignments reported in this conflict are somewhat unusual. Of the four groups involved, A, C, and D normally behaved as distinct clans by allowing their members to intermarry, but they were also considered by informants to have ties of common descent. They could thus be considered as branches of a single non-exogamous clan. However, in the fighting described above, C is said to have aided B, an unrelated group. According to the informant, this was because the two groups resided in the same part of the village and "considered themselves almost like brothers." The members of B itself belonged to two different sections of this clan that were living within the village.

informant's childhood and involved a woman from his own village.

A war once occurred because several men from Mbo village decided to enslave a woman from Guzaŋ in the next valley. They captured her, for no legitimate reason, while she was working at her hilltop farm. When the Guzaŋ people discovered what had happened, they played their drums and sent a war party out. Then warriors from the two villages began to fight. As it happened, three men on the Mbo side were killed. Two were shot with guns and the other was beaten to death as his comrades escaped. After several hours, the men from neighboring villages were coming to assist Guzaŋ, and those nearby Mbo were also mobilizing. But before the fighting could become widespread, a ritual specialist from the Mbo side ran into the midst of the combatants and planted a tall bamboo pole trimmed with *kiŋ*. He also made a ritual statement to the effect that anybody who continued to fight would suffer *ndɔn* if he killed a person. This stopped the hostilities for a time. The war might have begun again if the side that had sent the *kiŋ* had not had a reasonable proposal. In this case, however, a settlement was reached. When the chiefs came to talk, the people of Mbo agreed to return their captive. After a while they brought her forward with a goat tied to one arm. Then the notables sacrificed the goat and stated that anyone who subsequently crossed the boundary to enslave a person would find blood like that of the animal erupting from his stomach. Afterward, the meat was shared among all the notables and chiefs. They also blessed the woman by rubbing her with camwood and said, "Even though a war was fought and men died because of you, no *ndɔn* from this should ever affect you." This finished the matter, except that debts of *iɣi wit* are still observed between the two villages.

Leadership and Competition in the Wider Polity

Our understanding of life in the precolonial Meta' polity is further enriched by data about how leading village chiefs competed for influence and authority in the intervillage sphere. Here again, case histories provide the basis for reassessing the informants' ideal model in light of actual behavior. According to that model, precolonial Meta' was a loosely organized political community that became active mainly in response to security threats and problems of widespread concern. In this *ad hoc* association for mutual assistance, centralized authority is said to have played a minor role. Certain chiefs, it is true, enjoyed enhanced prestige as the hosts of important intervillage activities. Some also possessed unique *čam*-able properties and key ritual specialist roles. However, since their prerogatives were relevant only in limited contexts, these had not become the basis for a paramount chiefship in Meta'.

The decentralized nature of the "ideal" Meta' polity is likewise reflected in the fact that no single leader was credited with control over most of the broadly recognized honors. Although Chief Tabi of Zang village came the closest, several of his rivals also had significant claims. Two other village heads, for example, shared the status of *ɜsum* ("oathing site") holder, and the most widely attended intervillage assembly (*ikwiri kyɛŋ*) was held not at Tabi's village but in that of Fonnyen.

Based solely upon the informants' general statements, it would be difficult to go much beyond the preceding rather broad assessment of the role of centralized authority in the wider Meta' polity. However, by juxtaposing their idealized model with actual rivalries among chiefs, one can probe more deeply into the complex phenomenon of polity-level leadership. In fact, concrete case histories provide insights into several different questions regarding centralization at this level. Among other things they can:

1. Help us to assess the vigor of various chiefs' efforts to acquire power outside their own villages,

2. Shed light on the strategies through which aspirants to senior chiefship sought to gain their objectives,

3. Reveal which approaches were the most successful, and

4. Allow us to assess the strength of egalitarian or anti-centralization forces in the wider Meta' polity.

Turning to the first of these questions, several remembered case histories of intervillage warfare clearly demonstrate how fiercely some precolonial chiefs struggled to expand their power.[2] They also show that both villages and broader coalitions

2. In the following cases (15, 16, and 17), I have departed from the practice of employing pseudonyms by identifying those participants who were *fɔn*s attempting to establish senior statuses at the valley or polity level. The primary reason for this is that the affairs of these men became matters of public record when they put forth their claims to higher honors, and their identities would have been difficult to conceal in any event. Even so, in Case 16, I have disguised the name of the village and the private parties who were involved.

sometimes went to war to defend the honors claimed by their chiefs. One such war is said to have occurred during immediate precolonial times in a Meta' valley that was almost evenly divided into zones dominated by the two major chiefly clans. Here the most powerful local Mindik village chief had for some time claimed that leopards killed anywhere in the valley should be delivered to him. He in turn accepted the obligation to forward the chest portion of any such animal to his senior clanfellow, Tabi. However, in this instance, a war is said to have broken out when a leopard was slain by hunters in one of the neighboring Bɔnjɔ villages and its chief proclaimed his intention to retain it. According to two informants who gave detailed accounts of the conflict, it went on for several days, with at least one combatant being killed. At its peak, the war involved all of the Bɔnjɔ and Mindik villages in the valley. The rules of engagement seem to have been limited: women and children were not killed, enemy heads were not taken, and the actual fighting was restricted to the battlefront, even though it would have been extremely easy for either side to raid the settlements of the other. The war finally ended when persons bearing the sacred plant *kiŋ* appeared on the battleground. The Mindik chief then decided to drop his claim to the disputed noble game. One informant's description of the "Leopard War" was as follows:

CASE FIFTEEN

A war once broke out in the Bome valley over the skin of a leopard. The people of Funam, a Bɔnjɔ village, killed the beast and brought it to their chief. Since this was the first such animal taken in his area, there was uncertainty about whether he should keep it or pass it on to a more powerful village head. But he decided to retain the animal, and after butchering it, he placed the skin on a tall bamboo pole in order to taunt Fongu, the neighboring Mindik chief in Ku village. This caused Fongu to attack Funam and to wage war along the stream boundary between their two villages. The war lasted for two days, during which one person was killed on the side of Ku. Dane guns were used in the fighting, and men came from all the other villages in the valley to assist the principals. While Bɔnjɔ chiefs helped Funam to fight, the Mindik villages assisted Ku. The war finally stopped because nobody wanted to go on killing his neighbors. A man came between the two groups and placed *kiŋ* on the ground in order to halt the fighting. After this, people from both sides discussed how best to make peace. They determined that each group should bring a goat so that a *čɜp* (a supernaturally sanctioned prohibition on further combat) could be established. In creating this the leaders first put water in a calabash and then made a ritual statement in which they said that anyone who thereafter killed a person on the other side would be affected by the "bad water" (i.e., would suffer *ndɔn*). Then they smashed the calabash to the ground. Finally, the chiefs of Funam and Ku sacrificed the two goats, each giving the head of his animal to the other. This finished the case, although, later, people began to say that *ndɔn* might affect the man who had slain a fellow Meta' person during the war. The killer was then obliged to pay the village leaders two goats so that they would remove the curse from his head.[3]

In addition to showing how strongly some *fɔn*s were motivated to increase their influence in the intervillage sphere, the foregoing case illustrates the strategy that was employed by one chief who sought preeminence at the valley level. His was a composite approach of extending claims to chiefly honors outside his own village and then relying upon military means to impose them. The case also demonstrates the considerable strength of the forces opposing centralization. In this instance, the claimant was vigorously resisted by both a neighboring chief whose own status would have been correspondingly reduced and by the people of that *fɔn*'s village.

Other precolonial case histories reveal additional tactics that were used by expansion-minded *fɔn*s as well as the difficulties that they faced in consolidating broader powers. Two cases of this sort were obtained from an informant in the Medig valley area. Both involved Fonnyen who was the chief of Nyen village and one of the most influential leaders of Medig. Not only did he enjoy a senior genealogical position within the Mindik chiefly clan, but he was also the possessor of an *ɜsum* ("oathing site") and host to the most celebrated intervillage assembly in all of Meta'. The case histories are interesting in that they suggest that Fonnyen had sought to expand his authority primarily through appropriating control of the capital-punishment mechanism in nearby villages. In the first conflict, which has already

---

3. A second informant's account of this same war, though similar in most respects, did not mention the ritual performed to establish the *čɜp* after combat had been halted. This informant also reported that each side had suffered one death among its casualties.

been discussed in Chapter 8 (see Case 8), Fonnyen authorized the execution of a witch in a neighboring village. The latter was believed to have killed his sister's son, who resided in yet another community. One of the most noteworthy things about this case is that the procedures followed deviated quite sharply from ordinary expectations. Ideally, the decision-making in capital cases was handled entirely within the village of the accused. Furthermore, care was usually taken to consult the victim's agnatic kin, and the execution was carried out by an anonymous agent of the village leaders. However, as can be seen from the account given in Chapter 8, none of these criteria was met in the case at hand. Instead, Fonnyen simply approved a request from a clan section in a neighboring village to take revenge upon the supposed killer of its brother, who resided elsewhere. Interestingly, this striking departure from normal procedures was associated with an almost complete breakdown of the social order. The execution of the witch led to one of the most dramatic episodes of interclan fighting recorded in Medig as well as the temporary expulsion of the avenging clan section from the valley. Given such a denouement, one can only conclude that Fonnyen had overreached himself in the attempt to transform his already considerable valley-wide influence into actual legal authority.

The second conflict reported by the same informant reinforces this interpretation. In this case, which also involved an execution in another village, Fonnyen seems to have stayed on somewhat firmer ground by approving the killing only after conferring with the victim's chief. Perhaps partly for this reason, he and other chiefs were able to restore order after a riot ensued and to resolve the dispute by imposing fines. However, several other aspects of the incident do suggest that Fonnyen was seeking broader coercive authority than permitted by Meta' customary law. In addition to the fact that none of the parties resided in his own village, there was no attempt to consult the agnates of the witch or to employ the usual anonymous executioner (*tɜkɜnɜ*). A final noteworthy feature is the way in which this dispute permanently disrupted local trade. As the following account illustrates, fear of the *ndɔn* associated with an unwarranted execution could cause even a well-established market to be abandoned. This underscores the fragility of the Meta' market peace and the importance of the various institutions that were relied upon to maintain it.

CASE SIXTEEN

A fight once occurred at the market in X village of the Medig valley. It broke out because A, a royal from X who was suspected of witchcraft, was killed in the marketplace by B, a man from the chiefly lineage in the neighboring village of Y.[4] The chiefs of X and Y had sat down with Fonnyen to decide what to do about A. They determined that he should be killed, but to be certain of their decision they also performed rituals that would cause the executioners to miss if A was innocent. They did not consult the close agnates of A. Although the latter suspected A of witchcraft, they had no idea that he was to be executed. When B killed A he went undisguised and speared him in full view of the market. This caused a riot to break out. If the brothers of A had caught B, they would have killed him on the spot. Finally, some people intervened and stopped the fighting. Later they gathered at Nyen to settle this case. The chiefs of X, Y, and Nyen were all present. As it happened, each side had to pay many goats, which were then shared among the chiefs and notables. The lineage of B gave seven goats to free itself from any *ndɔn* induced by B's killing of A. The notables then made a ritual statement to protect B and his brothers: "B came from your house to kill someone who was a witch. He did this to avenge the witch's victims. Therefore you should suffer no *ndɔn* from his deed." The lineage of A itself gave seven goats because its members were also at fault. They paid this fine to dissociate themselves from A's witchcraft and so that no more witches would appear in their group. This settled the matter. However, after this incident people no longer attended the market at X and it closed. Everyone believed that the blood of the slain witch remained in the marketplace and that there would always be fighting and killing if people came there to trade.

Initiatives in Zang

A final illustration of centralization processes within the wider Meta' polity can be found in the history of the Zang Tabi chiefship in the Zang valley. This case differs from the preceding ones in several important respects. To begin with, our evidence

---

4. While it is possible that the killer from Y was just an assigned executioner, it appears more likely that he was a member of the group that had lost a person to the witch from X. However, this detail is unclear in the account given by the informant.

on the various Zang chiefs' efforts to enhance their status goes back over several generations and thus has much greater time depth. Whether this reflects an actual difference between Zang and the other villages or is simply the result of our possessing more complete data here, it is impossible to say. Yet it does indicate that centralization in Zang was occurring through a gradual process rather than an abrupt shift. It also appears that the Zang rulers' efforts to expand their powers were at once less aggressive and more successful than those of the *fɔns* previously discussed. By emphasizing service more than the imposition of authority, they managed to gain recognition from much of the Meta' polity rather than just a single valley.

Yet another unusual aspect of the Zang chief's situation was the wide variety of factors upon which his claims to seniority rested. In addition to possessing a renowned *ɜsum* ("oath-taking site") and being one of a select few chiefs who could host the type of assembly known as *ikwiri kyɛŋ*, Tabi was the head of the village in which Tɜɣɜnɩča—the heroic founder of the Mɩndɩk chiefly clan—had lived out his final years.[5] The majority of informants in fact regarded him as Tɜɣɜnɩča's successor, even though the same honor was claimed by Fonnyen of Medig during the unsettled days of early British administration.[6] Whatever the truth of the matter, Tabi's links to this legendary patriarch did lay the foundation for more unprecedented honors. Most significantly, they were at least in part the basis for his claim to the prestigious chest portion of leopards killed anywhere within Meta'.[7]

Tabi was also unique in the active role that he played in mediating disputes within the Mɩndɩk chiefly clan. According to

5. Tɜɣɜnɩča is said to have resided and been buried at Zangmbeng, a site some distance to the west of the present Zang chief's compound but still within the territory of Zang Tabi village.

6. See C. H. Croasdale, A.D.O., "Intelligence Report on the Menemo Speaking Families of the Widekum Tribe in Bamenda Division of the Cameroons Province," May, 1933, paragraph 29 (Buea Archives).

7. Although Tabi's possession of this particular right was denied by some village heads, others—including some outside his own valley—confirmed it both to me and to early colonial administrators (see Memorandum, From District Officer to Resident, Buea. No. 406/83/1922. October 12, 1922, "Native Administration. Bameta. District and District Head. Creation of." [File Ab18, Buea Archives]). This makes Tabi the only Meta' chief with a moderately credible claim to have received symbolic tribute from villages and valleys other than his own.

informants, he had intervened in several succession crises caused by rivalry between closely related chiefs during precolonial times. In one instance, he is said to have established a new *modus vivendi* between chiefs Tebe and Fonbah of Njekwa village, while in another he arranged matters between Fomukwen of Kwen village and Fongu of Ku. Now such peacemaking initiatives by an outside senior clansman are not unprecedented, even in nonchiefly groups. However, these examples were unusual in that the mediator had come from a different valley. While this may in part reflect the difficulty that rival chiefs who were neighbors experienced in resolving conflicts on their own, it also seems to indicate that Tabi enjoyed a special status within the dominant Mindik clan.

The final confirmation of Tabi's status as a senior polity-level chief of course came from his possession of the staff called ɔbɛne. As seen in Chapter 10, this object conveyed upon its possessor the power to cleanse the pollution of homicide and was therefore closely bound up with the definition of Meta' as a polity. It also conferred great prestige upon its holder and was a source of payments from those seeking absolution. In this context, it is very interesting to note that the ɔbɛne right had not always belonged to the chief of Zang. In point of fact, one of his predecessors is said to have obtained it as part of the settlement of a dispute. Accounts of this episode were presented to early British officers, and very similar ones were collected by the present writer in the Bome valley and Bosa.[8] According to these sources, the staff of ɔbɛne was originally possessed by one Njwi Ače or Tebogasa, forefather of the current chief of Bosa village, which is located between Tuanyang in the Bome valley and the town of Bali-Nyonga. In some versions, Njwi Ače is said to have shared the custody of ɔbɛne with the forefather of Fonyam, the present-day chief of Kobanyang village in Bome. But whatever the arrangements may have been, the control of ɔbɛne was trans-

8. My own informants in Zang Tabi itself did not mention the relatively recent acquisition of ɔbɛne by their fɔn. However, the substance of the story is said to have been accepted by Zang sources in colonial times. See C. J. A. Gregg, A.D.O., "Meta: An Assessment Report on the Meta Clan of the Bamenda Division, Cameroons Province," January 1, 1924, and C. H. Croasdale, A.D.O., "Intelligence Report on the Menemo Speaking Families of the Widekum Tribe in Bamenda Division of the Cameroons Province," May, 1933 (Buea Archives) for early colonial accounts of this historical event.

ferred when Njiazu?, a predecessor of Tabi, apprehended the son of Njwi Ače for the theft of a goat and held him captive. This occurred at a time when Njwi Ače had already migrated from Tadkon in Mogamo but was still living in the vicinity of Zang Tabi village. The event can be roughly dated through the genealogies of the chiefly lines concerned: two informants from Zang indicated that it was the second or third successor of Njiazu? who first saw the Germans, while according to the present Bosa chief, the fifth successor of Njwi Ače was ruling when the Germans first arrived. This would place the episode being considered here some two to five generations before colonial conquest. In any event, all the sources agree that Njiazu? released Njwi Ače's son only after receiving the staff of *ɔbɛne* as a ransom. Thenceforth Njiazu? became the sole ritual specialist cleansing homicides in Meta', while Njwi Ače traveled on to settle in Bosa.

A final change that affected Tabi's position in the intervillage system is implied but not fully documented in the available accounts. This was the Zang chiefs' reorganization of the Meta' homicide cleansing system. Although the various informants' testimonies differ somewhat on their identities, most are in agreement that during immediate precolonial times, there existed a number of intermediaries—usually chiefs and chieflets with ties of clanship to Tabi—who had the exclusive right of escorting killers to Zang. Now for such a system to have been in place at the dawn of the colonial era, the Zang chiefs must have seized the opportunity to reorganize the homicide purification institution soon after their acquisition of *ɔbɛne*. This involved creating a new network of agents, responsible to them alone, who were scattered throughout Meta' territory. While it is unclear whether a comparable system existed when the *ɔbɛne* power was still in the hands of Njwi Ače, either its invention or its refocusing upon Zang would have been an important step in the consolidation of the Zang chief's new role.[9]

As the foregoing discussion illustrates, centralized polity-level authority seems to have found its greatest expression in the

9. This expansion of political influence through a network of intermediaries escorting supplicants to a renowned ritual specialist resembles the development of networks focusing upon several famous oracles among the Ibo (Ottenberg 1958, Uchendu 1965: 100–101).

chieftaincy at Zang Tabi. However, there were also real limits to Tabi's influence in the intervillage sphere. Many of his extraordinary rights were simply honors rather than signs of actual authority, and even though he played an important role in conflict management, this seems to have been construed mainly as a service to disputants. One indication of this is the fact that the crucial initial steps in the resolution of homicides continued to be carried out by the leaders of the village in which a killing had occurred. In this context, Tabi's principal function was to remove the last traces of *ndɔn*.

Finally, just as in other cases of expansionist village heads, Tabi's power was also limited by the resistance of his fellow chiefs. This is amply demonstrated by the following accounts of a war that broke out between Zang Tabi and the nearby Bɔnjɔ village of Njah Etuh. The conflict is said to have occurred just prior to the resettlement of these groups in Bali-Nyonga by the Germans. It was reported independently by four informants and described in detail by two of them. Since the accounts of the latter differed in several important respects, both will be presented here.

According to the first informant, the Zang-Njah war was the direct result of the Zang chief's attempts to extract tribute and a recognition of his seniority from the *fɔn* of Njah. His description is as follows:

CASE SEVENTEEN (VERSION ONE)

The people of Njah once fought a war with Zang Tabi. This occurred because of Chief Tabi's demands for recognition. He thought that since he was the only one settling cases of homicide, others should accept him as the ruler of Meta' and present their tribute (*ngɔmi*). Accordingly, one day when he was returning home from a visit to the chief of Tuanyang in the Bome valley, he asked the Njah chief to give him some goats [lit. *čɔʔɜ wu*, "to pay for his feet" as he passed]. The latter was greatly annoyed at this, so that he and Tabi began to argue and insult one another. At one point the Njah chief fired his gun in the air and exclaimed, "If you ever come to demand another goat, then you will see." [10] When the Zang chief heard this, he and his party fired into the air as well. This started a skirmish in which two Zang people were

10. Like the various acts of symbolic aggression mentioned earlier, discharging firearms during a dispute was believed to cause *ndɔn*.

killed as they retreated homeward. The war ended after this encounter. There was no subsequent fighting because Tabi had been warned not to pass through Njah nor to ask for tribute, and he refrained from doing either. If the war had continued, Njah might have been assisted by Bosa and Kai as well the villages on the Bɔnjɔ side of the Bome valley, while Zang could have been helped by the Mindik villages in Bome. But it never came to this.

Like the preceding version, the second informant's account describes the Zang-Njah war as having erupted one day when the Zang chief was returning from a visit to Tuanyang. Yet it differs in a number of respects. Most significantly, it does not describe Tabi as having demanded tribute from Njah. It also portrays the war as merely one episode in a history of clashes between the two groups, and it pictures allies from various other villages as having come to the aid of the principals. Finally, in sharp contrast with the first account, it describes an elaborate ritual that was done to make peace between the two villages.

CASE SEVENTEEN (VERSION TWO)

The chief of Njah once traveled to Anong village in Mogamo, which was then at war with Zang Tabi. When Chief Tabi learned that the Njah *fɔn* had gone to visit his enemies, he waited on the path to block his return. However, the Njah chief took another route through the bush and managed to avoid him. Sometime later when the successor of this Njah chief was on the chair, he stopped Tabi while the latter was returning from a visit to Tuanyang. He confronted him and his escorts, telling them that since Tabi had forced his father to escape into the bush, he would not be allowed to pass easily through Njah himself. This caused an outbreak of fighting between the people of Tabi's party with their Tuanyang friends and the villagers of Njah. Later, people of still other places came to the aid of the parties. Njah was assisted by Bɔnjɔ villages such as Kai, Funam, and Njimetu, as well as by Bosa, and Zang was helped by Ngwokwong. People from the Medig valley area mostly remained neutral. As it happened, two men were killed on the side of Zang and many people from Njah were wounded. Later an Njah man died. The fighting was halted when a ritual specialist from Bessi village in Medig came with two assistants to intervene. He informed both sides that it was not good for them to be at war with each other. Then a ritual was performed. They faced two goats in opposite directions and killed the animals, giving one to each side. After this they drank a great deal of palm wine and feasted lavishly while the two chiefs who had fought each other drank from a single cup. They then left for home with the state of war completely ended.

It is of course impossible to resolve the discrepancies between these two accounts of the Zang-Njah war. Nonetheless, when taken together the different versions serve to underscore some important points. In addition to illustrating the actions, alliances, and tactics that were possible in such a conflict, they also show the potential strength of the opposition to any village head who sought paramountcy. While Tabi's honors and prerogatives clearly surpassed those of other village heads, their autonomous power precluded much further consolidation of his position.

Conclusion

In this chapter, I have presented various data concerning actual behavior within the wider Meta' polity, including both mundane social conflicts and cases of competition among the leading village chiefs. Although the need to employ a reconstructive methodology has made it impossible to present a full account of such behavior, a rather detailed picture has nonetheless emerged. This in turn provides the basis for some reassessment of the ideal model of Meta' polity organization (see Chapter 10).

In the informants' discussions of that model, we noted a great concern with the maintenance of law and order as well as a complex array of mechanisms for regulating conflict in the intervillage sphere. The case history materials provide an invaluable counterpoint to these images by revealing numerous instances in which conflicts over property or the security of persons broke down in violence. Now this does not necessarily mean that the polity-wide legal system described in the previous chapter was wholly illusory. Indeed, it was just such violence that often brought the regulatory system most strongly into play. However, it does illustrate how individuals and groups continually tested the limits of the system.

As regards leadership within the wider polity, several important conclusions have emerged. First, one must be impressed with both the vigorous efforts that several leading *fɔn*s made to expand their authority and the considerable support that they received. In some instances, villagers even went to war on behalf of their chiefs, a fact that reflects a powerful trend toward centralization. There was also a tendency for the initiatives of status-seeking *fɔn*s to be expressed in somewhat stereotyped ways. Thus, for example, political status frequently turned on *čam*-able properties. As seen in both the "Leopard War" and Chief Tabi's claim to receive the chests of such animals from all over Meta', pretensions to senior chiefship at the valley or polity level were often couched in terms of rights over noble game. Another commonly attempted route to enhanced political authority lay through establishing control over conflict-resolution processes. This can be seen in many of the examples we have considered, ranging from Fonnyen's apparently unsuccessful attempts to direct the decision-making in capital cases outside his own village, to Tabi's efforts as a mediator in disputes between Mindik chiefs, to his appropriation of the power of *ʒbɛne*. As all these cases show, supervision of conflict management, at least potentially, provided one of the most promising means by which enterprising village heads might expand their powers.[11]

Concerning the effectiveness of the different strategies for achieving paramountcy, the overall history of Tabi's chiefship supports the argument that a *fɔn* could somewhat enhance his status in the wider polity by providing needed services in areas such as conflict resolution. However, the example of Fonnyen suggests that this strategy could not be pressed very far, especially if it meant usurping the rights of other conflict-resolution agents or going beyond the constitutionally allowable exercise of power. Finally, the case-history materials presented in this chapter also reveal the impact of anti-authoritarian values on political leadership in the intervillage sphere. More than anything else, these data have shown that aspirants to senior chiefship faced serious obstacles from both the resistance of the public and the opposition of rivals. Thus, in the "Leopard War" as

---

11. Some studies in legal anthropology have pointed to similar conclusions. Collier (1976), for example, portrays control of village-level dispute-settlement processes as fundamental to the power of traditional politicians in Zinacantan, Mexico.

well as in the case of Fonnyen and the conflict between Zang Tabi and Njah, we have seen that claims to seniority, however well founded, were likely to be repelled in a violent fashion. This was clearly a factor that militated against centralization in the wider Meta' polity.

TWELVE

Conclusion

THIS STUDY began with a discussion of three contrasting approaches to the complex acephalous polities of precolonial Africa. We can now reassess these in light of data from an additional society. The preceding chapters have provided the basis for a model to explain the unique patterns of political organization encountered in Meta', and this may in turn suggest insights into the forces that encouraged the emergence of elaborate uncentralized systems more generally in Africa.

Methodologically, the way has been paved for such conclusions by a sustained focus upon three distinct kinds of data. While informants' general statements have been used to clarify Meta' political ideology, remembered case histories of conflict have shed light on actual political behavior. In addition, data concerning the articulation of Meta' with the broader regional system have revealed ways in which relations with neighboring groups may have influenced its political processes.

In this chapter, I shall first summarize the characteristics of Meta' political organization as revealed by each of the three types of data and then propose an overall interpretation of the Meta' system. This will make possible a synthesis reconciling the various approaches to complex acephalous groups discussed at the beginning of the book.

Ideology

Turning first to the ideal model of Meta' political organization, we have seen that both patrilineal descent groups and villages were important units in the local-level system. Clan sections were portrayed by informants as the most reliable political support groups, units within which members presumably owed absolute loyalty to one another. Such groups also determined access to nubile women, land, and other essential resources. Villages, by contrast, regulated interlineage disputes and defended members against outside physical and mystical attack.

Ranking was another prominent feature of the ideal political organization of both descent-based groups and territorial units. Within clan sections, for example, the possibilities for male career advancement were assumed to be strictly controlled by hereditary leaders. Without their support, it was believed, men could not attain compound headships or important titles, ritual prerogatives, or *čam*-able properties. In addition, marriage for most males was expected to be late, new compounds were only reluctantly established, and lineage segmentation was a complex ritualized process that occurred over several generations.

Relations among fellow villagers also turned on considerations of rank. Villages were governed by groups of lineage head/notables, one of whom possessed the preeminent role of *fɔn* or chief. These men derived authority from being identified as "original settlers" and from their possession of important *čam*-able properties. In addition to providing ritual and secular leadership, they were the focus of a network of economic transactions that increased both their wealth and their status within the village-level system.

Other themes of political ideology ran counter to the emphasis on rank. While the Meta' were in many ways preoccupied with hierarchy, there was simultaneously a strong element of anti-authoritarianism in their political thought. This was not so much a broadly based egalitarianism as a resistance on the part of established political actors, such as compound and lineage heads, to the infringement of their autonomy. The readiness with which individuals and descent groups used force to assert their vital interests was one expression of this. Another is seen in the role of the chief. Despite the fact that the Meta' credited chiefs with awesome mystical potency, they were absolutely opposed to their exercising power directly. Many Meta' customs—from the chief's use of a spokesman, to his avoidance of a direct judicial role, to his subjects' insistence on full bride-wealth for their daughters—are best understood in these terms.[1]

A final aspect of the ideal model of Meta' political organization was its elaborate system of inter-village organization. Members of the thirty-odd Meta' villages were bound to each other by multiplex ties of clanship and affinity. This encouraged mutual assistance in external warfare as well as the extension of protection to market-bound travelers and cooperation in the large-scale communal hunts that were sponsored by different chiefs. It also laid the foundation for the concept of Meta' as a moral community in which offenses against "brothers" were mystically dangerous and intervillage war was forbidden. The concrete expression of this was an elaborate polity-wide legal system that operated through a number of prestigious oathing sites and a network of experts in ritual conflict resolution. Meta' political ideology thus contained the formula for a large-scale polity that was decentralized and predicated upon cooperation rather than the imposition of authority. This gave rise to the mass gatherings known as *ikwiri*, in which the leaders of various villages joined the mystical power of their voices to ward off dangers confronting the polity as a whole. In this setting, consensus more than anything else was viewed as the basis for mystically powerful action.

Process

Our understanding of the Meta' political system is also enriched considerably by second type of data, actual case histories of conflict and competition remembered from precolonial times. For example, the corpus of disputes that has been presented prompts significant modifications of the ideal model of Meta' village organization. Although the cases do support the notion that parties resolved disputes by something approximating the ideal procedures, they likewise demonstrate that the situation

---

1. This interesting combination of ranking and anti-authoritarianism had important parallels among nearby peoples such as the Ibo. See Cookey (1980) and Uchendu (1965) for additional discussion of the Ibo, and Cohen (1978c) for some observations on the implications of egalitarianism for theories of political evolution.

was frequently volatile and unpredictable. Nearly every imperative of Meta' law—from the principle that agnates did not murder one another to the requirement for elaborate consultation before a habitual offender was put to death—was seen to have been violated in one or more instances. The actual cases likewise enhance our appreciation of how clan sections functioned as political support groups and often resorted to violent self-help. It is against this backdrop of realism that the specialized dispute-settlement procedures that form part of the ideal model of Meta' village organization must be considered.

In a similar fashion, the several extended village case histories presented in Chapter 9 permit reassessment of the ideal model of leadership within such communities. That model portrayed villages as cooperative groups supervised by single chiefs and councils of lineage head/notables. As the representative of a noble clan, the chief possessed unique rights and powers. He controlled the village's regulatory maskers, coordinated decision-making in many serious conflict cases, and supervised the processes through which villagers *čam*-ed for titles and honors. Finally, the chief was the center of a local-level redistribution system in which the villagers provided gifts, labor, and certain forms of tribute, while he organized important annual rituals and provided periodic feasts. If this rather streamlined image of the precolonial village is compared with the actual histories presented in Chapter 9, numerous discrepancies are apparent. Meta' villages are revealed as arenas of intense factional politics, based upon competition between clan sections and larger descent-based coalitions. Moreover, in at least some instances, notables from nonchiefly clans controlled most important village-level activities and *čam*-able properties. Finally, certain villages had multiple claimants to chiefship or associated with neighboring groups in key activities. The village was thus neither necessarily fully centralized nor distinctly bounded. Each Meta' community had an organizational pattern that was the unique product of a variety of factors that could override the ideal pattern of village organization. Most significant among these were the sequence in which various groups had arrived in the village, the sizes of its principal clan sections, and the possibilities for alliance formation to which these factors gave rise.

Case histories of competition within the intervillage sphere likewise suggest qualifications of the ideal model. In the wider Meta' polity, some conflicts, such as warfare between villages, were theoretically impossible, while others, like fighting, kidnapping, and homicide, were generally thought to be resolvable. However, remembered cases demonstrate that all of these types of disputes occurred with sufficient frequency to test the limits of Meta' "brotherhood." Such conflicts stemmed from many causes, ranging from attempts by village heads to enhance their prestige, to cases in which groups reacted violently to the infringement of their rights, to instances where innocent travelers were kidnapped in order to be sold.

The case histories also attest that, despite the convention that all Meta' chiefs were fully autonomous, there was no lack of aspirants to paramountcy. Some important chiefs tried to supervise the resolution of homicides or the decision-making in capital cases outside their own villages. Others contested violently with their peers over honors like the receipt of noble game and the submission of tribute. The aggressiveness with which these rights were pursued and the violence that this sometimes precipitated reflect fundamental contradictions in the Meta' political system. While aspirants to senior chiefship made strenuous attempts to expand their power, their potential subjects and satellites resisted just as vigorously. On balance, the case histories suggest that, although centralization had proceeded far within some Meta' villages, it was rather effectively blocked on the polity level.

The Meta' Polity in Regional Perspective

While information about political ideology sheds light on concepts and motivations, and case-history material injects realism into our view of precolonial politics, information regarding the role of Meta' within the wider regional system may help to explain the model of political organization that has just been summarized. Any hypotheses arising from such data can be tested preliminarily by comparing Meta' with other polities that articulated with the regional system in contrasting ways and had correspondingly different political institutions.

To lay the groundwork for the clearest possible comparison with the neighboring societies discussed in Chapter 3, I shall focus discussion upon the two factors that were there seen to have had the greatest impact on the political systems concerned: (1) the influence of the environment (natural and social) upon polity size and settlement pattern and (2) the effect of a polity's location within the regional system upon its members' participation in intersocietal exchange.

Consideration of the first criterion indicates that Meta' society had at once a distinctive form of political community and a unique environmental situation. To begin with, the Meta' polity was large, surpassing even some of the Bamenda plateau chiefdoms in size, while its settlement pattern was dispersed. This is a particular combination of traits that was not found among nearby peoples. Thus, in savanna groups, such as the plateau chiefdoms themselves and the acephalous societies of the Metchum valley, moderate-to-large polity size went together with compact settlement. Yet Meta' also differed from neighboring forest peoples such as the Ngi and Mogamo. While these did share its dispersed settlement plan, the size of the political communities that they were able to form was generally much smaller.

In environmental terms, what the Meta' pattern appears to correspond with is an intermediate level of risk. On the one hand, the Meta' polity was clearly threatened by several expansionist chiefdoms such as Bafut, Mankon, and Bali, which partially encircled it in the northeast. Not only did the Meta' represent an inviting pool of potential slaves, but they also controlled much of the supply of palm oil that the larger chiefdoms sought. This led to frequent intersocietal wars that in turn encouraged widespread military cooperation within Meta' itself. On the other hand, the Meta' terrain did afford considerable protection—in the form of secondary forest cover, streams, swamps, and steep hillsides—that was unavailable to the plateau groups. This was in fact what rendered scattered settlement viable in Meta'. Still, the defensive situation of the Meta' was not nearly as ideal as that of the forest villages in Ngi and lower Mogamo. The latter groups, being located deeper in the forest zone and protected by sizable mountains and escarpments, were in many instances also insulated from the plateau chief-doms by the Meta' themselves. Hence, while all forest peoples shared a dispersed pattern of settlement, only the Meta' re-quired a large-scale polity for defense.

Meta' was also unique in terms of the other major variable that influenced polity organization in Bamenda—mode of ar-ticulation with the regional system. While various neighboring groups shared one or another aspect of the pattern seen in Meta'—its degree of self-sufficiency, its role within the exchange network, the types of products that its people traded, and the manner through which its commerce was organized—none ex-actly fit the same overall profile. As regards self-sufficiency, Meta' compares quite favorably with most of the neighboring polities. Although its citizens did not mine and smelt iron or have direct access to the long-distance trade, they produced most other essential items that circulated within the regional system. The Meta' also occupied a key intermediary position in a westward extension of the intraregional exchange system. Sev-eral plateau chiefdoms received much of their palm oil through Meta', and many forest villages obtained their supplies of iron tools, livestock, and grain primarily from there.

It is likewise noteworthy that the products passing through Meta' in the greatest quantity were of a distinctive kind. For the most part, Meta' served as a conduit for heavy traffic in what are best described as items of "popular" commerce. These in-cluded commodities, such as palm oil and grain, that were pro-duced by numerous households as well as being bulky and re-quiring large amounts of labor to transport. Although there was some trade in goods that do not fit this description (e.g., live-stock, iron tools, and prestige items), these were costly, and in some cases came from a considerable distance. They therefore contributed less to the total volume of trade.

Finally, Meta' differed from the other Bamenda societies in terms of the way in which its commerce was organized. Whereas the majority of forest villages, lacking both specialized traders and highly developed networks of markets, had access to the regional system mainly through markets in Meta', the pla-teau chiefdoms and their smaller satellites to the east partici-pated in commerce primarily through professional traders and "big man" exchanges. The Meta', by contrast, relied upon a diffuse system of open village markets at which there was widespread participation by producer/sellers, petty traders, and professional merchants from the plateau groups. Although Meta' did have specialized traders of its own and village chiefs who participated in "big man" exchanges, transactions conducted by these agents were clearly not the dominant forms of trade.

When the overall pattern of Meta' articulation with the regional system is considered, it is plain that this polity bore only partial similarities to its neighbors. It somewhat resembled the small chiefdoms in the mountains to the east of the Bamenda plateau, since they too fulfilled middleman functions in the system of intraregional exchange. However, it differed from these groups in its focus on "popular" commerce and in its organization of trade through markets. The larger plateau chiefdoms were also like Meta', having possessed intermediary positions, yet they occupied more central roles in the regional exchange system and had direct access to the long-distance trade. In addition, they did not emphasize "popular" commodities to the same degree as Meta'. Finally, although the Meta' produced palm oil like the peoples of the Metchum valley, Ngi, and lower Mogamo, their role in interpolity trade was one of middlemen transferring forest oil to the plateau rather than that of primary producers situated at a terminus in the exchange system.

Of all the nearby populations, that of upper Mogamo seems to provide the closest parallel to Meta', in that it was relatively self-sufficient, an intermediary supplying oil to the plateau, and possessed of some village markets. However, the Mogamo markets did not form as complex a network as that seen in Meta', and they were less vital to intraregional exchanges than their Meta' counterparts were (see Map 3, p. 64). In addition, the trade in slaves and prestige goods, which played a dominant role in the Mogamo economy, was largely monopolized by the village authorities. This effectively precluded the sort of popular control of commerce seen in Meta'.

If the economic linkage of Meta' to the regional system was unique, this also appears to have encouraged the development of distinctive forms of political organization. In comparison with neighboring polities, Meta' was noteworthy for (1) its moderate yet unmistakable development of ranking and (2) its patterns of widespread cooperation in ritual and conflict resolution. Concerning the first point, it is evident that the Meta' system of ranking represented an intermediate level of development in Bamenda. Although fairly similar to that found in some Mogamo villages, it far surpassed anything seen in acephalous groups, such as those of the Metchum valley peoples and the Ngi. Yet it was also modest by comparison with the elaborate hierarchies of the central plateau chiefdoms. The status possessions of Meta' lineage heads paled in comparison with those of their counterparts on the plateau, and Meta' had nothing like the large palace complexes, with scores of chiefly wives and retainers, that were found in the major plateau groups. In addition, the political center of gravity also differed between Meta' and the plateau societies. Whereas in the latter groups chiefs and notables belonging to palace societies had consolidated control to the extent that they possessed a relatively autonomous power base, their Meta' peers were still representatives of their descent groups first and village notables only secondarily.

Such contrasts in hierarchy and the distribution of power were doubtless the result of many factors. However, they seem likely to have been influenced by the ways in which the various central, peripheral, and semiperipheral societies participated in the regional exchange system. As we have seen, the citizens of the central plateau chiefdoms were in the best position to profit from both the intraregional and the long-distance trade. They also occupied a zone in which exchange was a dangerous enterprise, organized through the active agency of small groups of specialized traders. These factors would have encouraged both the accumulation of wealth and its concentration within a few noble and chiefly houses. Peripheral societies such as Ngi and the Metchum valley polities, by contrast, had fewer opportunities for the consolidation of trade-based wealth. Since these groups were producers of a single important commodity and located at one end of the network, there was less chance for their citizens to profit from trading in general. Moreover, it was difficult for small elites to establish control of interpolity exchange because the major commodity, palm oil, was a "popular" item.

In Meta' society we find yet another permutation of these patterns. Here, where trade was still organized on an unrestricted basis, where items of "popular" commerce played a predominant role, and where the society occupied a moderately advantageous semiperipheral position within the intraregional exchange network, ranking had developed to an intermediate degree. The Meta' social hierarchy rested on the ability of descent group leaders to tap into the trade-derived wealth of junior agnates. The heads of lineages and clan sections accomplished this through their control of the system of *čam*-ing for honors and titles, as well as by arranging the transactions associated with kinship rituals. Such descent group leaders also formed alliances with peers belonging to unrelated clan sections in order to confirm their places within the village hierarchy and to have access to redistributions at the village level. However, the fact that ordinary compound heads exercised direct control over the processes of intersocietal exchange gave them a certain power as well. This obliged the notables to rely more upon ideologically sanctioned than coercive means in appropriating their trade-derived wealth.

Yet another factor that discouraged the development of stratification in Meta' was the dispersed settlement pattern. This obviously rendered it more difficult for notables to supervise their groups and therefore to retain control. However, several comparisons suggest that this was not an overriding influence. On the one hand, acephalous groups such as the Metchum valley polities resided in fortified towns but still had among the most egalitarian social systems in Bamenda. On the other hand, the Bangwa, who occupied a position similar to that of the Meta' on the edge of Bamiléké plateau to the southeast, demonstrate that forest groups with scattered settlement were not invariably uncentralized. Their crucial role as intermediaries in the long-distance trade in slaves and elite goods appears to have stimulated formation of several tightly centralized chiefdoms with rigid social hierarchies (Brain 1972, 1981; Brain and Pollock 1971; Fardon 1985). Finally, if O'Neil (1987: 29–31, 75–77, 80–81, 356–359) is correct in thinking that the authorities of some of the major slave-trading villages in Mogamo were consolidating their power in the late nineteenth century, similar processes may have been beginning among forest peoples much closer at hand.

The other noteworthy feature of Meta' political organization—

its elaborate polity-wide system of conflict management—is likewise more intelligible in light of this society's role within the regional system. In part, broadly based legal cooperation may have represented a collective response to insecurities that were exacerbated by the group's own means of adapting to that network. Even a cursory glance at Meta' shows that in terms of conflict management this society was unique. Its system of conflict resolution by ritual specialists and village-level notables permitted settlement of many disputes between Meta' belonging to different villages. It also did much to assure the security of the population in a situation where kidnapping and enslavement were constant threats. Finally, a complex of institutions—including the doctrine of clan loyalty, the concept of "lost man," the safeguards that governed sales of habitual offenders, and the emphasis upon polity endogamy—can be interpreted as a veritable population program through which the Meta' sought to protect their "human resources" in a predatory social environment.

Neighboring groups showed partial similarities at best. As Warnier's (1983: 445–468) discussion of conflict-resolution mechanisms on the plateau attests, some chiefdoms there shared the basic concepts and practices associated with ritual conflict resolution. In the plateau groups, however, this process of dispute settlement tended to be controlled autocratically by the authorities rather than through diffuse popular regulation as in Meta' (Warnier 1975: 228–230, 244–251, 256–258). Moreover, while the rulers of the larger chiefdoms used the "slave rope" system of licenses to regulate traffic in human beings, they had nothing comparable to the elaborate formal consultation procedures that preceded the sale of any Meta' citizen. They likewise possessed nothing resembling the Meta' custom of "lost man," which helped to assure the security of travelers, and they permitted numerous interpolity marriages by members of trading houses that wished to broaden their contacts. That many suspected witches were submitted to the poison ordeal (Warnier 1975: 251–253) provides a final indication of the potential for authoritarianism that was inherent in the plateau political systems. Given their doctrines regarding the sanctity of human life, the Meta' would have found such a practice abhorrent.

The various peripheral stateless societies also contrast sharply with Meta'. On the whole, their accomplishments in polity formation and regulation of intervillage conflicts were modest. The Ngi, for example, possessed an atomistic political organization in which villages of several hundred persons constituted hostile warlike isolates, while the Metchum valley peoples were only moderately more successful in political unification and cooperation. Although they employed some of the same conflict-management procedures seen in Meta' (e.g., ritual assemblies and the ritual resolution of homicide cases), the largest groups cooperating in such rites were only one-tenth the size of the Meta' political community. Ide, the best-known Metchum polity, also seems to have made little effort to assert societal control of its "human resources." Not only did its members fail to use clan ties as a basis for cooperation outside the range of the small polity itself, but they had nothing comparable to the Meta' institution of "lost man." Furthermore, in contrast with the relatively endogamous Meta', the Metchum valley peoples recognized one form of marriage to outsiders that involved the possibly complete alienation of the bride from her kin in return for a single payment. Thus, while the citizens of Ide may have desired a larger polity and taken some steps to achieve it, the obstacles to the establishment of such a system appear to have been too great. Finally, in Mogamo there are no reports of large-scale polities or conflict-resolution systems. Instead, with growing involvement in the exchange of slaves and elite goods, centralization within small villages and village groups seems to have overcome any impulse toward political consensus-building on the societal level.

If it is to be argued that the impressive Meta' polity was indeed a response to insecurity, it needs to be shown that the Meta' faced unique kinds of threats and that they could plausibly have responded to these in a collective fashion. Regarding the uniqueness of the group's problems, it must be stressed that more than any other Bamenda society, Meta' had specialized as an intermediary for trade by organizing popular participation in an open market network. This means that Meta' must have experienced mobility and interaction between strangers on a scale unknown elsewhere in the region. Traffic was also augmented by a variety of practices, ranging from frequent intervillage marriages, to the custom of locating farms at a distance from the village, to the cooperation of persons from many villages in communal hunts. Given also a semiforested environment in which the danger of kidnapping and molestation of travelers was increased, it was plainly in both the individual and the societal self-interest to collaborate in providing mutual security as well as in resolving disputes between members of different villages.

A system for achieving these objectives could easily have taken shape as individuals, in the effort to assure support from kin residing in other villages, elaborated doctrines relating to clan loyalty and the mystical dangers associated with the betrayal of affines. Under the fluid and unpredictable conditions that I have described, Meta' citizens would have also been motivated to accept the legal authority of notables and ritual specialists belonging to other villages as well as to insist on constitutional safeguards in the handling of slave transactions and capital cases. But the clearest example of collective action to promote security in the intervillage sphere is seen in the large ritual assemblies at which the representatives of many villages took steps to curse unknown offenders.

In conclusion, much of the complex polity organization encountered in Meta' society is most convincingly explained by reference to the group's environmental setting and its role within the regional trading system. None of the other nearby stateless societies had established a similarly elaborate polity, because none had the combination of dispersed settlement, a highly active network of small markets, and an intermediary position in the intraregional trade that encouraged these developments. At the same time, the adjacent chiefdoms on the Bamenda plateau possessed neither these features nor the vulnerabilities that spurred polity formation in Meta'. Within their close confines there were fewer problems in maintaining security, as well as greater opportunities for chiefdom authorities to control conflict management in autocratic ways. Finally, since their trade largely was in the hands of specialists, the latter could arrange for their own safety while abroad by forming individual alliances on an *ad hoc* basis, and in cases of serious violations of traders' rights, the home chiefdoms were free to retaliate with force.

This is not to argue that the Meta' political system had in any sense reached a state of stable equilibrium. Although we cannot document the changes historically, comparison with neighboring groups suggests that the particular compromise between statelessness and centralization that characterized Meta' had probably evolved in relatively recent times under the influence of a substantially altered regional system. It was also open to change. If the Meta' had occupied a more central position along the long-distance trade routes like their Mogamo neighbors to the south, powerful forces of centralization might have been released, while less involvement in trade and less exposure to predatory neighboring chiefdoms would have no doubt caused a shift toward greater statelessness. As it was, the role of Meta' as a secondary intermediary within a flourishing regional exchange system had permitted both moderate development of ranking and the consolidation of a large-scale polity with a complex system of conflict management.

Significance of the Meta' Case

The foregoing analysis has suggested that precolonial Meta' political organization was the product of a complex interplay of forces, including both the polity's own internal dynamics and its members' responses to problems posed by their relations within the wider regional system. Such an interpretation differs in several respects from the models that have been proposed by previous researchers working on comparable societies. As outlined in the Introduction, there presently exist three main approaches to explaining contrasts in the political organization of precolonial acephalous societies and the emergence of complex systems such as Meta'. First, Robin Horton's model relates variations in the overall integration of stateless societies—particularly the roles played by descent organization and cross-cutting institutions such as age sets, earth-cult groupings, and secret societies—to the influence of migration, settlement, and interpolity warfare. Second, there is the voluntaristic centralization model, which stresses the problems of conflict management that the members of acephalous groups were likely to face in situations of increasing population density, resource scarcity, and the expansion of trade. Advocates of this approach portray the emergence of stronger leadership and centralized authority as adaptive responses to these problems. Finally, there are the conflict theorists, who have reinterpreted stateless societies as systems of informal hierarchy based upon the control that elders exercised over crucial economic transactions among kin. From this last perspective, the more elaborate acephalous systems are merely polities in which elders have managed to consolidate more completely their power base and to expand the scope of their control.

Although each of the above models yields some insights into a political system such as Meta', none of them provides a full explanation of the patterns that we have encountered. Thus on first glance Meta' seems to correspond well to Horton's second type of stateless system. Not only did it have the dispersed settlement, the federation of unrelated lineages, the distinction between first settlers and latecomers, and the ritually based territorial community associated with this type, but it was also the product of the kind of "disjunctive migration" that Horton believes gave rise to such systems. However, precolonial Meta' political organization also possessed several important features not considered in Horton's model. For example, neither the very large size of the Meta' polity nor the elaborateness of its decentralized system of conflict management can be accounted for by the fact that Meta' lineages carried out disjunctive migrations. Horton's theory of Type Two systems is thus only the beginning of an explanation at best.

Similar dilemmas are inherent in the voluntaristic centralization hypothesis. Although the Meta' did confront just the sort of conflict-management problems envisioned in the theory, and although there was indeed a tendency toward centralization of authority on both the village and polity levels, it is implausible to link these two phenomena causally as in the voluntaristic centralization model. It is true that Meta' was a densely settled social field in which trade and other factors encouraged mobility and created a need for reliable institutions of dispute settlement. Public concern over personal insecurity had also encouraged development of an elaborate polity-wide system of conflict management. However, the data do not support a conclusion that chiefs were primarily responsible for the effectiveness of conflict resolution in Meta'. No centralized system of legal authority had developed at the polity level. Moreover, both the analysis of political concepts and case histories of actual disputes suggest that, although chiefs and notables sometimes rushed in to halt interlineage fights, the success of conflict management within the Meta' polity generally depended more upon a complex system of decentralized authority and multiple options for dispute processing than on interventions by particular village heads. Indeed, it was more the case that chiefs tried to use their legal role as the means of enhancing their power than a matter of the public seeking them out for unique forms of assistance when disputes proved beyond its control.

Finally, the data reveal that under normal circumstances the Meta' people expected their chiefs to play a rather passive role in dispute settlement. They were highly resistant to the expansion of chiefly power and unwilling to allow chiefs to exercise their legal authority directly. Thus, while problems of the sort emphasized by the voluntaristic centralization theory seem to have given rise to a complex polity, it was one of quite a different kind than anticipated by the theory. At the same time, centralization, to the extent that it was occurring, was promoted by forces other than the need for effective conflict resolution.

It is precisely here that the third major approach, conflict theory, can be of assistance, since it correctly identifies political competition as the basis for centralization in Meta'. As we have seen from numerous case histories, both individual aspirants to leadership positions and descent-based factions competed intensely to expand their power on the village and polity levels. Yet they were also met by stern resistance on the part of potential subjects who valued their autonomy highly. The overall result of this interplay of forces was a sociopolitical system that, though fundamentally acephalous, still had significant elements of centralization and a relatively formal hierarchy of rank.

All of these developments are fully consistent with the expectations of conflict theory. However, despite its plausible treatment of certain features of Meta' polity organization, conflict theory does not provide a comprehensive model. What the theory fails to account for is the more cooperative and consensual aspects of Meta' political organization. This study has documented that the Meta' had a well-developed sense of the common welfare and a strong collective interest in the control of conflict and disorder that had led to a complex polity-wide system of dispute settlement. For a model that counts competitive self-interest as the driving force behind most political behavior, such developments are difficult to explain.

What is called for is clearly a synthesis that combines (1) Horton's broad perspective on migration and intersocietal relations with (2) the understanding of political dynamics provided by conflict theory and (3) the appreciation of consensual politics that is implicit in the voluntaristic centralization model.[2] This is exactly what the present study has sought to provide. Crucial to the realization of this goal has been the use of a distinct mix of ethnohistorical information. While data on Meta' political ideology and remembered case histories of conflict have helped to weigh the forces of cooperation and competition that characterized the precolonial polity, information on the society's articulation with the wider regional system has been used to assess the influence of that relationship upon the group.

It should be noted that a considerable body of data from other areas appears consistent with the model that has been presented here. In both the region of northern Ghana (Goody 1957) and parts of southeastern Nigeria (Meek 1937, Netting 1972, Northrup 1978, Ottenberg 1958), for example, ethnographers and historians have recorded a close association between dispersed settlement in uncentralized polities, sizable moral and legal communities based upon mystical sanctions, and a pattern of frequent mobility due to market trade and other factors. While pursuing such comparisons is clearly beyond the scope of this study, an important role of ethnography is to develop plausible explanatory models that are well grounded in the complex specifics of particular environmental and regional settings. Here, I have not only attempted this, but gone on to support the resultant model by making limited comparisons within the Bamenda region.

2. Bloch (1977) and Moore (1975) have urged social anthropologists to integrate the conflict and integration perspectives (points two and three above) in their analyses of particular sociocultural systems, while Haas (1982) and Johnson and Earle (1987) have attempted to combine these two approaches with regional analysis (point one) in their recent discussions of political evolution.

Turning in conclusion to somewhat broader concerns, it is fair to say that this study of precolonial Meta' has helped to clarify at least some aspects of political life in preindustrial society. In particular, it has shown that despite strong tendencies toward violence, competition, and the formation of hierarchies, the members of some stateless groups still managed to create very large and cooperative political communities. In this regard, the late-nineteenth-century Meta' polity stands as a monument to human peacekeeping ability. Yet Meta' also demonstrates that the impulse toward peace is likely to be realized only in certain kinds of situations. It was most of all the special role that Meta' occupied within the Bamenda regional system that promoted peacefulness by making ritual collaboration and cooperation in conflict-management matters of collective self-interest. In numerous other African stateless societies, similar impulses toward community existed, but too many other factors discouraged their fulfillment. The challenge of peacekeeping is thus to so structure social and environmental relationships that this remarkable potential for the formation of cooperative political institutions can be released.

Reference Matter

List of Informants

The following inventory includes only those informants who provided information about precolonial Meta' social and political organization itself. Many others who gave data on contemporary Meta' ethnography have been omitted. Village affiliation and date(s) of testimony are given for each informant and, where it is known, the informant's clan affiliation as well. I have rendered the personal names of nonliterate informants with my best guess of what would be the conventional English spelling in Cameroon.

1. Chief Fongu (Mindik clan, Ku village): 1/13/70, 5/26/70, 7/1/71.
2. Chief Take (Bɔnjɔ clan, Funam village): 5/19/70, 9/15/70, 10/17/70 12/10/70, 1/8/71, 1/28/71, 5/14/71, 5/15/71.
3. Tabeng (Bɔnjɔ clan, Funam village): 5/25/70, 3/18/71, 7/1/71.
4. James Iya (Bɔnjɔ clan, Funam village): 6/12/70, 6/30/70, 8/23/70, 12/11/70.
5. Chief Fobang (Mindam clan, Tuanyang village): 6/19/70, 12/14/70, 1/11/71.
6. Mangana (Bɔrangɔp clan, Funam village): 6/23/70, 7/31/70, 9/3/70, 10/27/70, 10/29/70, 1/4/71.
7. David Mba (Bɔnjɔ clan, Funam village): 7/9/70, 9/3/70, 9/9/70.
8. Jeremiah Anyi (Mitiŋ clan, Funam village): 8/2/70.
9. Peter Fominyoh (Bɔnjɔ clan, Funam village): 8/5/70, 8/23/70, 9/7/70, 9/9/70, 10/7/70, 10/12/70, 10/27/70.
10. Meyu (Bɔrangɔp clan, Funam village): 8/22/70, 9/3/70, 9/15/70, 6/1/71.
11. I No Sabi Atam (Bɔrangɔp clan, Funam village): 8/22/70, 10/26/70.
12. Isaac Fomubat (Bɔnjɔ clan, Funam village): 8/25/70.
13. Tifano Kwehiwu (Miwum clan, Kobanyang village): 8/26/70, 12/30/70, 1/7/71.
14. Jacob Nji (Bɔnjɔ clan, Ku village): 8/31/70, 12/7/70.
15. Jonas Tabri (Mindik clan, Funam village): 9/2/70.

16. Simon Fomenjang (Mitiŋ clan, Funam village): 9/8/70.
17. Zetero Tete (Azonge) (Bɔrangɔp clan, Funam village): 9/10/70, 9/19/70, 10/18/70.
18. Kiyagha (Mitiŋ clan, Funam village): 9/14/70, 12/1/70.
19. Bakire Ni (wife of Chief Take, Funam village): 9/15/70, 6/18/71.
20. Nduku (Bɔrangɔp clan, Funam village): 9/19/70.
21. Thomas Awa (Bɔgwanik clan, Ku village): 10/5/70, 10/24/70.
22. Fomukom (Mindik clan, Ku village): 10/13/70, 10/17/70, 12/31/70, 3/31/71.
23. Lucas Mengwe (Miwum clan, Funam village): 10/15/70.
24. Reverend Sita (Bɔrangɔp clan, Funam village): 10/15/70.
25. David Gase (Bɔnjɔ clan, Funam village): 10/16/70.
26. Fomujong (Bogwanik clan, Ku village): 10/17/70.
27. Chief Aje (Fortu) (Bɔnjɔ clan, Njimetu village): 11/16/70, 1/5/71, 1/26/71, 2/16/71, 3/4/71, 3/8/71, 3/25/71, 5/7/71, 5/13/71, 6/1/71, 6/2/71, 6/21/71.
28. Petro Anyang (Bɔrangɔp clan, Njimetu village): 11/17/70, 12/22/70, 1/15/71, 2/11/71, 2/12/71, 2/23/71, 3/12/71, 4/1/71, 4/30/71.
29. Zachariah Anyong (Bɔrangɔp clan, Njimetu village): 11/19/70, 12/18/70, 1/14/71, 2/9/71, 3/5/71, 3/19/71.
30. John Mberi (Bɔnjɔ clan, Njimetu village): 11/20/70, 1/19/71, 2/8/71, 3/26/71, 5/26/71.
31. Moses Ndam (Njimetu village): 11/23/70.
32. Wunde (Bɔrangɔp clan, Ku village): 11/24/70.
33. Egwetang (Bɔrangɔp clan, Ku village): 11/27/70.
34. John Kun (Mutambi) (Bɔnjɔ clan, Funam village): 11/27/70, 3/2/71, 5/18/71.
35. Jacob Teghen (Mitiŋ clan, Funam village): 11/30/70, 12/21/70, 1/8/71, 2/16/71, 2/22/71, 3/20/71, 3/30/71, 5/7/71, 5/17/71, 6/12/71, 6/26/71.
36. Gwan (Bɔrangɔp clan, Funam village): 12/11/70.
37. Bafon Njoakut (Ɛzweɜzuʔ clan, Njekwa village): 12/14/70, 1/11/71, 1/25/71, 2/22/71, 3/18/71, 3/23/71, 4/29/71, 5/11/71, 5/21/71, 6/15/71, 6/19/71, 6/25/71, 6/28/71.
38. Manga (Mindik clan, Njekwa village): 12/15/70, 3/11/71.
39. Wara (Bɔgwanik clan, Njekwa village): 12/17/70, 3/1/71.
40. Yanda (Gundom village): 12/23/70, 1/12/71, 2/5/71, 3/9/71, 3/29/71.
41. Gando (Zang Tembeng village): 12/28/70, 4/9/71, 5/3/71, 5/6/71.
42. Afie (Nyen village): 12/29/70.
43. Ayo (Nyen village): 12/29/70.
44. Yahausa Teko (Kobanyang village): 12/30/70.
45. Fine Boy Mahecho (Mindik clan, Ku village): 12/30/70.
46. Fondere (Funam village): 1/4/71.

47. Fine Boy Mujung (Bɔnjɔ clan, Funam village): 1/4/71.
48. Ndiku (Njimetu village): 1/7/71.
49. Chief Akam (Bɔnjɔ clan, Kai village): 1/13/71.
50. Ndangong (Ɛzwɛзɔzuʔ clan, Njimetu village): 1/21/71.
51. Tita Njo (Bɔnjɔ clan, Njimetu village): 1/22/71, 5/12/71.
52. Bang (Bɔnjɔ clan, Njimetu village): 1/28/71, 2/1/71.
53. Petro Echo Adam (Mitiŋ clan, Tuanyang village): 2/25/71, 4/5/71, 6/17/71.
54. Andre Echo Adam (Mзnɔŋ clan, Njekwa village): 2/26/71.
55. Andreas Tundeh (Bɔnjɔ clan, Njimetu village): 3/15/71.
56. Menah (Tudig Village): 4/6/71.
57. Tabo (Bɔrangɔp clan, Njah Etuh village): 4/6/71.
58. Tita (Bɔrangɔp clan, Njah Etuh village): 4/8/71.
59. Abiku (Mitiŋ clan, Kai village): 4/12/71, 6/11/71.
60. Tendi (Mindik clan, Guneku village): 4/15/71, 4/28/71, 7/1/71.
61. Tasi (Mbemi village): 4/26/71.
62. Chief Fonnyen (Mindik clan, Nyen village): 5/20/71.
63. Tanah (Bɔnjɔ clan, Njah Etuh village): 5/20/71.
64. Chief Mbabit (Mindik clan, Mbemi village): 5/20/71.
65. Chief Fonong (Mindik clan, Njinibi village): 5/20/71, 7/1/71.
66. Chief Fobosa (Mahebo) (Miwum clan, Bosa village): 5/22/71.
67. Mukwang (Miwum clan, Bosa village): 5/22/71.
68. Gusa (Bɔnjɔ clan, Njah Etuh village): 5/24/71.
69. Fine Boy Mbahangwi (Bɔnjɔ clan, Zang Tabi village): 5/24/71.
70. Avu Peter (mother of Peter Fominyoh, Funam village): 6/9/71.
71. Isaac Tita (Bɔnjɔ clan, Kai village): 6/11/71.
72. Angwi Tebo (Gundom village): 6/14/71.
73. Asahengwa (Bɔgwanik clan, Njekwa village): 6/15/71.
74. Anna (father's wife of Chief Fonbah, Njekwa village): 6/16/71.
75. Tapita Agwa (Bɔgwanik clan, Njekwa village): 6/16/71.
76. John Nda (Bɔgwanik clan, Njekwa village): 6/18/71.
77. Tembon (Bɔgwanik clan, Njekwa village): 6/18/71.
78. Martha Anjoh (wife of Nyambi, Bɔgwanik clan, Njekwa village): 6/19/71.
79. Anagwa (Mindik clan, Ku village): 6/21/71.
80. Chief Fombu (Ngembo village): 6/28/71.

Group Interviews

1. Chief Akam, Teta Mba, Augustine Atoh, and Johnny Awi (Kai village): 12/20/69.

2. John Teko and Joseph Agu (both of Mitiŋ clan, Funam village): 6/12/70.
3. James Iya (Bɔnjɔ clan, Funam village) and Fomubat (Bɔnjɔ clan, Ku village): 6/25/70.
4. David Mba and Ba Aza (both of Bɔnjɔ clan) with Tinya Mukoro and Jegeri (both of Bɔrangɔp clan) (all of Funam village): 7/10/70.
5. Achu Anu and Tamukwen (both of Mindik clan and Funam village): 7/15/70.
6. Chief Fombi and John Kun (Mutambi) (both of Bɔnjɔ clan and Funam village): 7/24/70.
7. Jacob Teghen (Mitiŋ clan, Funam village), Simpson Njo (Bessi village), and Munango (Njinibi village): 8/5/70.
8. Zetero Tete (Azonge), Gwan, and Nduku (all of Bɔrangɔp clan and Funam village): 8/8/70, 8/16/70.
9. Peter Fominyoh (Bɔnjɔ clan) and I No Sabi Atam (Bɔrangɔp clan) (both of Funam village): 8/16/70.
10. Isaac Fomubat and Taken (both of Bɔnjɔ clan and Funam village): 8/21/70.
11. John Ehmuhu and Tinya Mukoro (both of Bɔrangɔp clan and Funam village): 8/21/70.
12. Zetero Tete (Azonge) and Nduku (both of Bɔrangɔp clan and Funam village): 8/24/70.
13. Jonas Tabri (Mindik clan) and Zetero Tete (Azonge) (Bɔrangɔp clan) (both of Funam village) with Jacob Nji (Bɔnjɔ clan, Ku village): 8/28/70.
14. David Mba (Bɔnjɔ clan, Funam village) and Chief Fonbah (Mindik clan, Njekwa village): 8/28/70.
15. Fomukom (Mindik clan) and Joseph Chek (both of Ku village): 9/4/70.
16. Chiefs Tebe and Fonbah (Mindik clan), Bafon Njoakut (Ɛzweɜuʔ clan), Tembon (Bɔgwanik clan), Mesagesah, and Wata (all of Njekwa village): 9/21/70.
17. Chief Fonyam (Mindik clan), David Ta Tepong (Ɛzweɜuʔ clan), and Martin Tenjoh (Bɔrangɔp clan) (all of Kobanyang village): 10/8/70.
18. Chief Fongu (Mindik clan) and Thomas Awa (Bɔgwanik clan) (both of Ku village) with Achu Anu (Mindik clan, Funam village): 10/12/70.
19. Fomukom (Mindik clan), Aza (Ɛzweɜuʔ clan), Fokum (Bɔrangɔp clan), and Godfrey Mokwa (Bɔgwanik clan) (all of Ku village): 10/13/70.
20. Anas, Fomujong, and Godfrey Mokwa (all of Bɔgwanik clan and Ku village): 10/21/70.

21. Monabet (Bɔnjɔ clan) and Ndiku (both of Njimetu village): 11/26/70.
22. Joseph Ache and Dan Fokoh (both of Mindik clan and Njekwa village): 12/17/70.
23. Moses Njibi and Werenyen (both of Bɔrangɔp clan and Kai village): 4/12/71.
24. Chief Tabi, Tabi One, and Simon Njam (all of Mindik clan and Zang Tabi village): 4/13/71.
25. Marcos Tembeng Ngya and Tasi (both of Mbemi village): 4/16/71.
26. Moses Njah Tabi and Matia Mbacham (both of Bɔnjɔ clan and Tonaku village): 5/24/71.
27. Chief Tabi and Tabi One (both of Mindik clan and Zang Tabi village): 6/10/71.

References Cited

Austen, Ralph A.
  1974 "The National Archives of Cameroon," *History in Africa* 1: 153–155.

Bloch, Maurice
  1977 "The Past and the Present in the Present," *Man* 12 (2): 278–292.

Bohannan, Laura
  1958 "Political Aspects of Tiv Social Organisation," in J. Middleton and D. Tait, eds., *Tribes without Rulers: Studies in African Segmentary Systems*, pp. 33–66. London: Routledge and Kegan Paul.

Bohannan, Laura, and Paul Bohannan
  1953 *The Tiv of Central Nigeria*. Ethnographic Survey of Africa, Western Africa, Part VIII. London: International African Institute.

Bohannan, Paul
  1957 *Justice and Judgement among the Tiv*. London: Oxford University Press for the International African Institute.
  1958 "Extra Processual Events in Tiv Political Institutions," *American Anthropologist* 60 (1): 1–12.
  1959 "The Impact of Money on an African Subsistence Economy," *The Journal of Economic History* 19 (4): 491–503.

Brain, Robert
  1972 *Bangwa Kinship and Marriage*. Cambridge: Cambridge University Press.
  1981 "The Fontem-Bangwa: A Western Bamileke Group," in C. Tardits, ed., *Contribution de la Recherche Ethnologique à l'Histoire des Civilisations du Cameroun*, Vol. 2, pp. 355–360. Colloques Internationaux du Centre National de la Recherche Scientifique, No. 551. Paris: Centre National de la Recherche Scientifique.

Brain, Robert, and Adam Pollock
1971   *Bangwa Funerary Sculpture.* Toronto: University of Toronto Press.

Brown, David
1984   "Warfare, Oracles, and Iron: A Case-Study of Production among the Pre-colonial Klowe, in the Light of Some Recent Marxist Analyses," *Africa* 54 (2): 29–47.

Burnham, Philip
1980   "Raiders and Traders in Adamawa: Slavery as a Regional System," in J. L. Watson, ed., *Asian and African Systems of Slavery,* pp. 43–72. Berkeley: University of California Press.

Chilver, E. M.
1961   "Nineteenth Century Trade in the Bamenda Grassfields, Southern Cameroons," *Afrika und Übersee* 45 (4): 233–258.
1963   "Native Administration in the West Central Cameroons, 1902–1954," in K. Robinson and F. Madden, eds., *Essays in Imperial Government: Presented to Margery Perham,* pp. 89–139. Oxford: Basil Blackwell.
1965a "Meta Village Chiefdoms of the Bome Valley in the Bamenda Prefecture of West Cameroon, Part 1," *The Nigerian Field* 30 (1): 4–18.
1965b "Meta Village Chiefdoms of the Bome Valley in the Bamenda Prefecture of West Cameroon, Part 2," *The Nigerian Field* 30 (2): 52–59.
1981   "Chronological Synthesis: The Western Region, Comprising the Western Grassfields, Bamum, the Bamileke Chiefdoms and the Central Mbam," in C. Tardits, ed., *Contribution de la Recherche Ethnologique à l'Histoire des Civilisations du Cameroun,* Vol. 2, pp. 453–473. Colloques Internationaux du Centre National de la Recherche Scientifique, No. 551. Paris: Centre National de la Recherche Scientifique.

Chilver, E. M., and P. M. Kaberry
1962   "Traditional Government in Bafut, West Cameroon," *The Nigerian Field* 28 (1): 4–30.
1968   *Traditional Bamenda: The Pre-colonial History and Ethnography of the Bamenda Grassfields.* Buea, Cameroon: Ministry of Primary Education and Social Welfare and West Cameroon Antiquities Commission.

Cohen, Ronald
1974   "Evolution of Hierarchical Institutions: A Case Study from Biu, Nigeria," *Savanna* 3 (2): 153–174.

1976 "The Natural History of Hierarchy: A Case Study," in T. R. Burns and W. Buckley, eds., *Power and Control: Social Structures and Their Transformation*, pp. 185–214. London: Sage Publications for the International Sociological Association.

1977 "Oedipus Rex and Regina: The Queen Mother in Africa," *Africa* 47 (1): 14–30.

1978a "Introduction," in R. Cohen and E. R. Service, eds., *Origins of the State: The Anthropology of Political Evolution*, pp. 1–20. Philadephia: Institute for the Study of Human Issues.

1978b "State Foundations: A Controlled Comparison," in R. Cohen and E. R. Service, eds., *Origins of the State: The Anthropology of Political Evolution*, pp. 141–160. Philadelphia: Institute for the Study of Human Issues.

1978c "State Origins: A Reappraisal," in H. J. M. Claessen and P. Skalník, eds., *The Early State*, pp. 31–75. The Hague: Mouton Publishers.

Collier, Jane F.
1976 "Political Leadership and Legal Change in Zinacantan," *Law and Society Review* 11 (1): 131–163.

Colson, Elizabeth
1953 "Social Control and Vengeance in Plateau Tonga Society," *Africa* 23 (3): 199–211.

Cookey, S. J. S.
1980 "An Ethnohistorical Reconstruction of Traditional Igbo Society," in B. K. Swartz, Jr., and Raymond E. Dumett, eds., *West African Cultural Dynamics: Archaeological and Historical Perspectives*, pp. 327–347. The Hague: Mouton.

Dillon, Richard G.
1973 *Ideology, Process, and Change in Pre-colonial Meta' Political Organization (United Republic of Cameroon)*. Ph.D. Dissertation. Department of Anthropology, University of Pennsylvania.

1976 "Ritual Resolution in Meta' Legal Process," *Ethnology* 15 (3): 287–299.

1977 "Ritual, Conflict, and Meaning in an African Society," *Ethos* 5 (2): 151–173.

1979 "Limits to Ritual Resolution in Meta' Society," *Paideuma: Mitteilungen zur Kulturkunde* 25: 35–39.

1980a "Capital Punishment in Egalitarian Society: The Meta' Case," *Journal of Anthropological Research* 36 (4): 437–452.

1980b "Violent Conflict in Meta' Society," *American Ethnologist* 7 (4): 658–673.

1981 "Notes on the Pre-colonial History and Ethnography of the Meta'," in C. Tardits, ed., *Contribution de la Recherche Ethnologique à l'Histoire des Civilisations du Cameroun*, Vol. 2, pp. 361–370. Colloques Internationaux du Centre National de la Recherche Scientifique, No. 551. Paris: Centre National de la Recherche Scientifique.

1985 "Chiefly Households in Precolonial Meta' Society," *Paideuma: Mitteilungen zur Kulturkunde* 31: 3–13.

Engard, Ronald K.

1986 *Bringing the Outside in: Commensality and Incorporation in Bafut Myth, Ritual, Art, and Social Organization.* Ph.D. Dissertation. Indiana University.

Evans-Pritchard, E. E.

1940a *The Nuer: A Description of the Modes of Livelihood and Political Institutions of a Nilotic People.* London: Oxford University Press.

1940b *The Political System of the Anuak of the Anglo-Egyptian Sudan.* London: P. Lund Humphries and Company for the London School of Economics and Political Science.

1947 "Further Observations on the Political System of the Anuak," *Sudan Notes and Records* 28: 62–97.

Fardon, Richard

1984 "Sisters, Wives, Wards and Daughters: A Transformational Analysis of the Political Organization of the Tiv and their Neighbors. Part I: the Tiv," *Africa* 54 (4): 2–21.

1985 "Sisters, Wives, Wards and Daughters: A Transformational Analysis of the Political Organization of the Tiv and their Neighbors. Part II: the Transformations," *Africa* 55 (1): 77–91.

Forde, Daryll, and G. I. Jones

1950 *The Ibo and Ibibio-speaking Peoples of South-eastern Nigeria.* Ethnographic Survey of Africa, Western Africa, Part III. London: International African Institute.

Fortes, Meyer

1936 "Ritual Festivals and Social Cohesion in the Hinterland of the Gold Coast," *American Anthropologist* 38 (4): 590–604.

1945 *The Dynamics of Clanship among the Tallensi: Being the First Part of an Analysis of the Social Structure of a Trans-Volta Tribe.* London: Oxford University Press for the International African Institute.

Fortes, M., and E. E. Evans-Pritchard

1940 *African Political Systems.* London: Oxford University Press for the International African Institute.

Fried, Morton H.
1967   *The Evolution of Political Society: An Essay in Political Anthropology.* New York: Random House.
1978   "The State, the Chicken, and the Egg: or, What Came First?" in R. Cohen and E. R. Service, eds., *Origins of the State: The Anthropology of Political Evolution,* pp. 35–47. Philadelphia: Institute for the Study of Human Issues.

Geary, Christraud
1979   "Traditional Societies and Associations in We (North West Province, Cameroon)," *Paideuma: Mitteilungen zur Kulturkunde* 25: 53–72.

Geary, Christraud, and Adamou Ndam Njoya
1985   *Mandou Yénou: Photographies du Pays Bamoum, Royaume Ouest-africain, 1902–1915.* München: Trickster Verlag.

Gluckman, Max
1956   *Custom and Conflict in Africa.* Oxford: Basil Blackwell.

Goody, Jack
1956   *The Social Organisation of the LoWiili.* London: Her Majesty's Stationery Office.
1957   "Fields of Social Control among the LoDagaba," *Journal of the Royal Anthropological Institute of Great Britain and Ireland* 87 (1): 75–104.

Haaf, Ernst
1971   "Religiöse Vorstellungen der Meta im Grasland von West-Kamerun," *Anthropos* 66 (1/2): 71–80.
1977   "Eine Studie über den Tod bei den Meta im Westkameruner Grasland," in H. Benzing, O. Böcher, and G. Meyer, eds., *Wort und Wirklichkeit: Studien zur Afrikanistik und Orientalistik,* pp. 163–178. Meisenheim: Hain.

Haas, Jonathan
1982   *The Evolution of the Prehistoric State.* New York: Columbia University Press.

Harris, Marvin
1979   *Cultural Materialism: The Struggle for a Science of Culture.* New York: Random House.

Harris, Rosemary
1962   "The Influence of Ecological Factors and External Relations on the Mbembe Tribes of South-east Nigeria," *Africa* 32 (1): 38–52.
1965   *The Political Organization of the Mbembe, Nigeria.* London: Her Majesty's Stationery Office.

296   *References Cited*

Hobbes, Thomas
    1651   *Leviathan: Or the Matter, Forme and Power of a Commonwealth Ecclesiasticall and Civil* (M. Oakeshott, ed.). Oxford: Basil Blackwell, 1947.

Horton, Robin
    1972   "Stateless Societies in the History of West Africa," in J. F. A. Ajayi and M. Crowder, eds., *History of West Africa*, Vol. 1, pp. 78–119. New York: Columbia University Press.

Johnson, Allen W., and Timothy Earle
    1987   *The Evolution of Human Societies: From Foraging Group to Agrarian State*. Stanford: Stanford University Press.

Kaberry, Phyllis M.
    1952   *Women of the Grassfields: A Study of the Economic Position of Women in Bamenda, British Cameroons*. London: Her Majesty's Stationery Office.
    1962   "Retainers and Royal Households in the Cameroons Grassfields," *Cahiers d'Études Africaines* 3–1 (10): 282–298.

Kaberry, Phyllis M., and E. M. Chilver
    1961   "An Outline of the Traditional Political System of Bali-Nyonga, Southern Cameroons," *Africa* 31 (4): 355–371.

Kopytoff, Igor
    1981   "Aghem Ethnogenesis and the Grassfields Ecumene," in C. Tardits, ed., *Contribution de la Recherche Ethnologique à l'Histoire des Civilisations du Cameroun*, Vol. 2, pp. 371–381. Colloques Internationaux du Centre National de la Recherche Scientifique, No. 551. Paris: Centre National de la Recherche Scientifique.

Latour, Charles-Henry Pradelles de
    1985   "Le Palais du Chef dans une Chefferie Bamiléké: Bangoua," *Paideuma: Mitteilungen zur Kulturkunde* 31: 31–47.

Levine, Victor T.
    1964   *The Cameroons: From Mandate to Independence*. Berkeley: University of California Press.

Lienhardt, Godfrey
    1957   "Anuak Village Headmen I: Headmen and Village Culture," *Africa* 27 (4): 341–355.
    1958   "Anuak Village Headmen II: Village Structure and Rebellion," *Africa* 28 (1): 23–36.

Masquelier, Bertrand M.
    1978   *Structure and Process of Political Identity: Ide, a Polity of the Metchum Valley (Cameroon)*. Ph.D. Dissertation. Department of Anthropology, University of Pennsylvania.

1979 "Ide as a Polity: Ideology, Morality and Political Identity," *Paideuma: Mitteilungen zur Kulturkunde* 25: 41–52.

Meek, Charles K.
1937 *Law and Authority in a Nigerian Tribe: A Study in Indirect Rule.* London: Oxford University Press.

Meillassoux, Claude
1978a "'The Economy' in Agricultural Self-sustaining Societies: A Preliminary Analysis," in D. Seddon, ed., *Relations of Production: Marxist Approaches to Economic Anthropology,* pp. 127–157 (translated by Helen Lackner). London: Frank Cass.
1978b "The Social Organization of the Peasantry: The Economic Basis of Kinship," in D. Seddon, ed., *Relations of Production: Marxist Approaches to Economic Anthropology,* pp. 159–169 (translated by Helen Lackner). London: Frank Cass.

Middleton, John
1960 *Lugbara Religion: Ritual and Authority among an East African People.* London: Oxford University Press for the International African Institute.

Moore, Sally Falk
1975 "Epilogue: Uncertainties in Situations, Indeterminacies in Culture," in S. F. Moore and B. G. Myerhoff, eds., *Symbol and Politics in Communal Ideology: Cases and Questions,* pp. 210–239. Ithaca: Cornell University Press.

Muller, Jean-Claude
1982 "Intertribal Hunting among the Rukuba," *Ethnology* 21 (3): 203–214.
1985 "Political Systems as Transformations," in H. J. M. Claessen, P. van de Velde, and M. E. Smith, eds., *Development and Decline: The Evolution of Sociopolitical Organization,* pp. 62–81. South Hadley: Bergin and Garvey Publishers.

Nader, Laura, and Harry F. Todd
1978 *The Disputing Process: Law in Ten Societies.* New York: Columbia University Press.

Netting, Robert McC.
1972 "Sacred Power and Centralization: Aspects of Political Adaptation in Africa," in B. Spooner, ed., *Population Growth,* pp. 219–244. Cambridge: M.I.T. Press.
1973 "Fighting, Forest, and the Fly: Some Demographic Regulators among the Kofyar," *Journal of Anthropological Research* 29 (3): 164–179.

1974   "Kofyar Armed Conflict: Social Causes and Consequences," *Journal of Anthropological Research* 30 (3): 139–163.

Nkwi, Paul N.
1976   *Traditional Government and Social Change: A Study of the Political Institutions among the Kom of the Cameroon Grassfields.* Fribourg, Switzerland: The University Press.

Nkwi, Paul N., and Jean-Pierre Warnier
1982   *Elements for a History of the Western Grassfields.* Yaoundé, Cameroon: Sopecam. Sponsored by the Department of Sociology, University of Yaoundé.

Northrup, David
1978   *Trade without Rulers: Pre-colonial Economic Development in Southeastern Nigeria.* Oxford: The Clarendon Press.

O'Brien, Dan
1983   "Chiefs of Rain—Chiefs of Ruling: A Reinterpretation of Precolonial Tonga (Zambia) Social and Political Structure," *Africa* 53 (4): 23–42.

O'Neil, Robert J.
1987   *A History of Moghamo, 1865 to 1940: Authority and Change in a Cameroon Grassfields Culture.* Ph.D. Dissertation. Department of History, Columbia University.

Ottenberg, Simon
1958   "Ibo Oracles and Intergroup Relations," *Southwestern Journal of Anthropology,* 14 (3): 295–317.

Pospisil, Leopold J.
1978   *The Ethnology of Law* (Second Edition). Menlo Park: Cummings Publishing Company.

Rey, Pierre Philippe
1979   "Class Contradiction in Lineage Societies," *Critique of Anthropology* 4 (13 and 14): 41–60.

Rousseau, Jean-Jacques
1755   "A Discourse on a Subject Proposed by the Academy of Dijon: What is the Origin of Inequality among Men, and is it Authorized by Natural Law?" in J. J. Rousseau, *The Social Contract and Discourses,* pp. 175–282 (translated by G. D. H. Cole). New York: E. P. Dutton and Company, 1950.

Rowlands, M. J.
1979   "Local and Long Distance Trade and Incipient State Formation on the Bamenda Plateau in the Late 19th Century," *Paideuma: Mitteilungen zur Kulturkunde* 25: 1–19.

Rudin, Harry R.
1938 *Germans in the Cameroons, 1884–1914: A Case Study in Modern Imperialism.* New Haven: Yale University Press.

Ruel, Malcolm
1969 *Leopards and Leaders: Constitutional Politics among a Cross River People.* London: Tavistock Publications.

Service, Elman R.
1975 *Origins of the State and Civilization: The Process of Cultural Evolution.* New York: W. W. Norton and Company.
1978 "Classical and Modern Theories of the Origins of Government," in R. Cohen and E. R. Service, eds., *Origins of the State: The Anthropology of Political Evolution*, pp. 21–34. Philadelphia: Institute for the Study of Human Issues.

Southall, Aidan W.
1956 *Alur Society: A Study in Processes and Types of Domination.* Cambridge: W. Heffer and Sons Limited.

Stevenson, Robert F.
1968 *Population and Political Systems in Tropical Africa.* New York: Columbia University Press.

Tardits, Claude
1980 *Le Royaume Bamoum.* Paris: Librairie Armand Colin.

Terray, Emmanuel
1972 "Historical Materialism and Segmentary Lineage-Based Societies," in E. Terray, *Marxism and Primitive Society: Two Studies*, pp. 93–186 (translated by Mary Klopper). New York: Monthly Review Press.
1979 "On Exploitation: Elements of an Autocritique," *Critique of Anthropology* 4 (13 and 14): 29–39.

Turner, V. W.
1957 *Schism and Continuity in an African Society: A Study of Ndembu Village Life.* Manchester: Manchester University Press on behalf of the Institute for African Studies, University of Zambia.

Uchendu, Victor C.
1965 *The Igbo of Southeast Nigeria.* New York: Holt, Rinehart and Winston.

Verdon, Michel
1980 "Re-defining Pre-colonial Ewe Polities: The Case of Abutia," *Africa* 50 (3): 280–292.

Warnier, Jean-Pierre
1975 *Pre-colonial Mankon: The Development of a Cameroon Chiefdom in*

Its Regional Setting. Ph.D. Dissertation. Department of Anthropology, University of Pennsylvania.

1979 "Noun-classes, Lexical Stocks, Multilingualism, and the History of the Cameroon Grassfields," *Language in Society* 8 (3): 409–423.

1983 *Sociologie du Bamenda Pré-colonial (Cameroun).* Thèse du Grade de Docteur ès Lettres, Université de Paris X.

1985 *Échanges, Développement et Hiérarchies dans le Bamenda Précolonial (Cameroun).* Studien zur Kulturkunde, 76. Wiesbaden: Franz Steiner Verlag.

Warnier, Jean-Pierre, and Ian Fowler

1979 "A Nineteenth-Century Ruhr in Central Africa," *Africa* 49 (4): 329–351.

Wilhelm, H.

1981 "Le Commerce Précolonial de l'Ouest (Plateau Bamiléké-Grassfield, Régions Bamoum et Bafia)," in C. Tardits, ed., *Contribution de la Recherche Ethnologique à l'Histoire des Civilisations du Cameroun*, Vol. 2, pp. 485–501. Colloques Internationaux du Centre National de la Recherche Scientifique, No. 551. Paris: Centre National de la Recherche Scientifique.

Index

In this index an "f" after a number indicates a separate reference on the next page, and an "ff" indicates separate references on the next two pages. A continuous discussion over two or more pages is indicated by a span of page numbers, e.g., "pp. 57–58." *Passim* is used for a cluster of references in close but not consecutive sequence.

Library of Congress Cataloging-in-Publication Data

Dillon, Richard G.
  Ranking and resistance: a precolonial Cameroonian polity in
regional perspective / Richard G. Dillon.
    p.   cm.
Includes bibliographical references.
ISBN 0-8047-1571-8 (alk. paper):
    1. Meta' (African people)—Politics and government.   2. Political
anthropology—Cameroon.   I. Title.
DT571.M47D55   1990   89-78332
323.1'1963606711—dc20   CIP

♾ This book is printed on acid-free paper.